FOLDING TECHNOLOGIES

Paper

• *Christophe Guberan (p. 150)*

DIRECT FOLDING
Without scoring (tools: hands, folder used by printers making rolled, simple, double, parallel, zigzag folds etc.).

MANUAL SCORING
(Tools: folding tool, scorer).

COMPUTER-CONTROLLED SCORING
(CNC tools: Cameo or Roland cutting plotter for paper).

MICROPERFORATION
(Tools: microperforator to create round holes or manual or CNC cutter to create dashes).

MOISTENING
Of the entire surface of the paper for crimping techniques, or moistening of the edge of the fold only.

CASTING OR WEAVING
Of paper with insertion of metal rods. The fold is formed by shrinkage of the paper during the drying process, or manually, with the metal causing the given form to remain.

Cardboard

• *Studio Nuy van Noort (p. 99)*

MANUAL SCORING
(Cutter, rounded tip, folding tool etc.).

COMPUTER-CONTROLLED SCORING
(Cutting plotter with specific point).

SCORING WITH PRESSES
And cutting forms (tools for shaping cardboard used in the packaging industry).

V MILLING
Of multiple-layer corrugated cardboard or of honeycomb cardboard, with double-blade cutter for foam board.

Plastic

• *Polly Verity (p. 36)*

SCORING
For certain plastics that can be folded cold (full and alveolar polypropylene).

V MILLING
For certain plastics that can be folded cold (cutter with 90° or 60° V angle on manual or CNC milling machine).

FOLDING WITH A FOLDING MACHINE
For certain plastics that can be folded cold (polycarbonate, polypropylene).

INJECTION MOULDING
Process that involves softening a plastic material in the form of granules or powder and injecting it into a mould to shape and cool it.

THERMOFORMING
Shaping technique for a material in slab form that involves heating it to soften and shape it with a negative or positive mould.

Metal

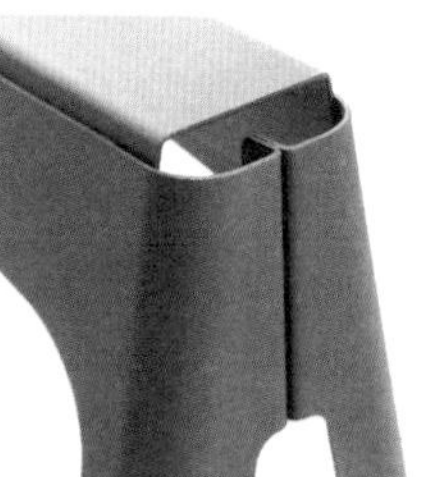

• *Normal Studio (p. 96)*

FOLDING WITH A FOLDING MACHINE
Manual or automatic (constraints: straight folds, limits on angles and distances).

STAMPING
Deformation of a sheet of flat and thin plate with a high-power press equipped with special tools, to obtain in particular a non-developable form.

ROBOTIC ARMS
For curved folds: two computer-controlled arms take hold of a piece of sheet metal on either side of the fold to be made, and they then move in space, mimicking the movement of a person's hands, but with more power and precision.

MOULDING
(Eg: moulds of folds in paper and a counter-mould).

PERFORATION
Of sheet metal along the folds (using a CNC milling machine or stamping) and manual folding without tools.

HINGES
(Assembled or made in the piece of metal itself).

Textiles

• *HOID (p. 76)*

FOLDING THROUGH SEWING
Pattern in one or several pieces, folded and sewn.

NEEDLE PLEATING
Passing of a needle above and below the accordion-pleated fabric.

PLEATING WITH A PLEATING FRAMEWORK
A process that involves manually inserting a piece of cloth between two sheets of folded Kraft cardboard that produce a male-female mould. This configuration is sometimes wrapped around a metal cylinder and placed into a gas-powered steamer.

PRINTING
Of patterns with inflatable ink.

MOUNTING
Of rigid parts forming the faces (thin pieces of cut wood veneer, for example).

Concrete / Plaster / Earth

• *Charlène Fétiveau (p. 56)*

PROJECTED
Requires fibres and various frames that give shape to the folds. This type of working of thin layers can be carried out by hand or with machines (Tyrolean style to project coatings). This requires a good mastery of repetition over a multistage production process. Climatic conditions during production influence the final result.

CAST
Requires a formwork (lost or otherwise) and a release operation. The formwork is a (negative) mould of the folded form. It must be sufficiently strong relative to the surge of the liquid, and have a surface that is easy to remove from the mould and that is usually oiled. It also requires fibres (straw, glass fibre, metal fibres, etc.) and frames (metal, wood, reeds, brambles, etc.).
High-performance concretes and plasters allow very thin folded surfaces.

COMPOSITE TEXTILE
Textiles soaked in plaster or concrete then shaped for drying. Composite textile, thin panels of concrete.

Glass

• *Erik and Martin Demaine (p. 34)*

HOT FORMED
Sticks or tubes worked over a flame with regular movement.

CAST
Liquid glass is pressed between two rollers.

BLOWN
The glass is blown at the end of a hollow steel rod.

Wood

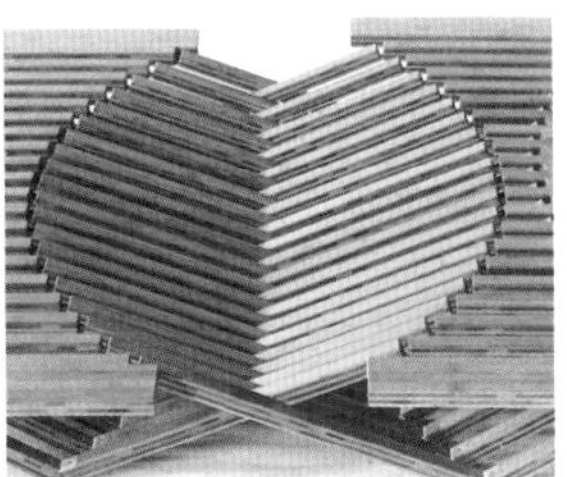

• *Robert van Embricqs (p. 109)*

BENDING
Process that involves softening the wood using heat or steam so that it becomes flexible enough to be curved. It is set on a mould to the desired shape and stabilizes during drying.

MOULDING
Process that involves gluing and positioning sheets of wood on a form and then hot pressing.

ASSEMBLING
Of panels along fold edges (gluing, screwing etc.).

HINGES
Assembly of two panels with metal hinges or those of another material, in order to maintain the fold's possibility of movement.

MOUNTING
On a foldable material (paper, textiles, etc.).

JEAN-CHARLES TREBBI

CHLOÉ GENEVAUX

GUILLAUME BOUNOURE

promopress

• *Éric Joisel.*

• *Paul Jackson.*

• *Géomorphos, Andres Gallego, Prof. Mauricio Velásquez Posada, Prof. Claudia Fernández Silva.*

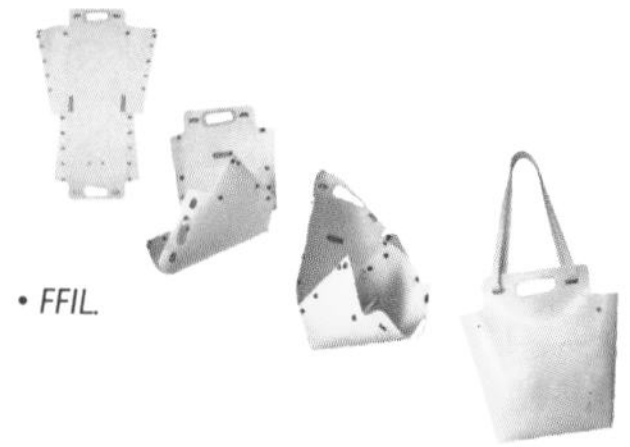

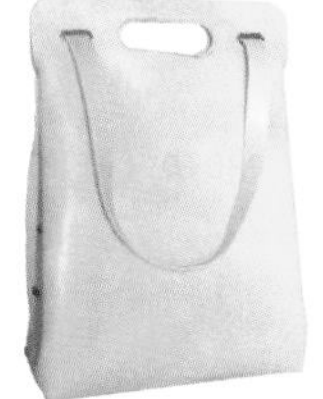

• *FFIL.*

Contents

• molo.

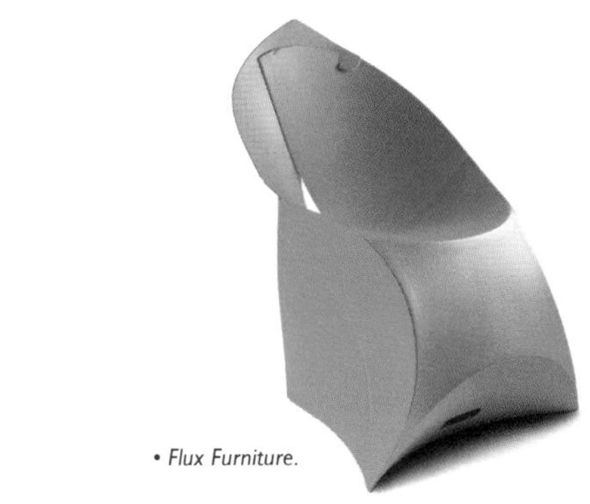
• Flux Furniture.

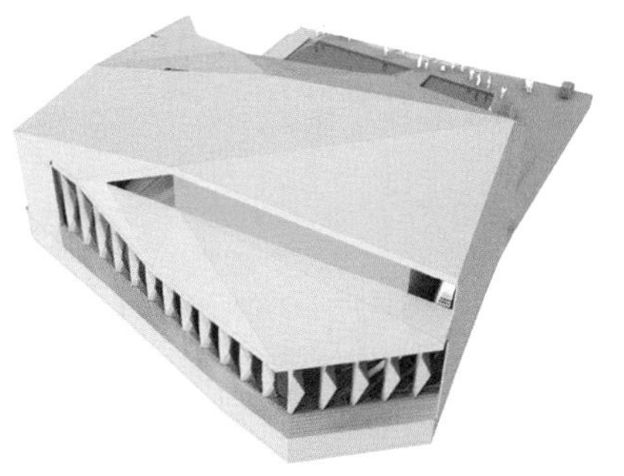
• Broissin Architects.

• Eric Olsen.

FURNITURE AND LIGHTING

ARCHITECTURE

INNOVATION

In memory of our friend and teacher Thierry Berthomier (1944-2010), who introduced us to the world of folding.

Chloé & Guillaume

A whole host of creators reveal their passions in this volume, from Éric Joisel with his *commedia dell'arte* characters to Polly Verity with her magnificent creations and Bernard Girault with the sensitive perspectives of his theatrical folds. And it taps into local traditions such as Anjou's cap pleating and into the potential of approaches and research involving our robotic origami-folding friends.

My coauthors Guillaume and Chloé are architects who have placed folding at the heart of their research activities. They created the company BOU-GE (www.bou-ge.com), which works on innovative products based on folding for the architecture and design sectors. In developing more technical aspects of folding, we have pooled our knowledge, and we thought it essential and useful to draw up an overview of folding techniques and types, which you will find on page 172 as well as on the inside of this volume's jacket.

We hope that you enjoy reading this book and that this new crop of quality creations proves to be a source of inspiration.

Jean-Charles Trebbi

WHY FOLD?

In a world made up of interacting elements—a world that is a theatre of evolutions of all kinds—metamorphoses will take place. Through a combined interplay of material strengths, spatial expanses and temporal omnipresence, which is governed by a few principles of order and minimums (concepts that are potentially synonymous with economy), transformations that are global or local and continuous or discontinuous are fostered at all levels. As a result of this interplay, within the two-dimensionality of surfaces (the favoured mediums for linear one-dimensionality, as well as the outer layer for three-dimensionality and its volumes), the fold—that remarkable singularity and site of exceptional behaviour—can come about.

Everything that exists is touched in this way, from the inert mineral kingdom to the living worlds of the plant and animal kingdoms, in which folding is a fundamental morphogenetic process that stamps its mark on the many structures whose birth and life it contributes to. By virtue of the balance between form and function, the characteristics of the generated forms correspond to capacities for preferred actions, though the protean may be accompanied by a certain versatility. Via the broad categories of primary properties (the inherent roles performed by basic folding: protective capacity, resistance through form, joint mobility), there is opportunity for many other potentially useful secondary effects to be produced.

Everything produced by man—for whom the exemplary nature of what nature has produced offers a lesson—for his own use corresponds to a similar rationale. But the aspirations particular to the human mind—the search for harmony and meaning—now must also be added to purely utilitarian demands. Folding is in its essence able to satisfy such purposes. In its multiple variables that humans are sensitive to, it possesses all of the sculptural qualities conducive to formative expressiveness (classic aesthetic contrasts of protruding or receding relief, shadows and lights, straightness and curvature, direction, texture, and so forth).

As for meaning, the law-like determinism of cause and effect that requires that a given configuration consistently results in a given role is such that each form can speak to us (such as the receptive invitation offered by concavity). And it is possible to understand in words like simplicity, complexity and explanation what certain configurations of folds are able to express as etymological truth.

An abundance of resources—which are occasionally playful, possibly magic and always spectacular—give folding eminently pedagogical virtues. Folding therefore offers the designer who seeks to format space and material for human use a real language to express tangible ideas. Through direct application to materials in activities ranging from basic and universally accessible artisanal practices to sophisticated techniques, folding is a permanent source of creativity. This activity, which is enriched with the cultural values of all eras and places, has offered countless gems in many fields—and it still produces new ones, as it will continue to do so long into the future. The creations presented here illustrate just this.

Jean-Marie Delarue, 2015.

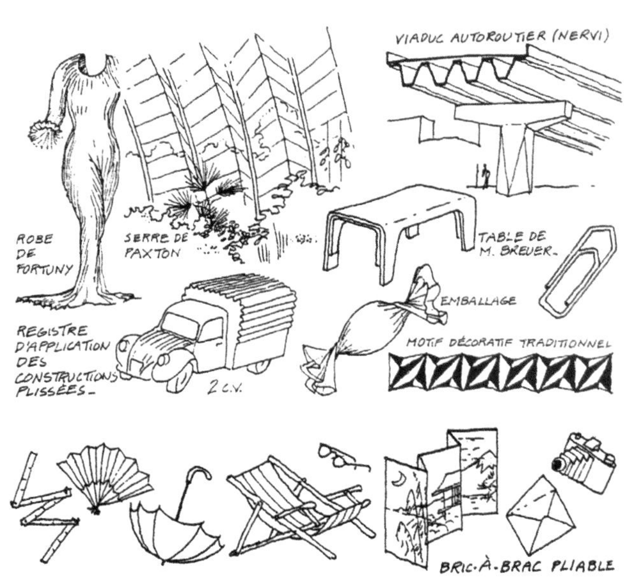

• *Jean-Marie Delarue, sketch illustrating the fields of application for folding as a result of its structural, technical, functional and expressive features, taken from the book* Plis, Règles géométriques et Principes structurants, *École d'architecture Paris-Villemin, 1997.*

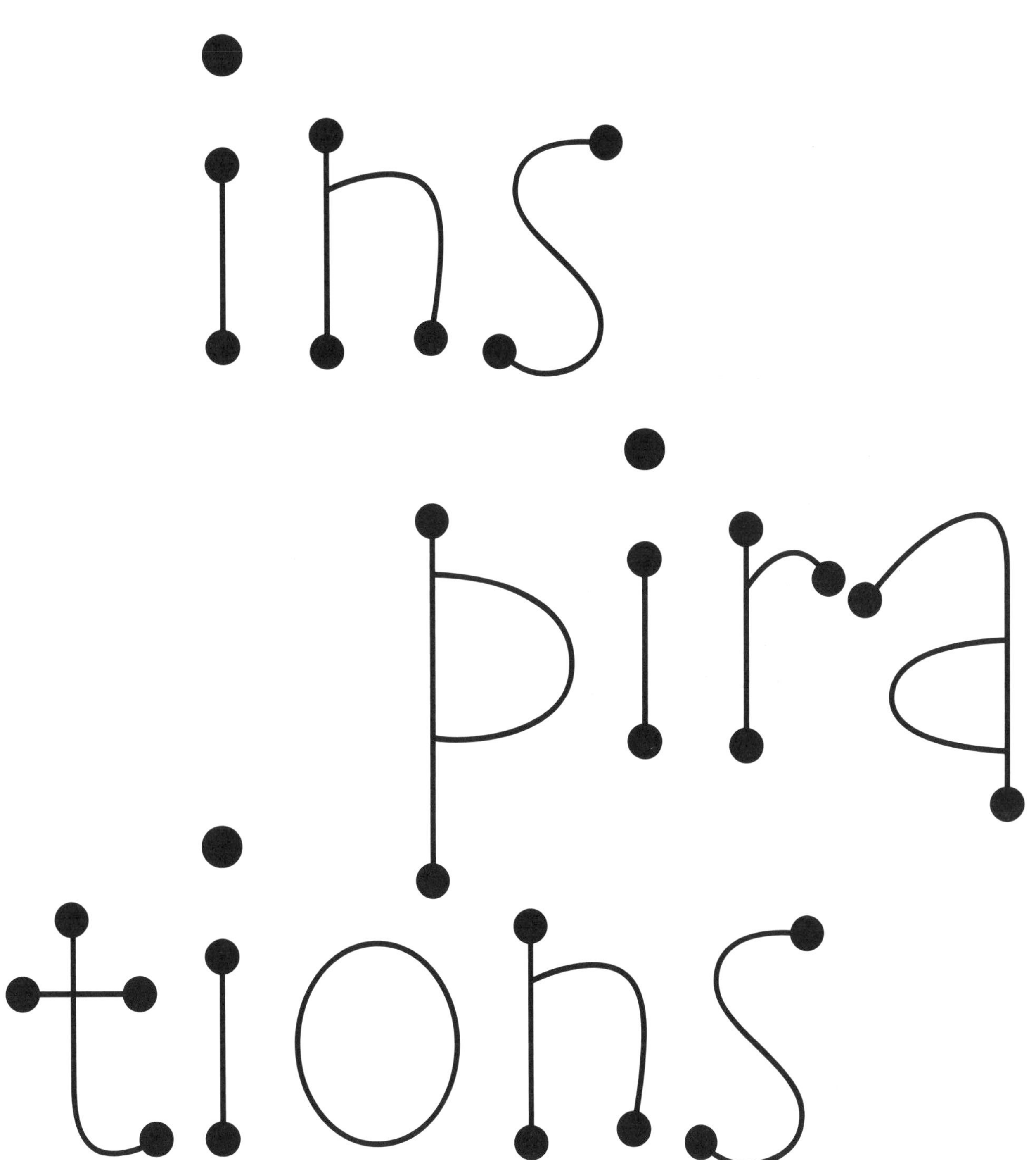

• *Vincent Floderer, leaves, crimping technique:*
Ailettes - Algues vertes, *display case*
26 x 39 x 5,5 cm (10 1/4 x 15 3/8 x 2 3/16 in),
exhibited at the Freising Gallery, Munich, Germany, 2008.

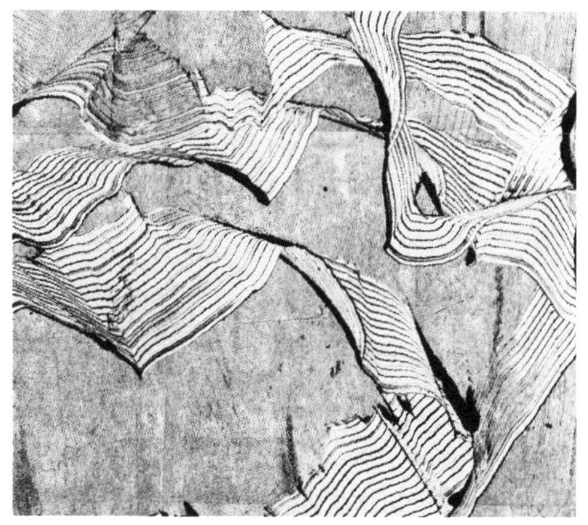

• *Richard Sweeney,* Monotype, *detail.*
• *Kunsulu Jilkishiyeva,* Anatolian orchid, *2012.*

INTRODUCTION

"But before explaining the organization of the world of forms any further, it seems important to me to stress that, in my opinion, the folding process opens up new avenues for understanding a whole universe of configurations for materials."
J-M Delarue, in II 27 Natural building, *1980.*

Folds have many functions in the organization of beings and things. According to Jean-Marie Delarue, folds entail a universal process of morphogenesis that governs the mineral, plant and animal kingdoms.
Everywhere in nature, folded forms emerge harmoniously, and they are the outcome of many interacting factors. The same configuration of folds can satisfy several functions. Folds' structuring role—that is, giving rigidity through form to a small amount of material—is only one function among others. Without creating an exhaustive list, one might think of folds as a processes for bringing about growth or increasing complexity, or as a hatching mechanism. "The metamorphoses that the embryo undergoes—for example, the generation of defined organs—take place through folds that give rise to multiple interfaces for energy exchanges, compactions of proliferating expanses, consolidating nervurations, hatching mechanisms and moving and articular folds (...). Later, these folds also give rise to shrivelling and its wrinkles." Folds are also characterized by their ability to contain owing to the manner in which they give form to matter and encompass and envelop. But folding is also unfolding. At the moment that they are made and owing to the endogenous or exogenous forces that they involve, folds also become movement.

In geological terms, for example, the folds of the Earth's crust are the visible trace of thrusts caused by the continents' drifting. These folds are the result of a compression of matter and constitute the Earth's relief. They are in certain respects the marks of time.
Whether on an infinitely small or infinitely large scale, folds structure material, carry genetic information and are perhaps even part of the morphology of the universe. In *L'Univers chiffonné***, Jean-Pierre Luminet describes a topologically crimped space that nevertheless has no edges or corners, calling to mind a flexible fabric.

Who never glimpsed or hoped for, through the fabulous progress of twentieth-century humanity, the beginnings of a new world? Each of us folds and unfolds our existence like paper tissue: memory, time and space as we conceive of them seem to be shaped by conceptual deployments and folds that are true jumps of intelligence toward infinity. What is the key for interpreting this mysterious alphabet? Folds may in essence be the shortest path towards what is distant in terms of ideas and facts.

* Research report entitled *Constructions plissées, figuration graphique et recherche structurale*. Research under the scientific supervision of J.-M. Delarue with the collaboration of J.-F. Brossin. 1981-87. Ministère de l'Equipement, du Logement, de l'Aménagement du Territoire et des Transports, direction de l'architecture et de l'urbanisme, sous-direction de l'architecture et de la recherche. ADRI, École d'architecture Paris-Villemin.

** Luminet Jean-Pierre, *L'Univers chiffonné*, Folio, 2005.

THE PLANT WORLD

The great diversity of the plant kingdom presents a complete and exhaustive panoply of the fold's main functions. Man's many efforts and accomplishments were not invented from scratch. The plant kingdom is a special field of study, and if we look at it from the original perspective of folding, it allows us to understand many things. In his research report *Constructions plissées**, Jean-Marie Delarue studies the main roles played by folds in nature. "Folding occurs at each stage of plant development (blooming, growth, wilting), and it is involved in each type of organ (in a particularly evident way in external and relatively extended two-dimensional elements such as leaf blades and flower petals)."

The kinetic dimension of folds is very important in nature. It is a process of adaptation and change that is based on both needs and growth. We might consider, for example, a leaf's development process. It first grows in the limited space of the bud or germ. This is vernation. The leaf is arranged in the bud based on folds that allow it to take up a minimum of space until it becomes ready and unfolds in the open air.

Unfolding is a key principle in the process of growth and blooming, but some leaves or flowers can also fold themselves back up. This is part of a process of adaptation to weather conditions, or one that governs, for example, the different phases of reproduction.

ANATOMY

Because they are present on both the outside and inside of our body, folds are familiar to us and are a part of our identity. As with animals, they are found where our joints are located, allowing mobility (think, for example, of the elbows, neck and hands, that mobile and agile tool par excellence).

Similar to our fingerprints, they are specific to each individual. Folds are also engraved into our skin. These reliefs create a nonslip surface that improves the sensitivity of our touch.

They are also one of the elements of our expressiveness. Expressions of joy, sadness and pain differ in each of us, and they are marked by a particular number of folds located in different places (around the eyes, mouth, forehead and so on). In the long run, they create an imprint of a person's character on the face, and they increase gradually in number as we age and our skin sags.

The inside of our body makes great use of folds, which perform different functions. From the moment we are formed, during the phase of cell differentiation, cell proliferation generates folds that become the site for the various organs. In addition, in order to increase the surface for exchange between two distinct volumes, the membrane that separates them consists of multiple folds. This allows an increase in the exchange surface within a minimum of space.

We might liken this principle to the design of a finned radiator, which through its folds has a large exchange surface, thus improving the radiator's performance. Folds are also found in the places through which nutrients pass, a process that is momentaneous and repetitive and that to a greater or lesser extent involves volumes. This requires conduits that can open and close as well as fill and empty, depending on the given needs.

Present in the deepest parts of ourselves, the fold is intimate in nature, and sometimes it gives us the sensation of a harmonious organization of matter.

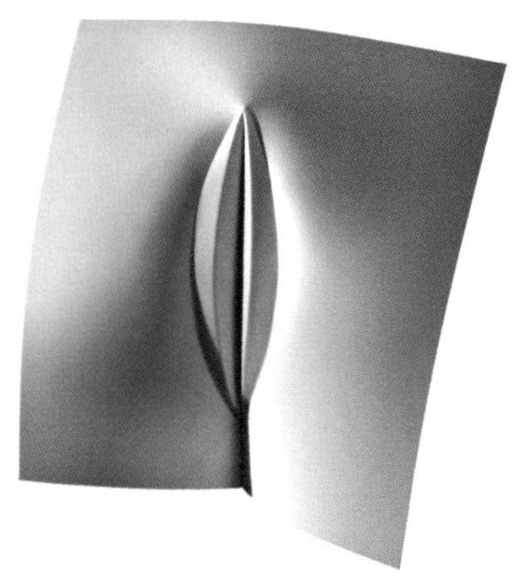

• *Stefan Weber, mask.*
• *Victor Cœurjoly, studies of curves.*

THE ANIMAL WORLD

Among other things, animals use folds because of their kinematic properties, particularly in order to adapt to different situations. The wings of the bat, for example, occupy a significant area when they are unfolded, which provides the lift necessary for flight. They fold back into a small volume at rest.
Shellfish are interesting to observe owing to the structural characteristics of their shells. Their protective outer skeleton is through its natural constitution an adapted response to development conditions and to the crustacean's environment. These natural shells are distinguished by three components: their microscopic (stratified, crystalline and multidirectional) structure, the distribution of the general curves of the shell, and the presence of secondary folds or many waves.

The carapaces of insects, which are sometimes genuine ribbed shields, illustrate folds' structuring and motor functions, thanks to a natural composite material called chitin. This "resin" can be flexible, rigid or even sharp within the same expanse of material. The thin and light wings of flying insects are stiffened by folds, which allow better resistance to bending and an economy of material that is essential for these living beings with an ephemeral existence.
Folds are also a component of the internal anatomy of most animals. Within a small volume, they allow a great length of "piping" to be arranged, as well as large exchange surfaces between different organs.
When they allow several entities to be articulated, folds can take on a motor function. One example of this can be seen in the way in which caterpillars move.

At the level of joints, a significant stretch of membrane is required to be able to freely evolve in many directions of space. We may observe in this respect that the very hard skin of elephants is particularly creased at spots that movement places especially heavy demands on. The presence of folds provides the flexibility necessary for living beings and therefore for their mobility.

- *Éric Joisel,* coq.
- *Robert Lang,* Fiddler crab.
- *Victor Cœurjoly,* Vaca y buey de Belén.

LIGHTS AND SHADOWS

Through the different superpositions and changes to planes that they create, folds bring about a stark or subtle play of shadows and lights.
The shadow's qualities are particularly relevant in Japanese culture, a subject that Junichirô Tanizaki talks about in his book *In Praise of Shadows**: "Such is our way of thinking—we find beauty not in the thing itself but in the patterns of shadows, the light and the darkness, that one thing against another creates. A phosphorescent jewel gives off its glow and colour in the dark and loses its beauty in the light of day. Were it not for shadows, there would be no beauty."
The sense of beauty that we obtain from properly ordered folds comes directly from the interplay of light and shadow that enlivens a surface and makes it change. Shadow slips an element of mystery into each fold, giving birth to a poetic dimension in places that by themselves are meaningless.

VISUAL EXPRESSION

The way in which things hang often creates the body's equivalent expression to facial wrinkles. It betrays emotion or tiny tensions of the soul that artworks try to mirror. It is perhaps through such hanging that the painter projects on the canvas a reflection on painting itself, in a kind of painting of painting. As they are revealed by the effects of chiaroscuro, folds becomes volume, animating the canvas and revealing a depth.
Folds have the particularity of being associated with continuity and discontinuity, a feature described by Leibniz's metaphor that "the division of the continuum must not be considered to be like that of sand into grains, but like that of a folded sheet of paper or tunic, such that there may be an infinity of folds."**

• *Andres Diaz Arboleda, as part of* Geomorphos, *course led by Mauricio Velásquez Posada and Claudia Fernández Silva at the School of Architecture and Design, Universidad pontificia Bolivariana, Medellin, Colombia, 2008-2012.*
• *Paul Jackson,* Fourplanes.

* Junichirô Tanizaki, *In Praise of Shadows*, Leete's Island Books, 1977.

** Leibniz, Pacidius Philalethi (C, p.614-615), in *Le Pli, Leibniz et le baroque*, p 9, "Critique" collection, Les éditions de minuit, 1988.

• *Metal folding, Pioes Sia company, Latvia.*
• *Andrey Ermakov, Egg box.*

THE FOLD'S KINETICS: "FOLD, UNFOLD."

Many everyday objects that are manufactured to meet various specific human needs make use of the fold's transformational ability. We use it to save space and increase mobility.

THE FOLD AS STRUCTURING PRINCIPLE

The principle of strength through form rather than through the amount of material used is what characterizes the structuring role of the fold. The starting point is a two-dimensional surface, which through folding takes on volume and organizes space in three dimensions. The fold can be seen as a means of organizing the void that it encompasses. Responding to a natural need for material and energy savings, it brings toughness to a surface that otherwise would remain flexible and unable to hold.

FOLDING TECHNOLOGY

In general, all materials lend themselves to being given folds through moulding or assembly processes, but this is not the case for forming or folding. Concrete, for example, is impossible to fold, but some of the moulding techniques for it have been inspired by folding.*

Folding is a permanent plastic deformation—that is, the fold does not disappear when the effort applied comes to an end.

When they are folded, materials undergo a stretching (tension) in the outer convex part and a pushing back (compression) in the concave inner part. The surface shared between these two zones is called "neutral fibre"; it retains its original length.

The structure of the material (plasticity), the property of resilience and the section (thickness and diameter) will determine the boundaries of the fold.

The thickness of folded materials varies from very small dimensions (a few microns in the case of the aluminium foil used in the partitions of planes, or in nano-origami in the field of nanotechnologies), to dimensions limited by machines, the curvature radius and stretchability limits –10 cm (4 in) for plastics, 5 cm (2 in) for metals–.

Nowadays, many products, objects and buildings are created according to principles of folding. In a research report entitled *Technologie du pliage*,** Jean-François Brossin describes the main techniques for folding materials.

According to Brossin, "We can distinguish three distinct folding processes for materials:

– forming consists of folding or bending a semifinished product such as a tube, a sheet or a bar by force;

– moulding, in which the material in its plastic state occupies a cavity and solidifies.

– assembly, which involves fastening parts together through different techniques.

It is interesting to note that the structural properties of folds also apply to materials that cannot be folded in the strict sense of the term, like a corrugated brick wall or a folded concrete structure produced through formwork (moulding)."

* See Trebbi Jean-Charles, *L'Art du pli, v1*, p.110. éditions Alternatives, Paris, 2008.

** Jean-François Brossin, "Technologie du pliage," in *Constructions plissées*, research report, MELATT, Paris, 1981, op. cit.

• *Hauser and SPIN, RoboFold fabrication,*
Trifold *table*
(www.trifoldtable.com).

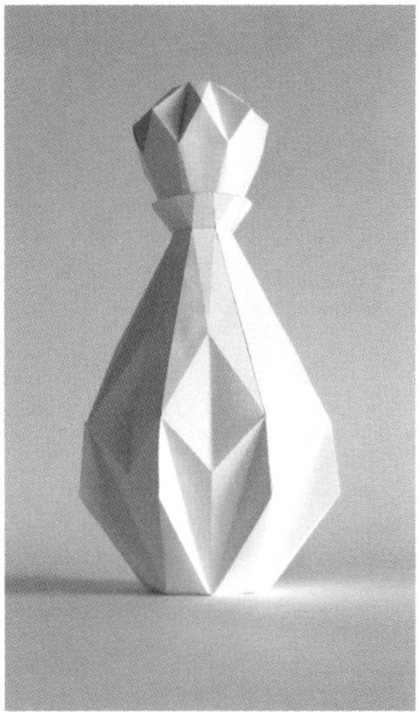

• *Charlène Fetiveau, paper prototype.*
• *Make Architects, folding kiosk, 2014.*

• *Maori Kimura, bag folded using foam printing.*

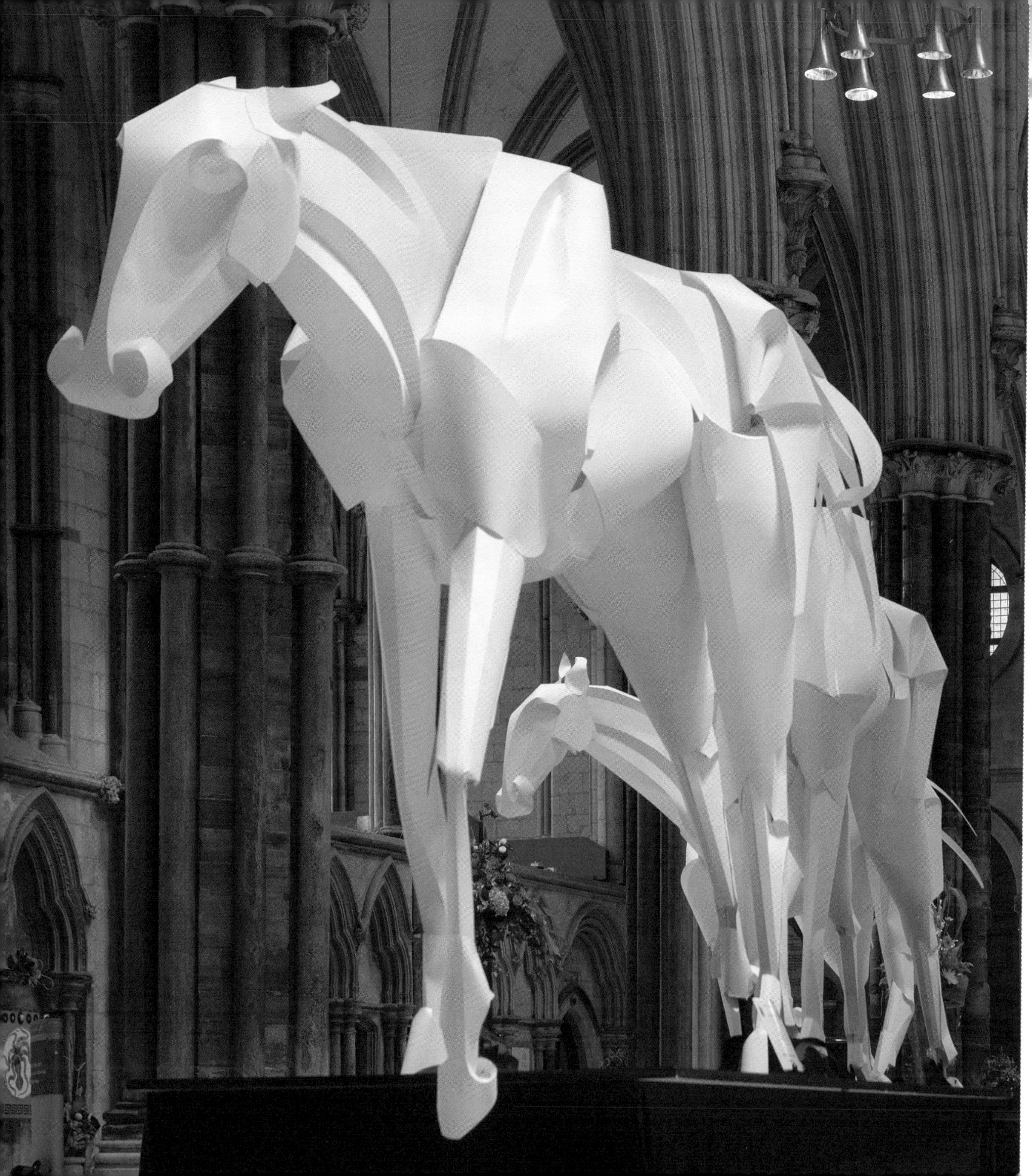

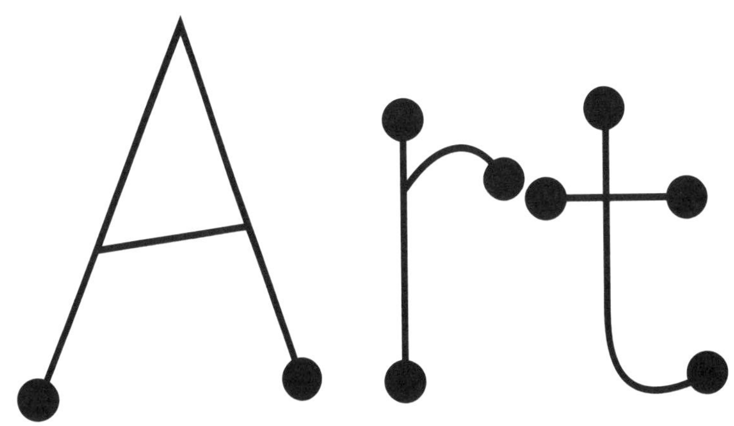

• *Richard Sweeney,* Olympic Horses, *Lincoln Cathedral, 2012.*

ART AS FOLDING

"The constraints of origami (folding a square without cutting or pasting) encourage simple figuration, compelling one to leave behind the superfluous and move towards the essentials. Origami's credo of 'no cutting or pasting' is almost the reverse of the technological world's credo of 'copy and paste'."*

• *Eric Gjerde*, Stacked triangles.
• *Eric Gjerde*, Biopaper.

Folding has been part China's paper arts since the sixth century, and it became part of Japan's a thousand years later. This refined popular art grounded in ritual practice is the expression of a very geometric simplification of objects. Minimalist art in the twentieth century in the West was strongly influenced by the uncluttered nature of Japanese culture.

The word "origami" comes from Japanese; it refers to the traditional art of folding paper.

Its basic principles constitute a codified definitional model for shaping paper. In the present era, new forms of origami have emerged.

The use of metallic paper and other new materials or the technique of using wet paper (wet folding), for example, indicate a transition. Origami has found a new format!

But it is not the only expression of folding in contemporary art. Art pushes boundaries and gives shape to ideas, and ideas to forms. Through the intermediary of the artist, it has seized upon folds as something that can give meaning to works. Folds are both a form of expression and a source of inspiration for art.

Discovering the world of talented creators whose works are sometimes stunning by analysing similarities and differences is not sufficient to understand the relationship between beauty and folding. One has to go beyond the material form of the fold to understand its intention and purposes, whatever the form may be. Intention is what carries meaning—a dashed line on a sheet of paper, for example. Purpose is what makes the material breathe: the space that allows the fold. Folds are not merely an art form; they are a part of art!

Debates on art should not overshadow its true function: revealing that "what is essential is invisible to the eyes."

Folding as art opens a window onto the beauty of the world. Only the idea of beauty is interpreted—is haggled over, perhaps—but this is still only the surface of things. Beyond any scheme, beauty in this world remains a fundamental principle that sheds light on the folds of our soul. Beauty is manifested as an invisible force that pushes us to become aware of reality. Art is a deployment of beauties, so to speak; in this respect, like any fold, it firstly allows one to guess at only a small part of its true scope...

* Excerpt of an interview with Étienne Cliquet by Viviane Berty, president of the MFPP, in *Le Pli* n°135, "L'origami à l'intersection de multiples domaines de création. Pliages de papier et dépliés dans l'œuvre d'Étienne Cliquet."

ORIGAMI, A GIFT TO HUMANITY

"Is origami for some people just an activity that involves folding paper to pass the time and make approximate reproductions of existing things?
I will recall some of its different attributes, which, I hope, could trigger more detailed studies on this or that point.
Origami allows people to develop geometric sense and concentration.
Origami gives a taste of the pleasure of working as a team, together or separately, in order to produce a model, while not spoiling individual freedom.
Origami, both at the level of its approach and at that of its creations, does not discriminate based on age. (When I was younger, I could teach what I found out to older people, at the same time as I could be taught by those same people.)
Origami is yoga for the mind, in that it brings great serenity and great enthusiasm.
In terms of education, origami is a selfless sharing.
Origami releases us from the tyranny of the single act, which makes us believe that we can achieve a result in one go, whereas it is generally necessary to try again several times.
Origami demonstrates, from an ecological standpoint, that it is good to salvage ancient teachings, that the slightest piece of paper can be used for a great and often amusing work, that the surface does not need to be huge or valuable, but that it can be always used—at best, something can be applied to anything by analogy.
All that the world has given you is an expired metro ticket: you can make it into an elephant!
That is the ecology of salvaging!
And this leads to optimal use, with no waste!"

Excerpts from multiple reflections by Alain Georgeot, folder, member of the MFPP, Mouvement français des plieurs de papier (French Association for the Promotion of Origami), 2012.

www.mfpp-origami.fr

• "Jeu de patience" fortune teller, François Dulac collection.
• Traditional tessellations and folds, J.-Ch. Trebbi.
• Le Chat, wet fold by Yves Clavel based on a model by Giang Dinh.

Photo by Makoto Yamaguchi (Origami House)

• *Éric at work.*
• *A series of busts that are characteristic of his technique.*
• Buste souriant.

Éric Joisel

FRANCE (1956–2010)

This great master of modern origami developed a very special technique that deftly mixes folding and paper sculpture to produce outstanding works. A generous man, this magician of the fold took great pleasure in humorously conveying his knowledge at the annual conventions of associations that bringing enthusiasts together, such as the MFPP in France, the CDO in Italy, the BOS in England, OrigamiUSA, the associations of Germany and Japan, and the AEP, the Spanish association that wanted to pay tribute to him by dedicating a permanent exhibition to him in the halls of its museum in Zaragoza.

"Seeking to create a break with traditional, generally flat origami, I strive to create fully three-dimensional objects using the techniques of pleat folding and wet folding."

Éric Joisel

"As a teenager, Eric studied drawing, painting, modelling, pottery and later sculpture with wood and stone. Then he enrolled in art school...

He began doing origami in 1983, and four years later he exhibited for the first time at the Espace Japon de Paris with Usataro Kimura, a Japanese artist who introduced him to the art form. In 1992, he became a professional origamist, registered with the Maison des artistes association as a sculptor. From that date, he devoted his life to origami. To create his first animals (hedgehogs, snails, turtles, seahorses and pangolins), he used the pleat-folding technique. He firmly favoured an 'economy of paper': the fewest folds hidden inside a model, and the most paper on the outside.
The wet-folding method, inspired the Japanese master Akira Yoshizawa, allowed him to create models with curved folds in three dimensions. These truly were sculptures, and far removed from the models of classic folding. In his final pieces, *Le Seigneur des anneaux* and *La Commedia dell'arte,* he created his models in a single burst, improvising some aspects and details during the creation process. He also revisited the raw material, handmade paper, seeking 'colours' through relief in the motifs. Always looking for finer renderings, he was introduced to the wet folding technique and shaping sheets of handmade paper coated in methylcellulose.

Éric Joisel is known worldwide for having created very realistic models—real paper sculptures—some of which have been sold in Japan, the USA, Spain and other countries. He also spent nearly 20,000 hours teaching novices of all ages and group leaders in schools, libraries and shopping centres."

Remarks from Alain Joisel, who oversees the management and appreciation of his brother's works, November 2014.

www.ericjoisel.com
- "3D masks & busts," Éric Joisel, 58 pages, BOS, 1999.
- "Le tissu prend le pli," David Larousserie, *Sciences & Avenir,* August 2007, pp80-83.
- *Between the Folds - the Science of Art, the Art of Science*, documentary on origami directed by Vanessa Gould, 2008, Peabody Award winner, 2010 (greenfusefilms.com).
- *Éric Joisel: the magician of origami*, Makoto Yamaguchi, Origami House, Japan, November 2010.
- *Le Pli* the journal of the MFPP, n° 118-119-120, Éric Joisel special, 2011.
- *Éric Joisel, le magicien de l'origami*, catalogue of the Musée du Papier d'Angoulême, 2012.

• *These wonderful characters inspired by commedia dell'arte are based on a plethora of cleverly applied folding techniques.*

Photos by Makoto Yamaguchi (Origami House)

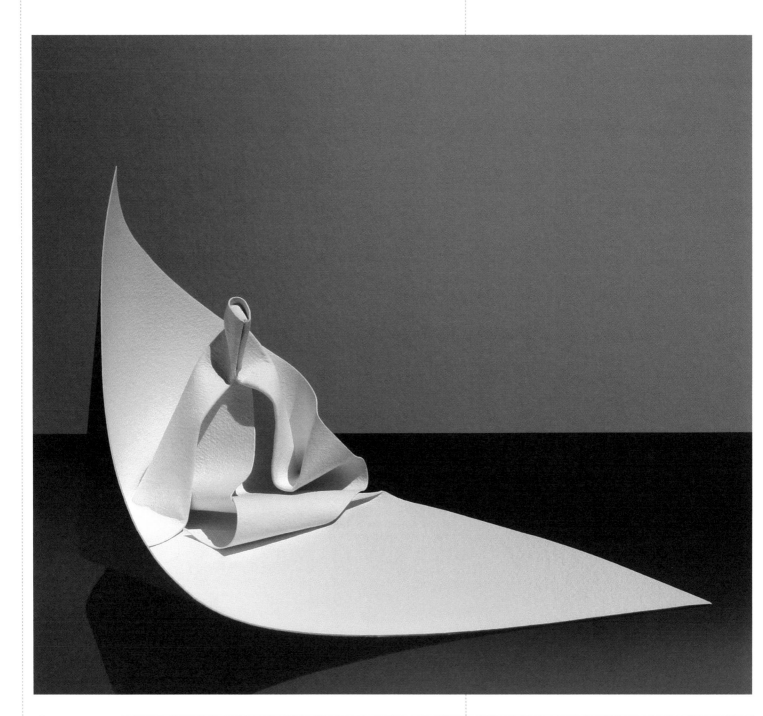

• Dreamer, *wet fold of a sheet of watercolour paper in triangular form, created in 2011, folded in 2014.*

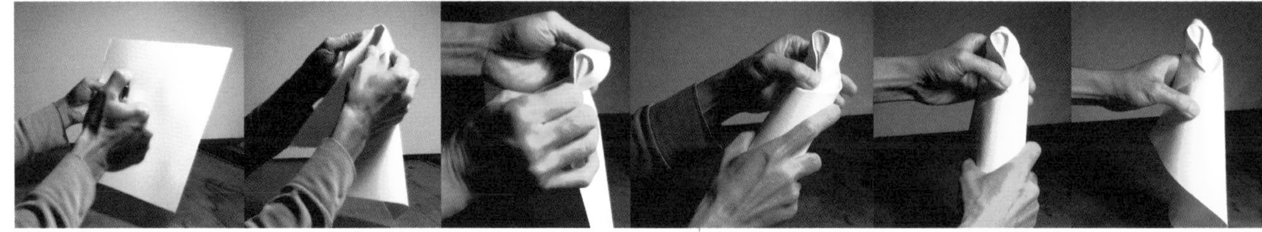

Giang Dinh

VIETNAM

Born in 1966 in Vietnam, Giang Dinh currently lives in Virginia, where he works as an architect.
He has been folding since he was a child, and he started producing origami in 1988. In his view, origami is a special type of sculpture that is only to be made through manipulating a sheet of paper—no more, no less. He strives for his artistic output to be simple and elegant.
His favourite quotation is: "It seems that perfection is attained, not when there is nothing more to add, but when there is nothing more to take away." (Antoine de Saint-Exupéry*).

"I always try to capture the essence of the subject with the fewest folds possible and the greatest spontaneity.
Most of my works are folded using moistened paper, a thick watercolour paper or hand-made paper. This technique known as wet folding involves dampening for the purposes of shaping. For certain pieces, when I need to combine different colours, I use acrylic paint instead of water or I paste two sheets of paper together with methylcellulose glue, which is made out of wood."

Remarks from Giang Dinh, October 2014.

* Antoine de Saint-Exupéry, *Terre des hommes*, Gallimard, France, 1939.

http://giangdinh.com

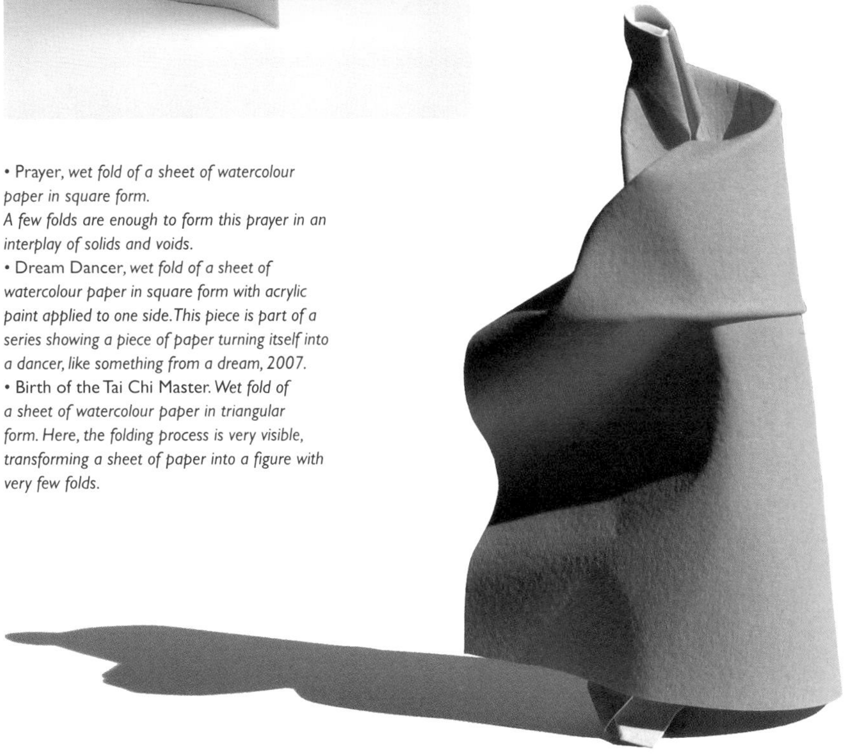

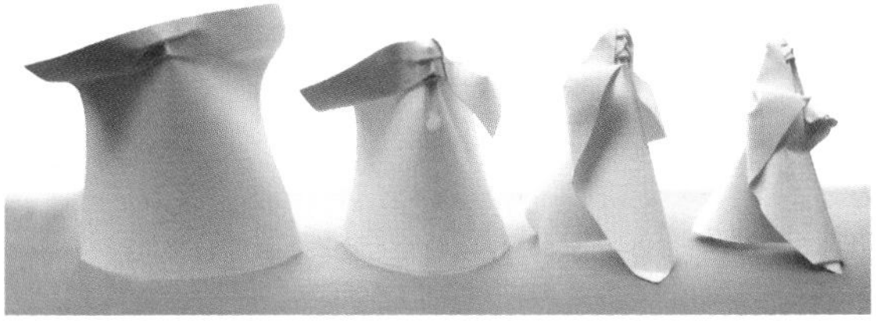

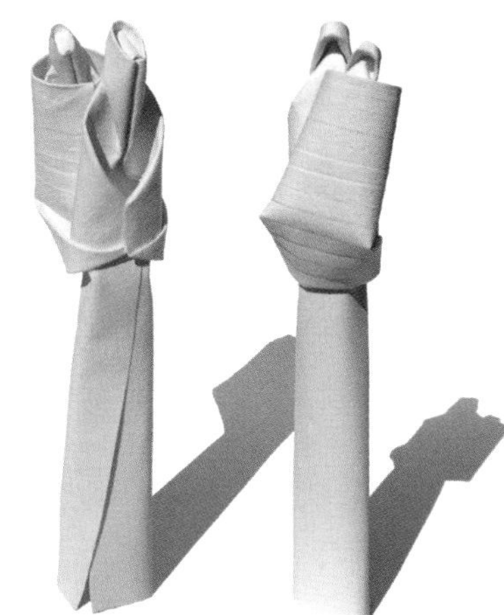

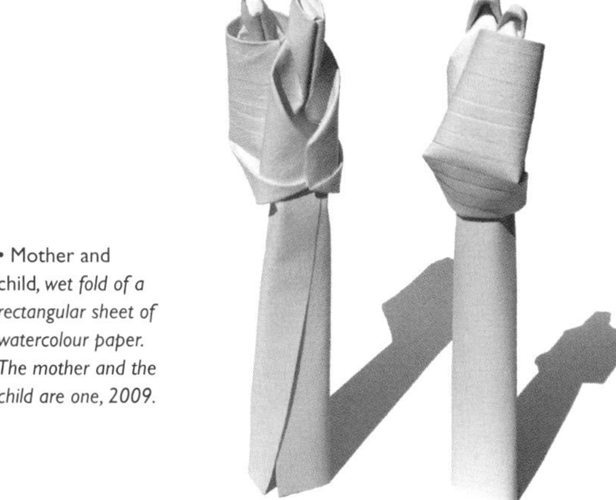

• Mother and child, *wet fold of a rectangular sheet of watercolour paper. The mother and the child are one, 2009.*

• Prayer, *wet fold of a sheet of watercolour paper in square form. A few folds are enough to form this prayer in an interplay of solids and voids.*
• Dream Dancer, *wet fold of a sheet of watercolour paper in square form with acrylic paint applied to one side. This piece is part of a series showing a piece of paper turning itself into a dancer, like something from a dream, 2007.*
• Birth of the Tai Chi Master. *Wet fold of a sheet of watercolour paper in triangular form. Here, the folding process is very visible, transforming a sheet of paper into a figure with very few folds.*

Li Hongbo

CHINA

Chinese artist Li Hongbo's sculptures are made entirely out of tissue paper. At first sight these busts, bodies and skulls appear solid. But they are made of hundreds of layers of stacked paper, and they are actually soft and unfoldable. Taking inspiration from traditional Chinese toys made from paper, this artist reproduces everyday objects and shapes. They can move, bend or stretch out.

"When I started to study painting seriously, I began by working with plaster models, and throughout my years of study, I have continued to do so. The models would stand there indefinitely, without saying a word, and I could manipulate them as much as I wanted to. Sometimes, I painted them beautifully, whereas at other times they looked hideous and even broken. But they never complained. To this day, they are my most loyal friends.

I sought out the most sensitive and warmest way to remember this period. I used paper, the material that I am most familiar with, to remake these study tools, so as to revive those memories in my heart. The static models from my past were immutable and impassive. However, by pasting, cutting and polishing my material, I made sculptures that resemble my old models in all respects—appearance, profile and even colour—while they remain in a static state. However, some basic essentials have changed; they are not frozen like plaster models any more. They can now be stretched, reversed, and transformed in the hands of those who manipulate them. And they have now returned to me as friends, even after all these years. They have become the new medium for my artistic creation, as well as the beginning of new opportunities."

Remarks from Li Hongbo for the Klein Sun Gallery, November 2014.

✏ Li Hongbo has also exhibited at the Klein Sun Gallery in New York.
✏ www.kleinsungallery.com/artist/Li_Hongbo/works/

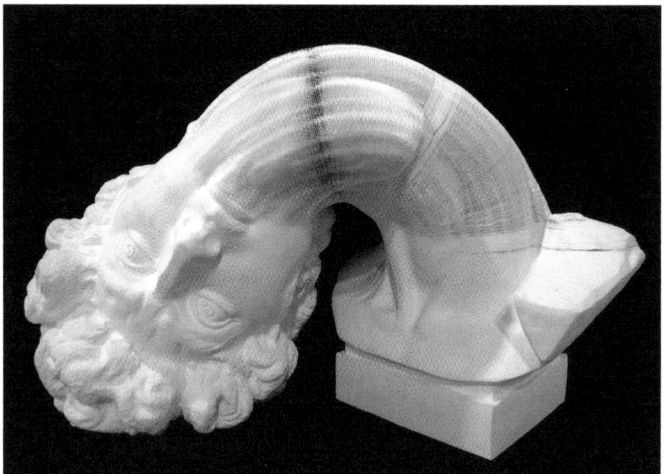

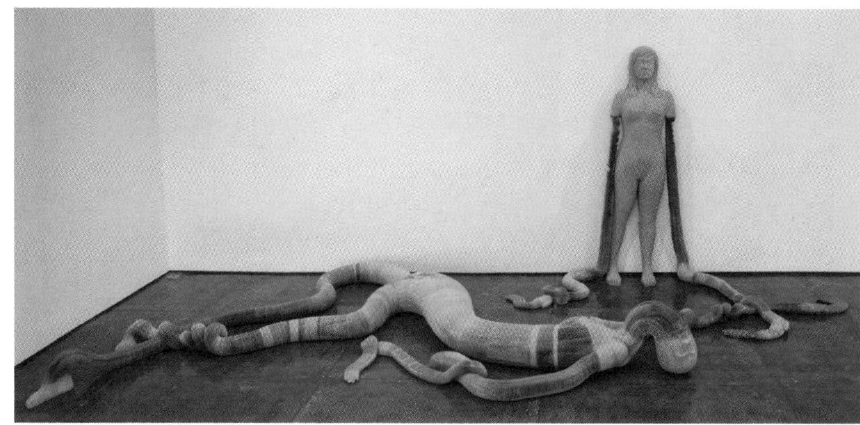

• *Bust of David and its spectacular unfolding, paper, 2012.*
• Girls, *paper, 2010.*

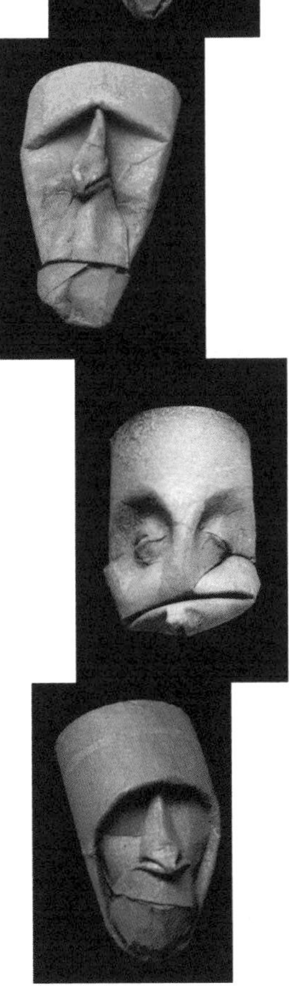

• *Masks made from rolls of toilet paper.*

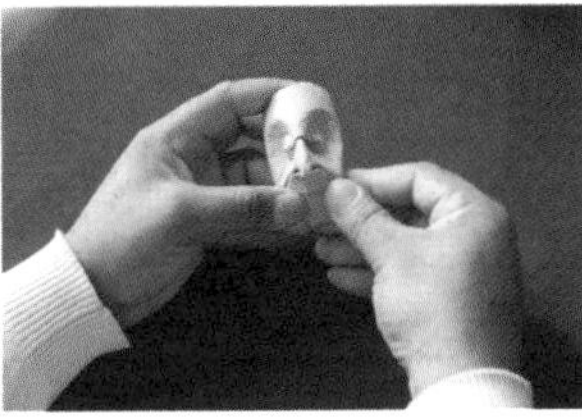

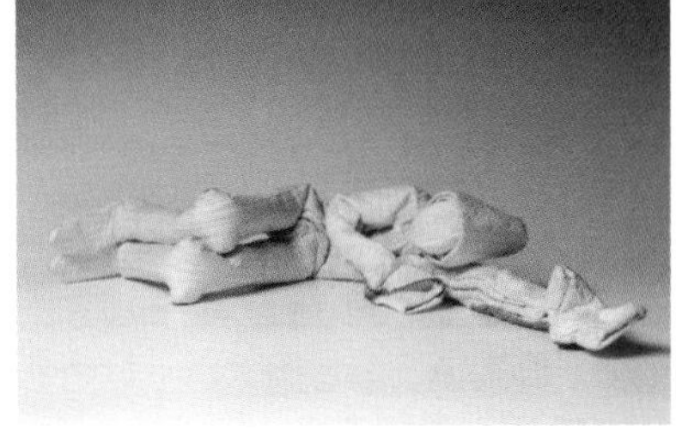

• *Paper man.*

Junior Fritz Jacquet

FRANCE

Oznoon: the fold as mirror of the soul

The masks emerged from a wacky project between origami friends: making use rolls of toilet paper. This is an obvious reference to the "upcycling" world: the roll, the most measly material imaginable, must be enhanced through the technique. This artist took seven years to familiarize himself with this technique: "Knowing how to make a roll of toilet paper smile" is what makes this adventure unique.
For Junior, the key is having a skilled eye, with a given type of material dictating the form:
"Creativity is born out of raw materials," he says. This creator sees folds as a necessity. As part of the genesis of his creations, he allows the surfaces through which forms with multiple expressions are born to be divided. The word "ply" means "fold," and as such, he says, "We often forget that multiply means to ply several times."

Remarks from Junior Fritz Jacquet, January 2015.

* CRIMP, Centre de recherche international de modélisation par le pli.

www.oznoon.fr

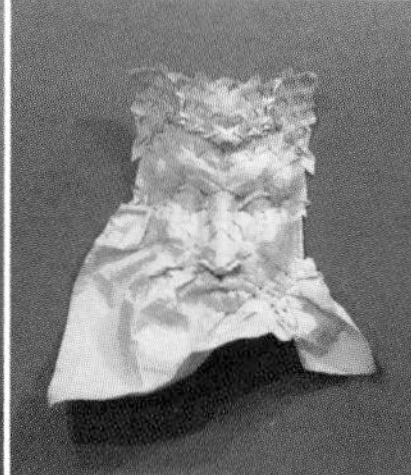

Joel Cooper

USA

Joel Cooper studied fine arts at the University of Kansas, and in particular traditional painting techniques and bronze casting. He had done origami as a hobby since childhood, but he had no idea at the time about incorporating this practice into his other artistic activities.

"Around the year 2000, I was introduced to 'tessellations,' which apply pure geometry to the art of paper folding. This appealed to my love of mathematics and engineering, and for the first time, I started to create my own original origami works. Although, by definition, 'tessellation origami' involves the regular division of a two-dimensional plane, I soon discovered that the techniques of folding and twisting could be used to create three-dimensional surfaces. My initial training had placed emphasis on figurative work, and so it came naturally to me to use these new origami techniques to create human forms. My first masks date from 2003. For each model, new elements are introduced and reworked until a satisfactory combination is reached. I do not use any diagram, written outline or computer program—only folding.

There are no cuts or glue, but the technique is unusual because the mask is not built from the inside like most origami is, but from a central base form. I think of these masks as 'topological origami'. There is no point of departure or steps to follow. I can start at any place on a sheet of paper and work outward until the entire surface is transformed."

www.joelcooper.wordpress.com

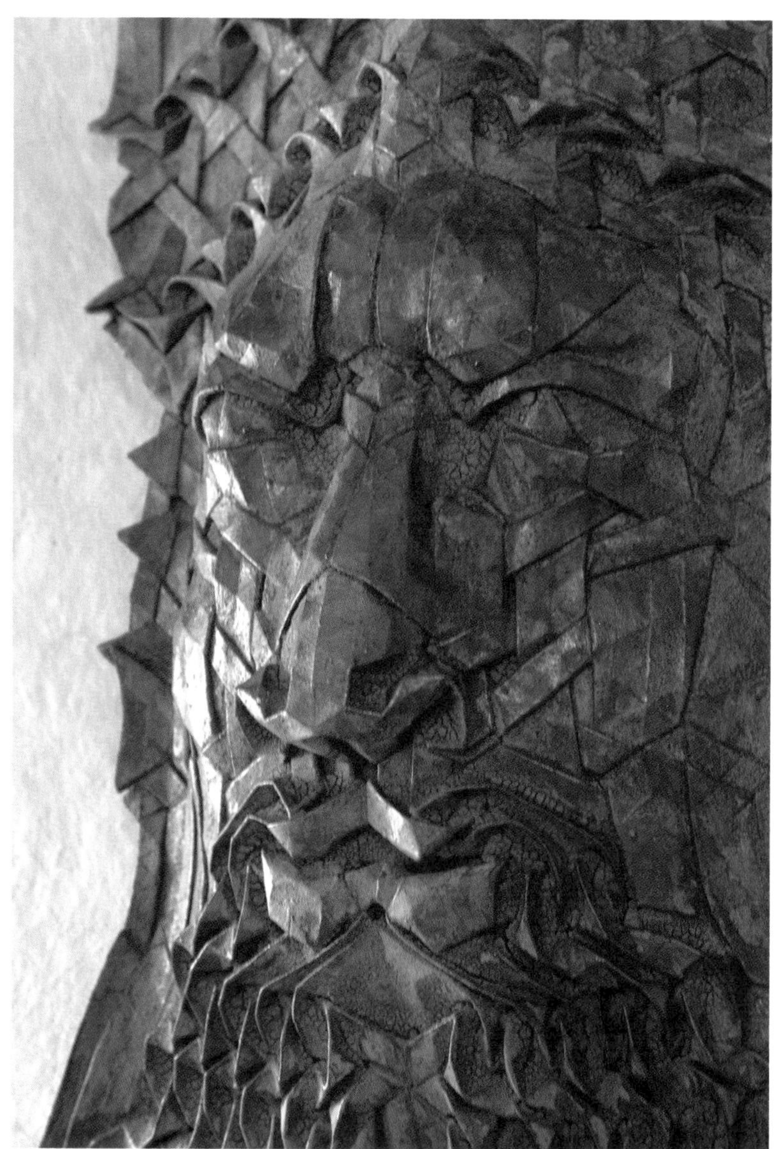

• The shape of the mask is created through the tension and strength of the paper, so a certain rigidity is required. The paper is folded and refolded on the same lines, and it must be strong and flexible. Joel works with paper that is normally used in bookbinding for flyleafs. It is well suited to wet folding. Each piece is completed through the addition of paints, dyes, inks and lacquer that prevents the paper expanding or opening up over time.

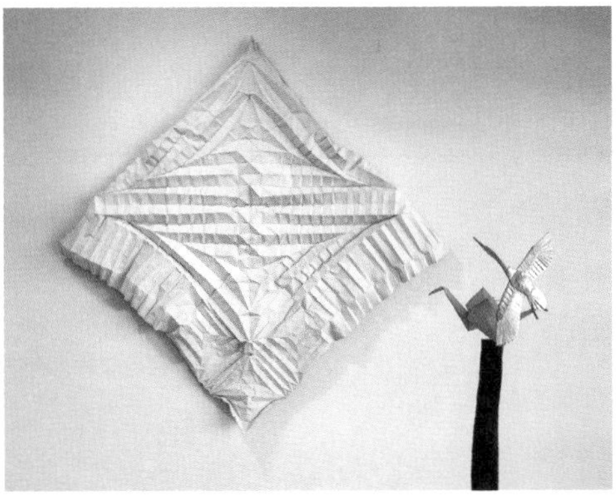

• *Robert J. Lang and Kevin Box,* Phoenix Rising, Opus #563, *Crease pattern of a crane and a metal creation of it, Selby Fleetwood Gallery, 2013.*
• *Robert J. Lang and Kevin Box,* Flight of Folds Monument, *moulded stainless steel with a powdered finish, Selby Fleetwood Gallery, 2013.*
• *Robert J. Lang and Kevin Box,* White Bison Monument, *metal sculpture, 2011.*
These sculptures by Robert J. Lang were turned into bronze castings, which he has made since 2008 in collaboration with Kevin Box. The technique employed is a variant of the lost wax process that has been adapted to use the folded paper originals rather than wax or clay models.

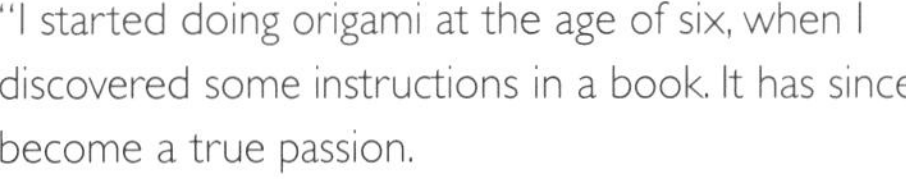

Robert J. Lang

USA

"I started doing origami at the age of six, when I discovered some instructions in a book. It has since become a true passion.

For me, art, origami and science are inextricably linked. I use mathematical principles to create many of my models, and conversely, many of my mathematical explorations of origami are guided by aesthetic or artistic objectives.

Working as a consultant, my goal is to develop the folding model that meets the needs of the application. Product development of any kind in the real world often requires a great deal of engineering and expertise in many areas. Origami is usually a small part of the sum of what is required, even if it often provides the most effective, most compact or most low-cost solution to an engineering problem.

For my creations of so-called 'natural' subjects, I find particular inspiration in nature itself; for my more geometric or abstract works, a mathematical principle is often the trigger. I want to create a new class of structure that requires a sort of mathematical problem to be solved.

For my figurative creations such as animals, I begin with the subject, and I then break it down into the different elements that constitute it. I then make choices about the way in which the parts will be represented. After that, I move on to tracing 'patterns' of all the individual pieces on a sheet of paper, in the most economical way possible.

From this sketch, I construct a folding diagram, which I use as a guide. For abstract geometric works, I develop a mathematical model for the desired shape, while for works of figurative art, I break the form into several 'construction blocks' that I can represent through mathematical models."

Interview with Robert J. Lang, January 2015.

- www.langorigami.com
- www.outsidetheboxstudio.com
- www.selbyfleetwoodgallery.com

Madjid Esfini

FRANCE

Niloufar: *alchemy of the fold.*

"From iron to paper, I explore the writing of ephemeral architectures." *Madjid Esfini, January 2015.*

Madjid Esfini is an artist who is inspired by materials and architecture. In his works, he combines paper and metal and recreates an almost organic symbiosis. In his workshop in Montpellier, he casts paper as though it were specialist concrete. The setting process produces a tension over an iron framework that curves. The folds are caused by a subtle alchemy that the sculptor combines with constantly repeated movements that are nevertheless reinterpreted each time.

Niloufar are fragile and solid apparitions driven by the movement of air. On the border between poetry, architecture and music, these folded sculptures express the tension of heaviness and lightness.

Having left Iran during troubled times, Madjid Esfini arrived in France and studied architecture. Through light installations, he tells us about his journey into art. A poet of forms, he invents an organic language through the mechanism of a paper skin that stretches out and becomes flesh on a metal skeleton. This slow process of morphogenesis is the result of constant attention at the moment of transforming the material.

It's a very different approach to folds than dry folding.

Here, the fold is created in a mould, and armatures produce it: but it is when the paper paste sets that the folded surface is formed through shrinkage.

www.madjidesfini.wix.com/atelier

• Niloufar, *paper and metal, 2015.*

Andrey Ermakov

RUSSIA

For Andrey Ermakov, origami is an art form that allows self-expression and the discovery of an "unknown world." His strange insects express movement and the protective function of the fold. Andrey usually uses Xuan Chinese rice paper or Hanji traditional Korean paper when folding his models. He also uses papers that have been treated with methylcellulose or that consist of multiple layers glued together with polyvinyl acetate (PVA).

Remarks from Andrey Ermakov, January 2015.

www.flickr.com/photos/origamiru/
International Origami Olympiad: www.snkhan.co.uk/forum/viewtopic.php?f=16&t=12530

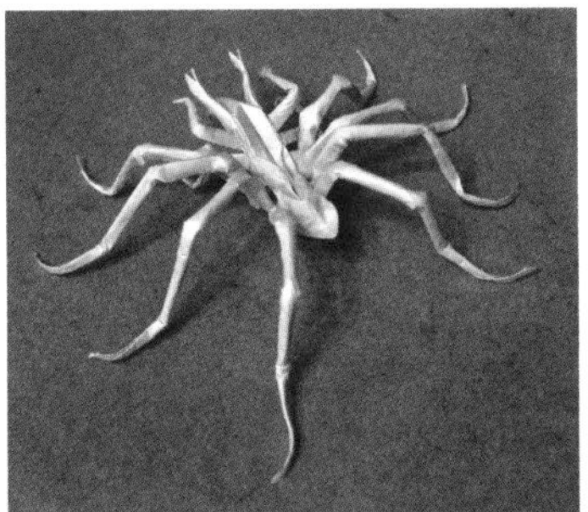

• Butterfly op.25 vers. 2. *Each of the butterfly's folds is arranged in a way that emphasizes the notion of fragility.*
• Arthropods op.80#1 (Pantopoda). *Because the legs are extremely fine and long, the model is folded using very thin paper.*

• Pleurottes de l'olivier.

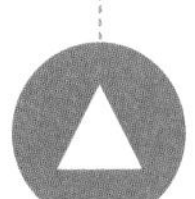

Vincent Floderer

FRANCE

Vincent Floderer is one of the founders of the CRIMP (Centre de recherche international de modélisation par le pli).

"From his intimacy with the paper, a soft, docile and resistant material made of folds, bends, air, light and sometimes colours is born. Under the pressure of his fingers and under his watchful eye, it is transformed into a multitude of creations. Vincent Floderer reappropriates nature or gives birth to new forms. From his hands, frogs, fish, shellfish, mushrooms, grains of pollen, corals, sponges, branches and other extravagant things emerge. Whether tiny or gigantic, all these creations are inhabited and this inner life that moves them makes them infinitely alive and fragile to us."

Text by Aline Jaulin, Paris, October 2013 (excerpt).

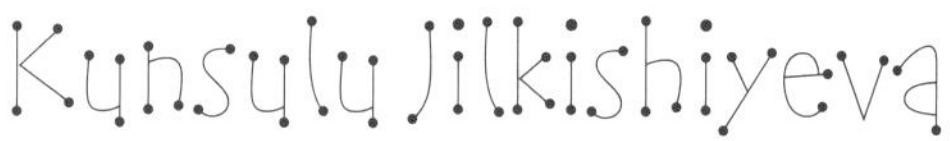

TURKEY

"Learning how to design an origami model is a never-ending process: the more you learn, the more you realize how little you know.
The International Origami Olympiad organized by Andrey Ermakov really helped me to flourish. It opened the doors of the magical world of this art to me, and origami subsequently became not only a hobby but also a lifestyle.
Once the inspiration has come, the technical part of the design begins. For the main layout of the template, I use the TreeMaker software developed by Robert Lang. This tool helps me to place the template in the square of paper."

Remarks from Kunsulu Jilkishiyeva, January 2015.

www.flickr.com/photos/sunny_marmalade

• *Kunsulu Jilkishiyeva in her studio.*
• Horselaugh *Designed and folded for the monthly challenge of the Origami Forum (http://snkhan.co.uk).*
This model is technically not very complex, but the challenge was to express the emotion of laughter in the face, January 2014.
• Hermit Crab *inspired by Éric Joisel's shell, playing with logarithmic spirals, October 2014.*

Victor Cœurjoly

SPAIN

Victor Cœurjoly has been folding since the age of six or seven; it's something that he grew up with. "My inspiration came from my passions, music and mathematics. And then in discovering other interests I have able to fold more mature pieces. I learned technical drawing, which I almost always use to design my works. Rarely, though more and more frequently, I fold in a disorderly manner by improvising. I have been able to experience very deep sensations through folding, and, looking back, I feel that my works are part of me.
Regarding the processes and materials that I use, over time I have lost the fear of experimenting. The more knowledge of techniques that I gained, the more I ventured into new ways of folding and new materials. Currently, I use thin or thick paper, plastic or metal. The things that I fold with include tools, folding machines, chemicals and hot air."

Remarks from Victor Coeurjoly, January 2015.

www.flickr.com/photos/31034209@N04/

• Ciérbol. *"Some of my works are self-portraits, not in terms of form but of depth. This was made at the time when I started to have faith in my decisions and my actions."*
• *This sheep model explores the technique of wrinkling.*
• Manazas *or the instinct of a being that wishes to express itself with its hands.*

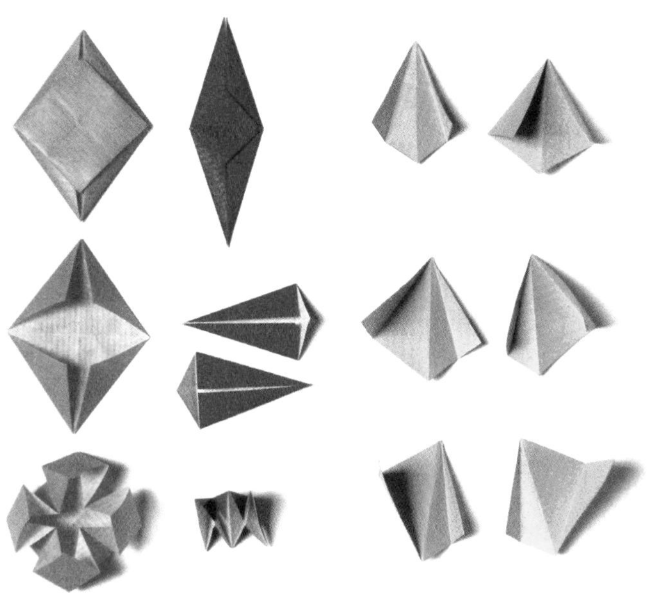

• Quilts Penrose rhombic quilt *(opus LIX), kraft paper.*
• *Tessellation variant* Penrose.
• Aller/retour *Beige tessellation created from a square of elephant-hide paper.*
• Les Oies sauvages *Tessellation, detail, created from a triangle of elephant-hide paper.*
• Migration fractale, *variant of* Oies sauvages *from a triangle of elephant-hide paper.*

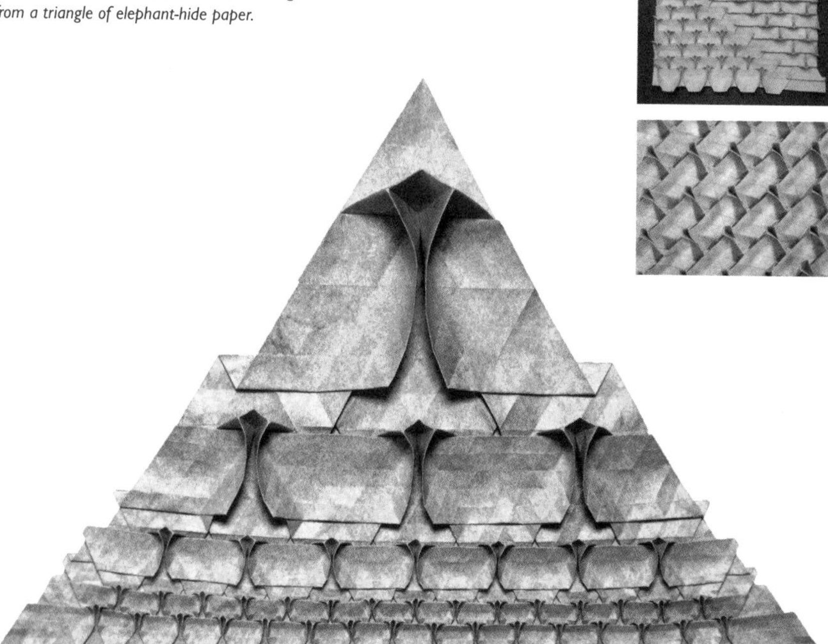

Christiane Bettens (alias Mélisande)

SWITZERLAND

"In Latin, is the word *tessella* refers to geometric fragments that comprise a mosaic. Tessellation refers to paving, to the whole formed by the tessellas.
I discovered this type of origami during my research on nonfigurative foldings. At the time (2004-2005), information was scarce and scattered: an image-based tutorial of Fujimoto's pyramid of squares (his pamphlets had not yet been republished), and images and information on the sites of Tom Hull, Andy Wilson, Alex Bateman, Peter Budai, Helena Verrill and Chris Palmer. With a bit of perseverance, these resources allowed me to master the basic techniques. I felt that there was still great unexplored potential in this area, so I started to do the groundwork on my own. And then one day I came across a certain Éric Gjerde's photo gallery—and bingo! There was someone across the Atlantic whose quest overlapped with mine. I got in touch with him, and so began an adventure whose magnitude we were not expecting; there was a Flickr group of over 1,000 members, a book and meetings on three continents. Art and architecture are inexhaustible sources of inspiration. Roman mosaics, tiles in churches, decorations in mosques: geometric patterns are everywhere, and all we have to do is open our eyes. One day, while rummaging around the digital archives of the University of Wisconsin, I found an old black-and-white image of a dome of a mosque in Toledo, whose vaulting formed an irregular octagonal star (which is my avatar on Flickr). In continuing my investigations, I learnt that this mosque, built in the year 999 and currently used as the narthex of a church, has nine domes.
I will not give up until I have a picture of each of them—they are all different. Finally, I folded the nine patterns and I hope to have the opportunity to go to Toledo to see this building one day."

Excerpt from an interview in Le Pli, *"L'origami des tessellations," n°133, 2014.*

www.origami-art.org/blog/
www.flickr.com/photos/melisande-origami

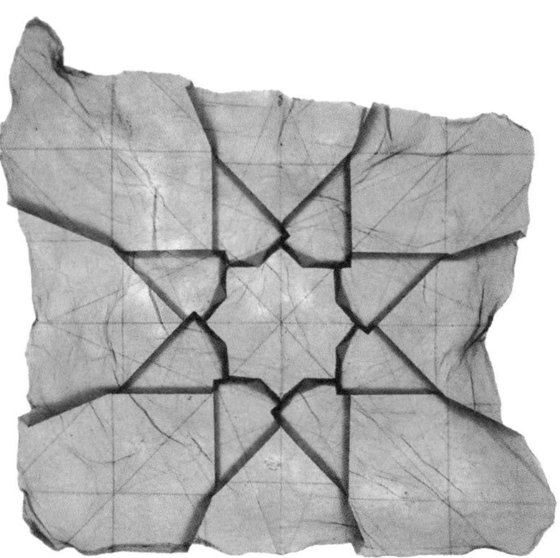

Éric Gjerde

USA

The transparency of tessellations

Éric Gjerde chose to return to his childhood love: paper. He works mainly on the geometric folds of tessellations, produced with a single sheet of paper. A repetitive base frame (equilateral triangles, squares, hexagons and so on) is first marked with folds, and the sheet is then unfolded. The stage of folding of the tessellation itself then takes place on this base frame: folds overlap and are superposed in a twisting motion. In his works, Éric frequently plays with the transparency of the paper, which, through the superimposed layers, subtly highlights the geometric design.

For some time now, he has been developing a new process for manufacturing organic paper, which he uses for his creations.

www.ericgjerde.com
www.origamitessellations.com

- Gnosis.
- Hexakaidecagon.
- *Biopaper experiments.*
- *Studies inspired by Voronoi polygons.*

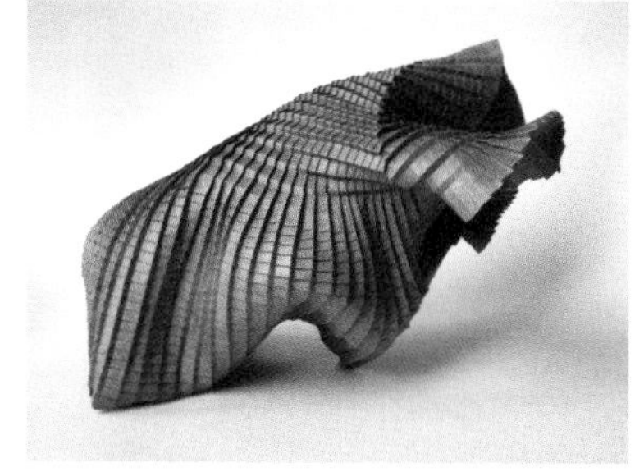

• This 2014 series is made from metallic elephant-hide paper, and each model is on average between 23 and 45 cm (9 and 18 in) in height.

Goran Konjevod

CROATIA

"A mathematician by training, I started to design my own pieces long after I had started folding complex origami. Initially, I needed to understand how the order in which the folds are made has a bearing on the tension in the folded model, thus producing a three-dimensional shape.
I like to break origami's usual rules. I do not fold slowly and cautiously; I almost always work as quickly as possible. I have come to intentionally ignore errors of accuracy, including even in the order of folds. sometimes I use inappropriate material—for example, paper that is too thin or too thick. I increasingly work with metal. This includes the casting of sculptures in bronze and iron for which paper serves as the original model, as well as working directly with metal using traditional techniques (straightening/forming with a hammer) and other more modern ones such as foldforming."
This technique, invented at the end of the 1980s by Charles Lewton-Brain, involves working sheet metal in several stages: the metal is folded repeatedly, forged several times and annealed, and then unfolded, at which point a new three-dimensional form has generally been achieved.

Remarks from Goran Konjevod, January 2015.

www.organicorigami.com

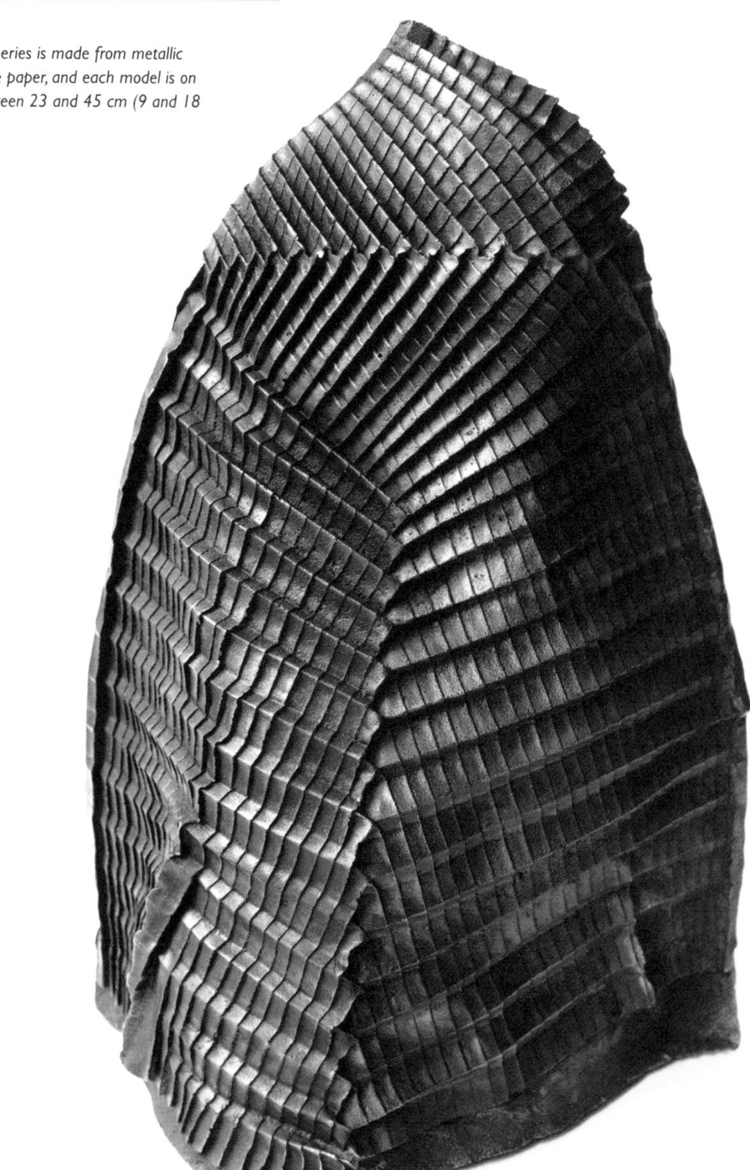

• Cliff. Bronze, *45x33x20 cm (17 3/4 x 13 x 7 7/8 in in). Casting based on an original paper model.*

Paul Jackson

ENGLAND / ISRAEL

The folder's "digital" art.

Initially, Paul Jackson made origami as a creative pastime while he was still a child. While studying art in London in the 1960s-1970s, one of his teachers wanted to see his folding. He rejected all of it: "Back then, origami was not considered to be part of the canons of art, which was a surprising position for a liberal institution like an art school: I decided to become an origamist out of rebellion!"

In 1981, nobody was doing anything serious with origami in Europe. There were just amateur hobbyists who were interested a bit by its exoticness. However, Paul decided to make it his profession. Because he had a good understanding of the mathematical principles behind folding, he contacted many design schools specializing in jewellery, architecture, furniture and so forth to offer his services as a teacher. Through doing so, he clinched his first commissions, such as the production of a stop-motion film for Citroën.

As a sculptural artist, this methodical approach to form has oriented him towards abstraction and allowed him to make connections with many movements such as the systemic movement in England and minimalist art. "We give ourselves rules that we make part of the creative process and conceptual reflection on art," he says.

For Paul's art, design or architecture students, who are surrounded by computers nowadays, folding is a simple and fun way to understand mathematics and forms "because you can do it yourself with your hands." Etymologically, "digital" means made with digits on our hands; we think that we live in the "digital" age, but origami is the original "digital" art!

www.origami-artist.com

Paul Jackson is an artist, teacher and prolific author. His great interest in educating has led him to publish a considerable number of origami books. His titles include: *Tricks and Games with Paper*, Angus & Robertson, 1985; *Step-by-Step Origami*, Acropolis Books, 1993; *The Art and Craft of Paper Sculpture* Quarto, 1996; *Incredible Action Origami*, Michael O'Mara Books, 2000.

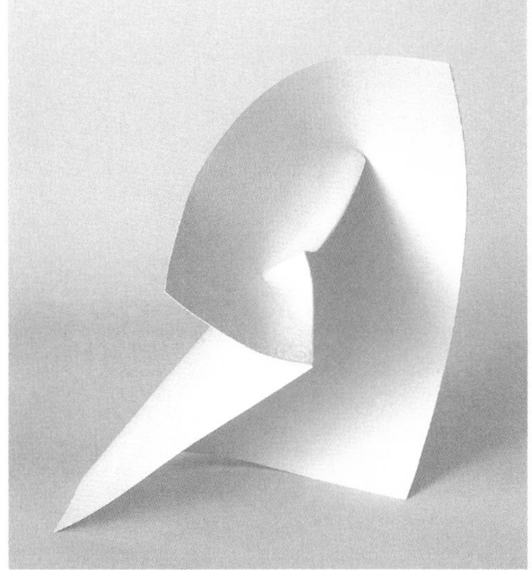

• *Works from the* Organic Abstraits, *series, comprising over 250 pieces (1990-2015). These pieces, made from newsprint stained with dry pastel, are inspired by forms such as bacteria or shells. Each model measures on average between 10 and 20 cm (4 and 8 in) in height.*
• One Crease *series, an exploration of the formation of a single fold on a sheet of paper. Square copier paper with 20 cm (8 in) sides.*

"From the moment when the curved folds are formed, the paper takes on a form of natural equilibrium. These equilibria are still poorly understood. We are studying what forms are possible in this kind of self-folding origami, in particular in order to consider applications for deployable structures and structures of other kinds."

• Part of Ocean Series, *Mi-Teintes watercolour paper, 2012. This series of around 20 pieces was exhibited, with Theo Jansen's work, at the Simons Center for Geometry and Physics Art Gallery, Stony Brook, in New York in 2012.*

• *Piece from the* Curved crease sculpture *series, elephant-hide paper, 2011.*

• *Duncan McClellan Gallery, St. Petersburg, Florida, 2013.*

Erik and Martin Demaine

USA

Erik Demaine is part of the Computer Science and Artificial Intelligence Laboratory at Massachusetts Institute of Technology (MIT).

His great curiosity that combines scientific and playful approaches led to his being made a professor at MIT at the age of just twenty.

"I became interested in folding when I started my PhD in 1996. Folding offered difficult geometric problems that could nevertheless be solved with calculations. Folding is exciting for me nowadays because this is the ideal area for combining science and art. We regularly explore folding problems without knowing what we will produce: research or sculpture, or ideally both. I always work collaboratively, most often with my father, Martin Demaine. We use our mathematical research to inspire new sculptures, and we use sculpture to help us to understand research problems.

We do a lot of back and forth on each piece, combining our two 'voices' in something that neither of us could make individually.

We work primarily with watercolour paper, often using machines (plotters and laser cutting machines) to assist us in the production of the models, but currently all our sculptures are made entirely by hand."

Remarks from Erik Demaine, December 2014.

www.erikdemaine.org

Jun Mitani

JAPAN

Jun Mitani is a professor in the Department of Computer Science at the University of Tsukuba in Japan.

He began studying geometric modelling in the field of computer graphics in the late 1990s.

"Since 2005, I have been designing origami works with my own software. I am interested especially in curved origami, which is difficult to produce without a computer. The combining of mathematics and computer science is what has allowed me to create my origami works.

I always use curved folds to design my three-dimensional works. For me, the process of designing new origami starts with the development of new software. Since I began working with 3D origami, I have therefore developed several computer programs. Creating a universal modelling tool remains a very difficult challenge. As a result, each of my software packages can handle a specific area of aspects of origami. With the help of a computer, I can quickly perform tests on screen without folding paper for real. This is a significant advantage when it comes to studying the feasibility of a model."

Remarks from Jun Mitani, October 2014.

www.mitani.cs.tsukuba.ac.jp/en/

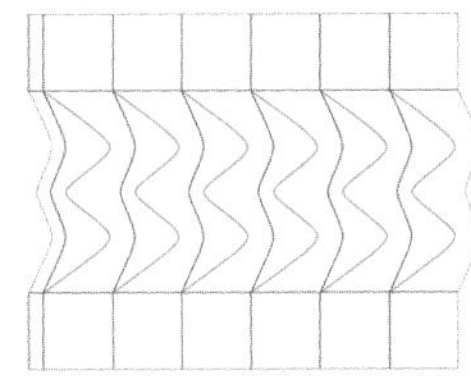

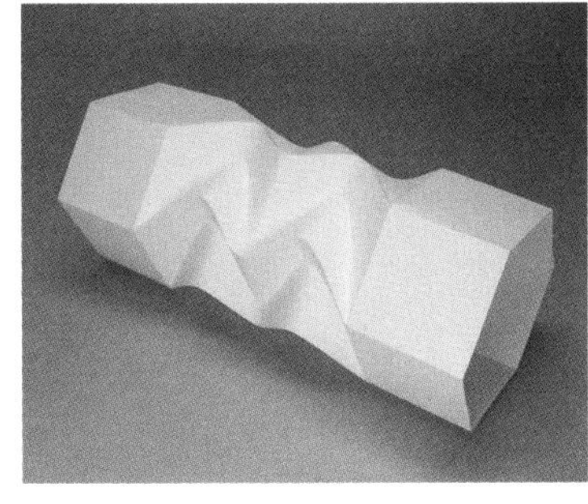

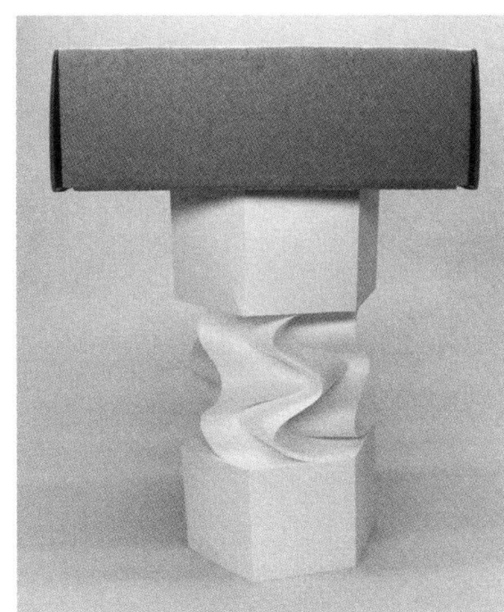

- Relief of helix.
- *Assemblage of two spheres.*
- Origami spring *and its pattern.*

Polly Verity

ENGLAND

"As the daughter of artists, there was always a large selection of paper at hand, and from my childhood I grew up enjoying folding. I use this material because it is a delicate and non-deformable (elastic) support medium. Its properties of rigidity and inelasticity mean that there are certain rules to follow when folding. These rules can be derived from mathematical formulas or found by experimentation, the method that I have chosen. In theory, there is an infinite number of possibilities when it comes to folding a sheet of paper. I look to make works with strong visual geometric dynamics.

The more that I can repeat a pattern, the better it is. First of all, I fold many models to find a curved form that appeals to me. I carefully unmake the model and record the folds using a line drawing on the computer. When the outline of folds is ready, I send the drawing to a CNC cutting machine (whose tiny blade can cut paper very gently). I then fold along the incised lines and examine the resulting fold. I redo the process until I am satisfied with the result. Paper and card are delicate and light. Sometimes, the job calls for something more robust, and so I use a sheet of polypropylene.

Having first worked with straight folds, I enthusiastically discovered curved ones. I always find this process unpredictable. Many of my experiments with curves fail, but when something works, a relief will jump out in such a sudden and surprising way. The observer will find it difficult to believe that it is simply folded into a flat and uncut sheet."

Remarks from Polly Verity, December 2014.

www.polyscene.com

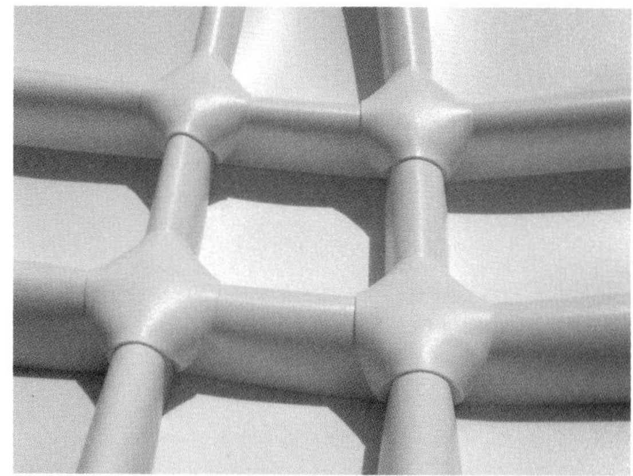

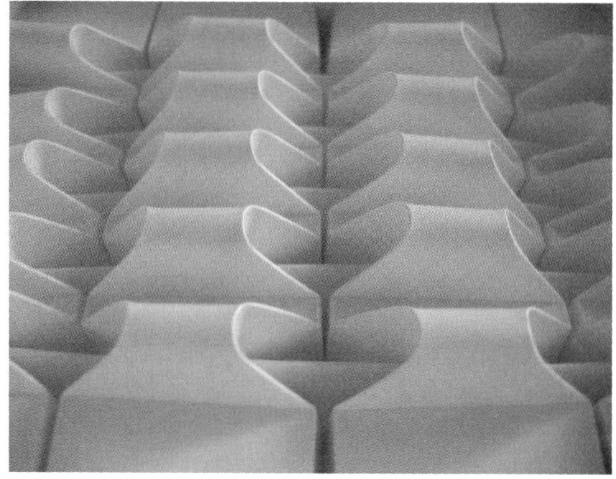

- *Tubes and connections.*
- Twisted Band.
- Nested Curves.

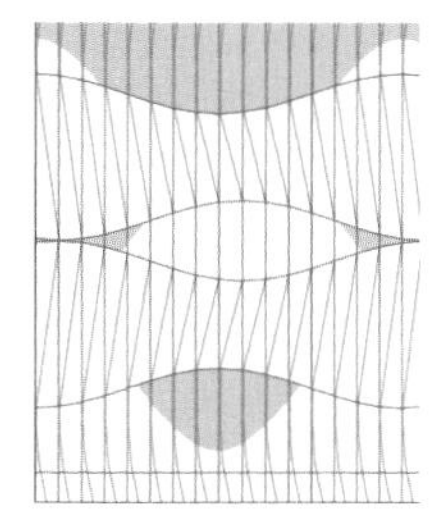

Stefan Weber

GERMANY

"At the age of thirty, tired of a monotonous life, I wanted to live outdoors, and origami allowed me to earn some cash. In the street, I would fold animals when I was asked in the space of a few minutes. It was not possible for me to use diagrams because the folding of most existing animals required too many steps to be accomplished in five minutes, or the animals were not realistic enough for people to pay even a few euros for them. I therefore developed my own models without any knowledge of origami techniques. Within three months, I was able to make a whole set of animals or flowers in less than ten minutes. While I was in the street, origami artists who discovered my creations were so surprised about the rapidity with which I could fold any animal that they invited me to participate in a major origami conference.
I've lived exclusively off origami for fifteen years, as a street entertainer, living outdoors like a homeless person. Thanks to origami, these have been beautiful and unforgettable years."

Remarks from Stefan Weber, January 2015.

www.origami-live.de/main.html
www.youtube.com/user/origamilive

• *Sculpture.*
• *Bird.*

• Double Diagonal Shift Vase 3
and corresponding framework of folds.

Rebecca Gieseking

USA

Drawn to both origami's aesthetic qualities and a mathematical challenge, Rebecca creates series of vases from paper, using straight and curved folds. The precise design of the model on graph paper allows her to predict the future dimensions of the piece and the way in which the folds will fit together. Before folding, Rebecca paints the paper with diluted acrylic paint, which is applied based on the position of the folds. The sinusoidal lines drawn on the flat paper then turn into straight lines on the folded surface.

Remarks from Rebecca Gieseking, November 2014.

www.rebecca.gieseking.us
www.rebecca.gieseking.us/2013/07/tutorial-folding-pleated-forms/

Richard Sweeney

ENGLAND

Richard Sweeney works with paper, particularly through the use of curved folds. His output is varied. Depending on the commission, his expertise allows him to express himself through drawing, sculpture or photography. His works are both geometrically controlled and sensual.

From this marriage between logic and sensitive intuition, emotion is born. The curved fold is something "magical" because our mind is not familiar with the relationship that is possible through folding between the continuous flat surface of paper and the curved surface turned into a volume by the artist.

Richard wishes to maintain an experimental approach in which working by hand has its place. His sculptures have as their starting point the intrinsic properties of the material that will be given form. Inspired by nature, the forms that he produces seem to have their own unique existence.

www.richardsweeney.co.uk

• Bone.
• Cube Press.
• Icosahedron II.

Thierry Berthomier

FRANCE (1944–2010)

Thierry Berthomier was an architect and a professor at the École d'architecture de Paris-Villemin, where he rubbed shoulders in particular with Jean-Marie Delarue and became involved in the MFPP. He then worked in Montpellier between 1991 and 2010, where he contributed to the creation of the Archiwaste collective.

Thierry Berthomier worked on folding and geometry based on a very particular angle of approach: the folded straight strip, a point of departure that caught his attention. "A pencil for drawing in space," is how he expressed his interest in the folding of paper strips. He methodically explored the many ways to fold a strip of paper and to assemble them together. To make "his arrays," he worked out and produced many polyhedra, alternating between different methods: he sometimes assembled the strips at the edges of the polyhedra, and sometimes at their vertices. The strips were sometimes folded in half lengthwise, then forming chevron folds.

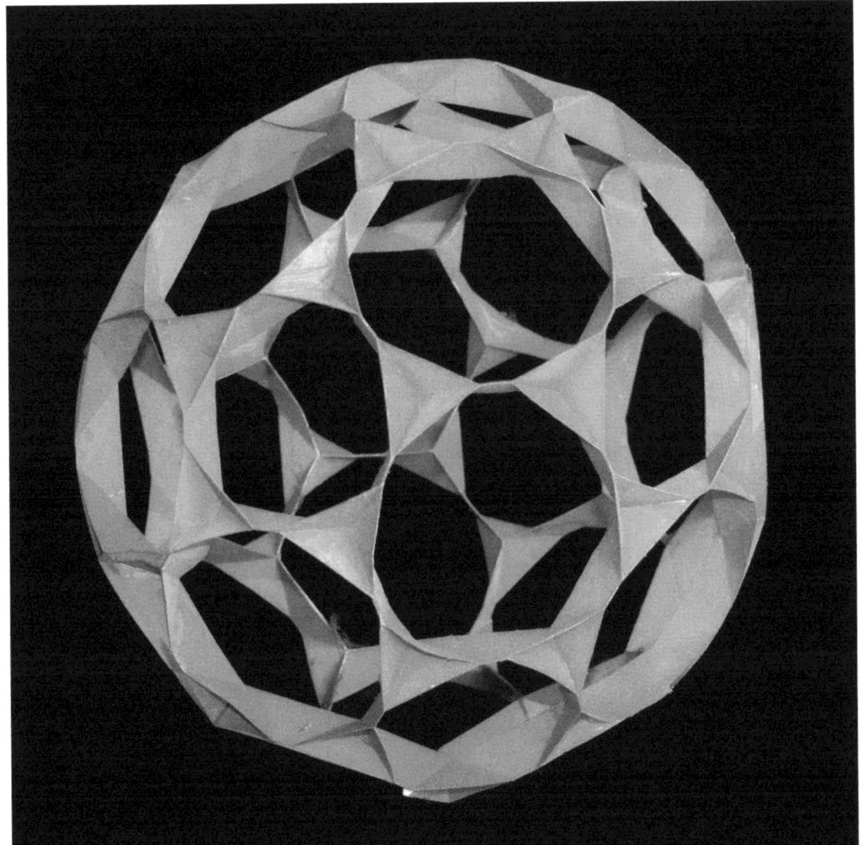

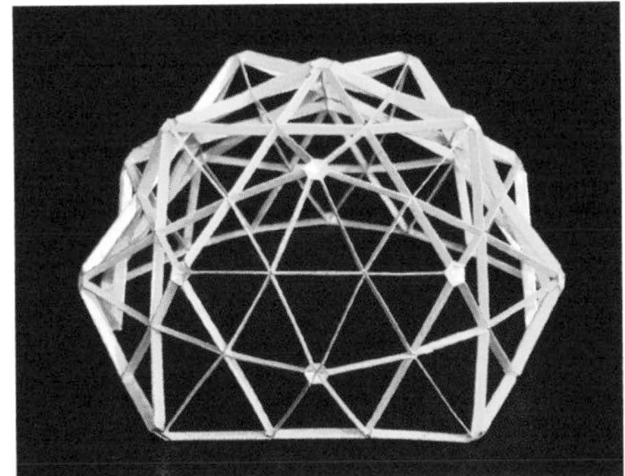

These polyhedra models, made from folded straight strips, were essentially intended to verify previously made calculations of angles.

- *Cuboctahedron.*
- *Truncated icosahedron.*
- *Pyramidation of truncated icosahedron allowing it to be produced only from folded strips based on two simple folds and a double fold.*

- *Node created from the assembly of folded parts.*

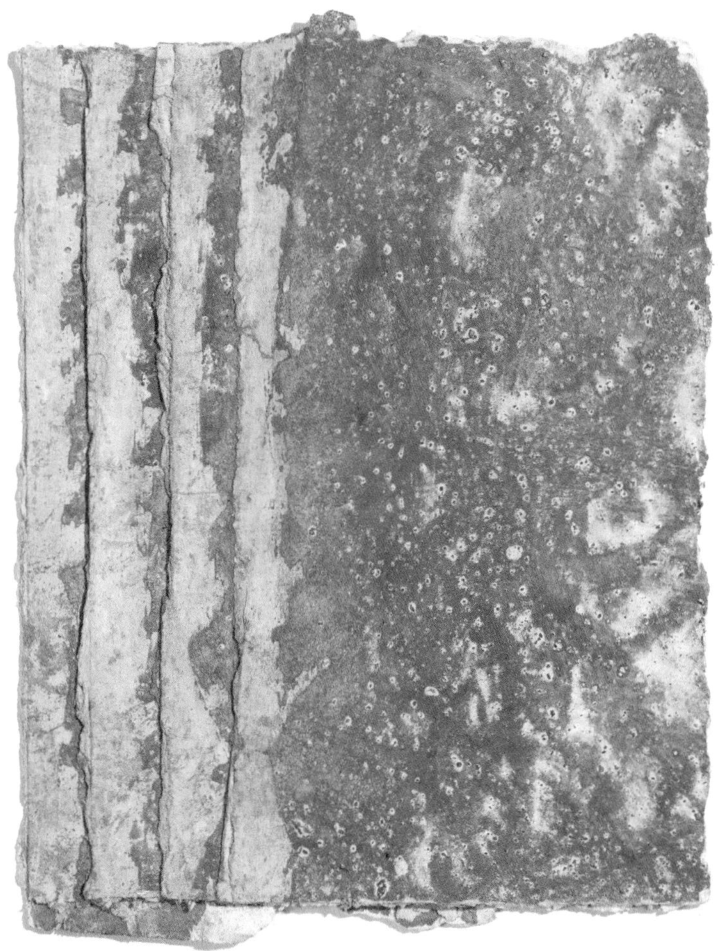

Marcel Robelin, Christian Renonciat and Damien Daufresne

FRANCE

Galerie Sabine Puget, Plis Exhibition

Sabine Puget's ***Plis*** (***Folds***) brought together artists who for some people are big names in contemporary art—for example, Hantaï and Degottex. The diversity of the works presented and the relevance of its reflection on folds made this exhibition,* accompanied by texts by the writer Bernard Chambaz, a reference in the field. Each artist offered his or her own particular expression. But why folds?

"Because folds, which are supremely polymorphic, never cease to extend to all areas of the visual and the invisible, and this has been the case since the dawn of time. They are clever and sculpt appearances. They become ornamentation, trimmings and drapery. They are a symbol of power, beauty and luxury. They bewitch the material that they model according to the imagination of artists and their wildest whims. They adapt to what they adorn, to the image desired by the person who made the commission, whether a churchman, king or courtesan. They convey the air and the fashion of the time. They describe the way of being in the world. Nothing—neither wear, nor destitution, nor old age—escapes them. They lose their haughtiness. They rumple, bunch up, degrade and get messed up. They become heavy from the dust of time, lose their colours and give us shivers."

Sabine Puget, 2014.

* "Plis," exhibition, July/September 2014.

www.galeriesabinepuget.com

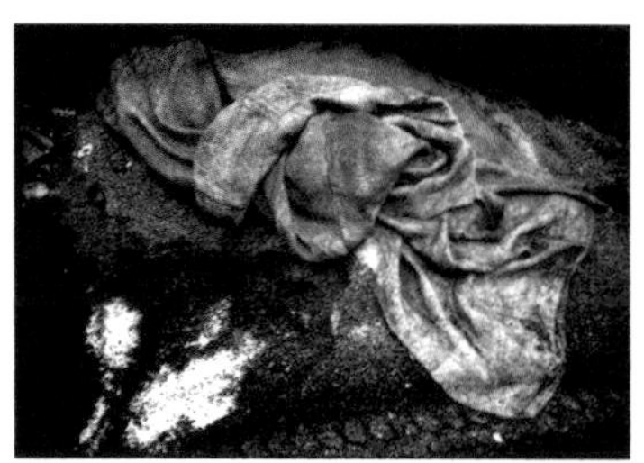

• Marcel Robelin, acrylic and ash on paper, 25 x 20 cm (9 13/16 x 7 7/8 in). 1995. Marcel Robelin, who was taken from us in 2013, crimped paper and covered it in ash, thus creating in the folds the places for remembrance for architectures that are open testimony of passing time accompanying the reveries of this solitary wanderer.

• Christian Renonciat, 4-fold unfolded paper, ayous wood, 68 x 74 cm (26 3/4 x 29 1/8 in). A virtuoso of illusion through fine wooden reliefs, Christian Renonciat offers a close and surreal view of folds once in fabric or paper.

• Damien Daufresne, photography, Vienna, 2014. Damien Daufresne seizes folds from ephemeral moments—mist, rain, the night—reinforcing this black and grey with shots that already seem corroded by oblivion.

Patrick Crossonneau

FRANCE

Patrick Crossonneau, or the shapelessness of thought

"In my sculptural research, I work with the concept of shapelessness through ink and paper, and through stains and folds. Ductile ink flows through wet paper. The stain unfolds, contorts and spreads out. There are dilutions and imperceptible movements on the sheet. Then everything appears to freeze; material chaos stabilizes, acheiropoietic images let the imagination make its choices as to the possible referents, drawings made of black and grey secretions like fractal objects.

Shapes emerge from the shapeless. The stain has no form in itself; the most improbable shapes are born out of the shapelessness. It is then time for folds to structure the sheet of paper and counteract the freedom that the ink gave itself. A new organization is created on the material support.

The process can be reversed: after being folded first, the paper will then receive the ink, and then finally be unfolded.

I play the role of 'klexograph' (someone who folds and inks a sheet of paper). The paper is mounted on another sheet or on canvas stretched on a frame. The folds made previously do not completely disappear. Traces of them remain, like ghosts that continue to structure the literal space of the pictorial support.

First of all two-dimensional, my sculptural productions now take on volume, and the paper used is sometimes already printed. The 'convocation' in my usually traditional folding pieces, which are sometimes very personal (though each time I discover in them a principle developed by one or more of the masters of folding), reveals new concepts that I put in place through installations and sculptures. Paper, light and folds are ubiquitous in them."

Remarks from Patrick Crossonneau, October 2014.

www.patrickcrossonneau.fr

• Plié-déplié, *2013.*
• Damier, *2012.*

Anne Bouin

FRANCE

The tradition of folding, calligraphy and haiku are the expression of a culture where the development of the individual is turned toward simplicity and purity of means. For the Japanese, origami is also a refined method of developing *ki*, a subtle form of vital energy used in martial arts and medicine. Folding is therefore both a method of meditation and the expression of calm and inner beauty.

Haïkimonos: artist's books

"In creating these poetic kimonos, I sought to bring together robe, book and poetry in a single object.
When hanging on a wall, the very simple and geometric form of the kimono has presence.
This form contains its own poetry and words.
The haiku, a very simple poem, naturally has quite a close relationship with the kimono.
When the kimono is folded, the robe disappears. That presence goes back into itself and into the privacy of a book. Because the kimono is double sided, two small collections of poems are formed.
The kimono can be carried around easily, something that evokes another idea that is dear to me, namely travel, and that recalls the wandering Japanese poets of centuries gone by. Bamboo rods fit together to create the rod that allows the kimono to be hung.
The kimonos are made with indigo blue paper, which is used as chicory packaging and which I have been salvaging for a long time from the shop in my village.
This deep blue paper, which recalls ancient kimonos, is waxed, and beautiful markings are left behind on it when it is crumpled. After being cut into rectangles, the paper is mounted on a nonwoven material that is very lightweight but strong.
The haiku and motifs are painted with Posca felts (acrylic)."

Remarks from Anne Bouin, March 2015.

www.librairieduciel.com/catalogue/index.php?id=20

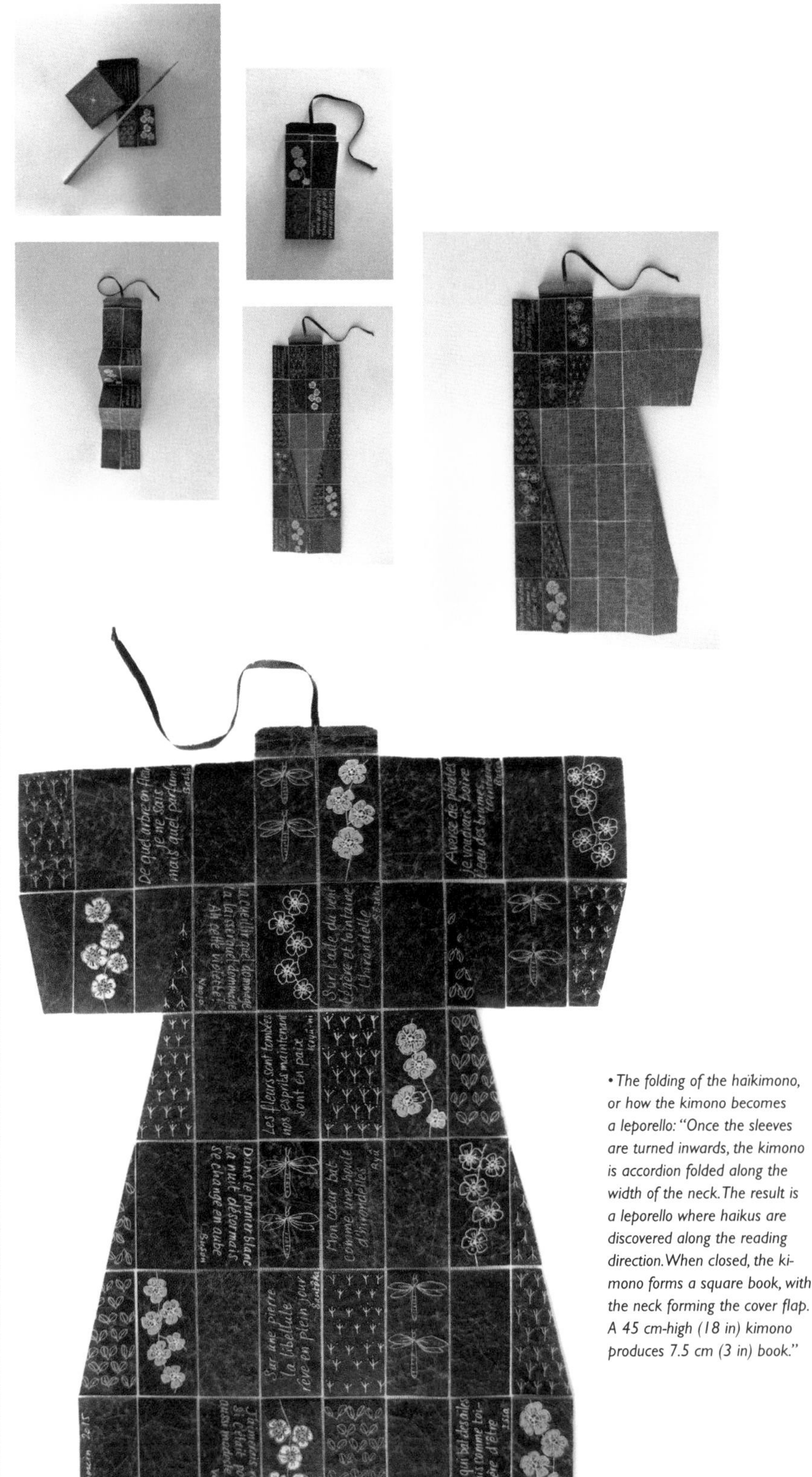

• The folding of the haïkimono, or how the kimono becomes a leporello: "Once the sleeves are turned inwards, the kimono is accordion folded along the width of the neck. The result is a leporello where haikus are discovered along the reading direction. When closed, the kimono forms a square book, with the neck forming the cover flap. A 45 cm-high (18 in) kimono produces 7.5 cm (3 in) book."

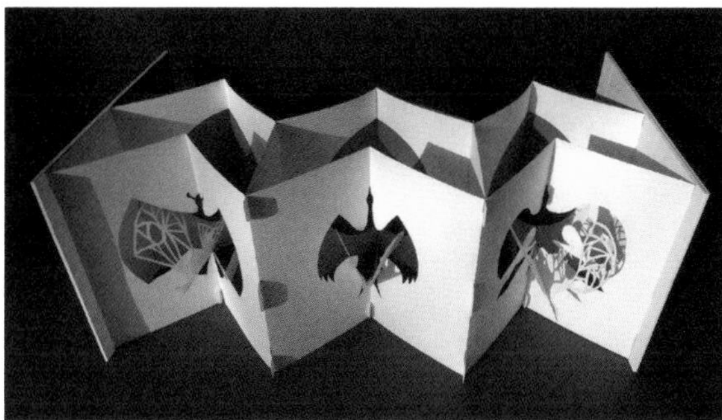

• Envol blanc, *2013. Leporello artist's book with a white background of translucent sulphite paper. Double tunnel/pop-up book design that becomes illuminated when presented in front of a window.*

Jean-Charles Trebbi

FRANCE

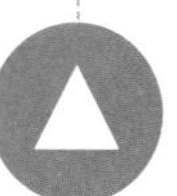

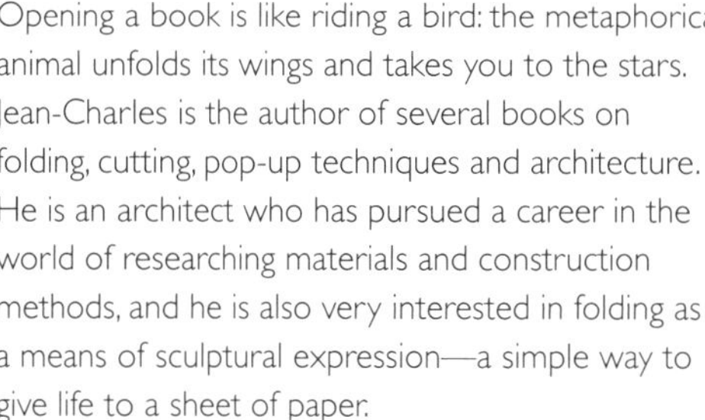

Opening a book is like riding a bird: the metaphorical animal unfolds its wings and takes you to the stars. Jean-Charles is the author of several books on folding, cutting, pop-up techniques and architecture. He is an architect who has pursued a career in the world of researching materials and construction methods, and he is also very interested in folding as a means of sculptural expression—a simple way to give life to a sheet of paper.
For Jean-Charles, folding is the lexicon of books without words. In *Petite envolée*, he offers up a whole range of flying animals from countries where the wings of dreams beat alone.
The support medium of his works is mainly paper, and for his artist's books he creates architecture that is different each time due to his ingenious mechanisms.

"The book is static by nature, and foldings techniques, supplemented by cuts, offer me the opportunity to work with shadow and light as a material that can be modelled. This is also why I called my site Orilum, a word made from the Japanese *ori*, meaning fold, and from the Latin *lumen*, meaning light, hence folding light through paper.
My areas of interest focus on the articulation of pages and the production of movement to provide an emotion. Folds are a tool that allow me to discover sculptural expressions that correspond to my aspirations. Research on innovative structures is the pretext for creating one-off books, artist's books, livres objets, miniature theatres or tunnel books like *Venezia* and *Matera*.
In my *Envol* series, which showcases imaginary insects and birds, I was inspired by a branch of origami called *kirigami*. I experimented with the inversion of folds to create a volume while giving the birds movement as the pages open."

Interview with J.-Ch. Trebbi, November 2014.

www.orilum.com
www.librairieduciel.com/catalogue/index.php?id=29

• Matera, une cité dans la roche, *2014. Panoramic pop-up theatre book.*
• Rêves en blanc, *2014. Tunnel book with an original structure. Illustrations and goffering by Frédérique Le Lous Delpech. 1.80 m (71 in) unfolded.*
"For the book Rêve en blanc, *which was created jointly with Frédérique, who did the illustrations and engravings, I wanted to create an unusual tunnel book. Tunnel books usually involve frontal monovision. In this project, the innovative structure has a double longitudinal reading, while the lateral reading becomes totally abstract. The accordion folding of the bellows, a classic technique for tunnel books, disappears in this creation. Here it is replaced by an interlocking of the faces. The fold becomes articulation for the creation of the book's volume. which is turned into a fully collapsible structure."*

Jean-Claude Correia

FRANCE

Jean-Claude Correia was born in Casablanca in 1945. A graduate of the École nationale supérieure des arts décoratifs and the founder of the Mouvement français des plieurs de papier (MFPP) in 1978, this internationally renowned artist has produced a remarkable body of work.

Dreams lie in the light captured by folds, which act as both screen and reflector. Dreams are in the illusions of forms when they suggest organizations close to minerals or the fossils of prehistoric animals, just before memory. Jean-Claude Correia would have loved to rub shoulders with Henri Michaux, who wrote: "The child is born with twenty-two folds. (...) The man's life is then complete. He dies in this form. There are no more folds for him to undo. A man rarely dies without having a few more folds to undo. But it does happen. Alongside this operation, a man forms a nucleus. (...) Some see the nucleus more than they do the unfolding. But the Wise Man sees the unfolding. The unfolding alone is important. The rest is just epiphenomenon."*

Remarks from Jean-Claude Correia, taken from L'Art en pli, *Centre de congrès d'Angers, 1985.*

* Henri Michaux, *Au pays de la magie*, p. 135, *in* Ailleurs NRF, Gallimard, 1984.

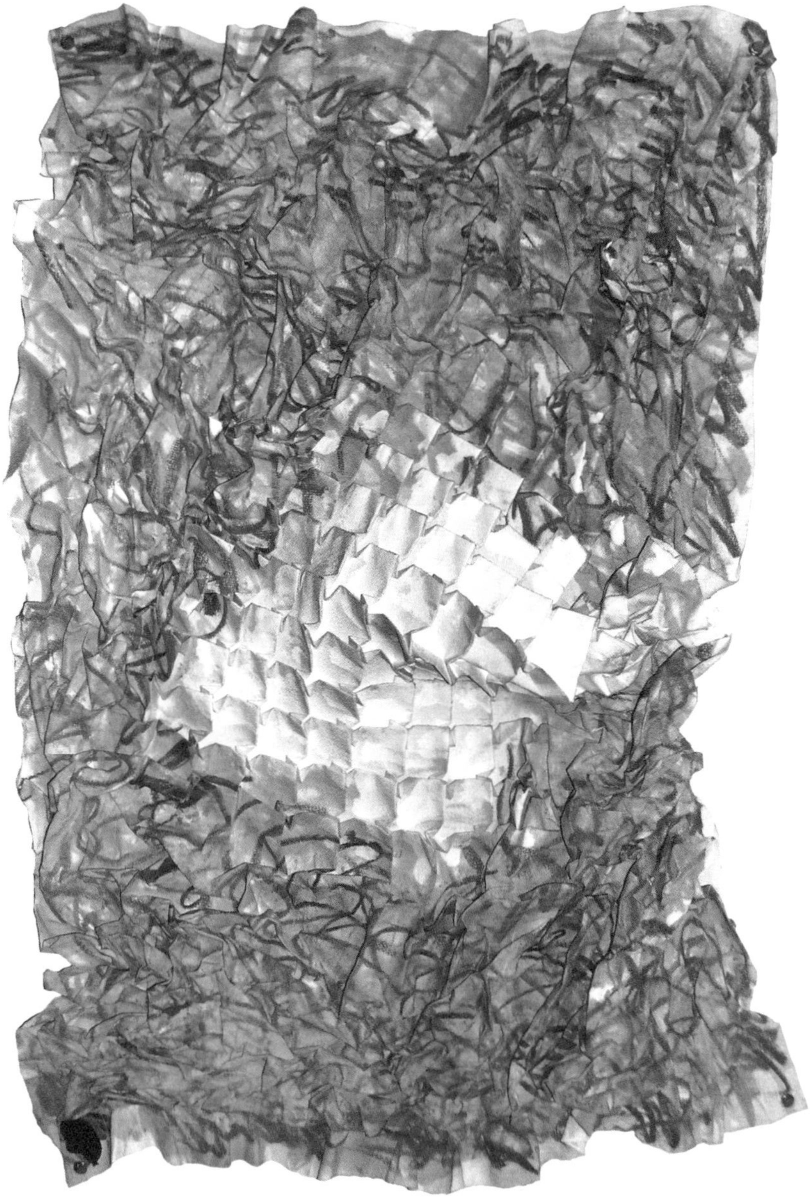

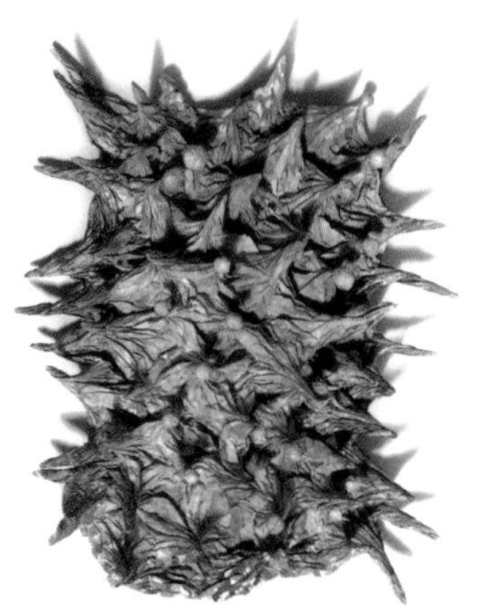

• Écume 99, *folded piece, Ingres paper, 73 x 82.5 cm (28 3/4 x 32 1/2 in) sheet dimensions, acrylic and pastel, 1999.*
• Plis et boulettes, *folded piece, Valopaque paper, 40 g, watercolour, 70 x 39 cm (27 9/16 x 15 3/8 in) sheet dimensions, 2002-2003.*

Jean-Paul Moscovino

FRANCE

Moscovino has been folding for a long time, and his sculptures all stem from a single flat surface (a sheet of paper for the templates and then sheet steel or aluminium). Research using paper is exciting, even though the weaving of forms and counterforms can be thankless when each new fold destabilizes and calls into question the previous ones. Difficulty stimulates creativity, and in pursuing form, the artist takes pleasure in reinventing the anatomy and architecture of his characters. When a model seems interesting, he will transpose it into steel –8/10 or 1 mm (1/16 in) thick–. Cutting, folding by hammering and welding with thin sheets require experience. It is tiresome work that is not far off metal fabrication. For monumental sculptures, the skilled help of another person is necessary because cut aluminium sheets –4-6 mm (3/16-1/4 in) thick– need to go through a large-size hydraulic folder. TIG* welding also requires know-how gained over the course of different projects. But the result is what the viewer sees, and Moscovino carefully erases all the traces of labour using a solid colour (often blue) without the addition of further detail, simply suggesting the space and elegance of lightness.

This interplay of folding generates reflection on surfaces and outer layers because by playing with the boundary between mass and void in this way, one is led to question the very nature of this limit sculpted from the fingertips, and this "skin" can only be colour. This ubiquitous phenomenon in the perception of space is as intriguing as its influence on form (an object will not have the same impact "dressed" in red as in blue).
On a large scale, sculptures (often the bodies of seated women), constructed like tepees or cathedrals, encourage circulation: it is possible to cross through or shelter under them and perceive how the arms, legs and torso join in a vault and project shadows that the artist integrates into the calligraphy of the whole.

Remarks from France M. Dehelly, November 2014.

* TIG: specialist arc-welding process.

www.moscovino.com

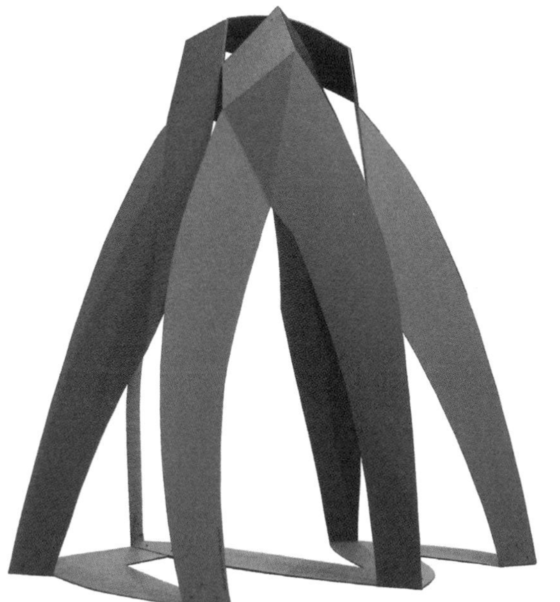

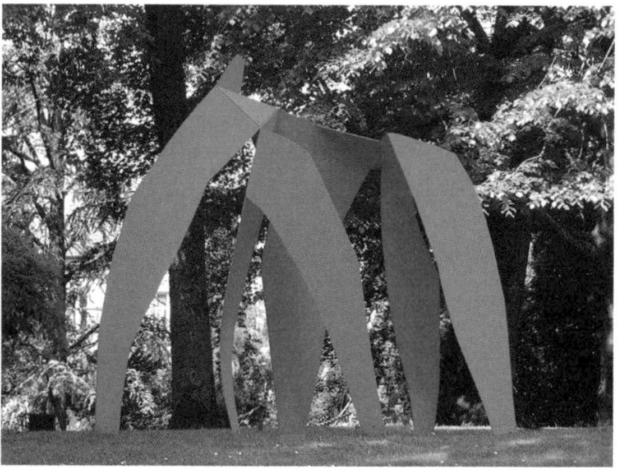

• Inter-ception, *raw state of structure.*
• Inter-ception, *red ochre on aluminium,*
2.70 m x 2.10 m x 2.70 m (106 x 83 x 106 in) height.
• Entre mêlée, *blue on aluminium,*
2.97 m x 2.05 m x 2.70 m (117 x 81 x 106 in) height.

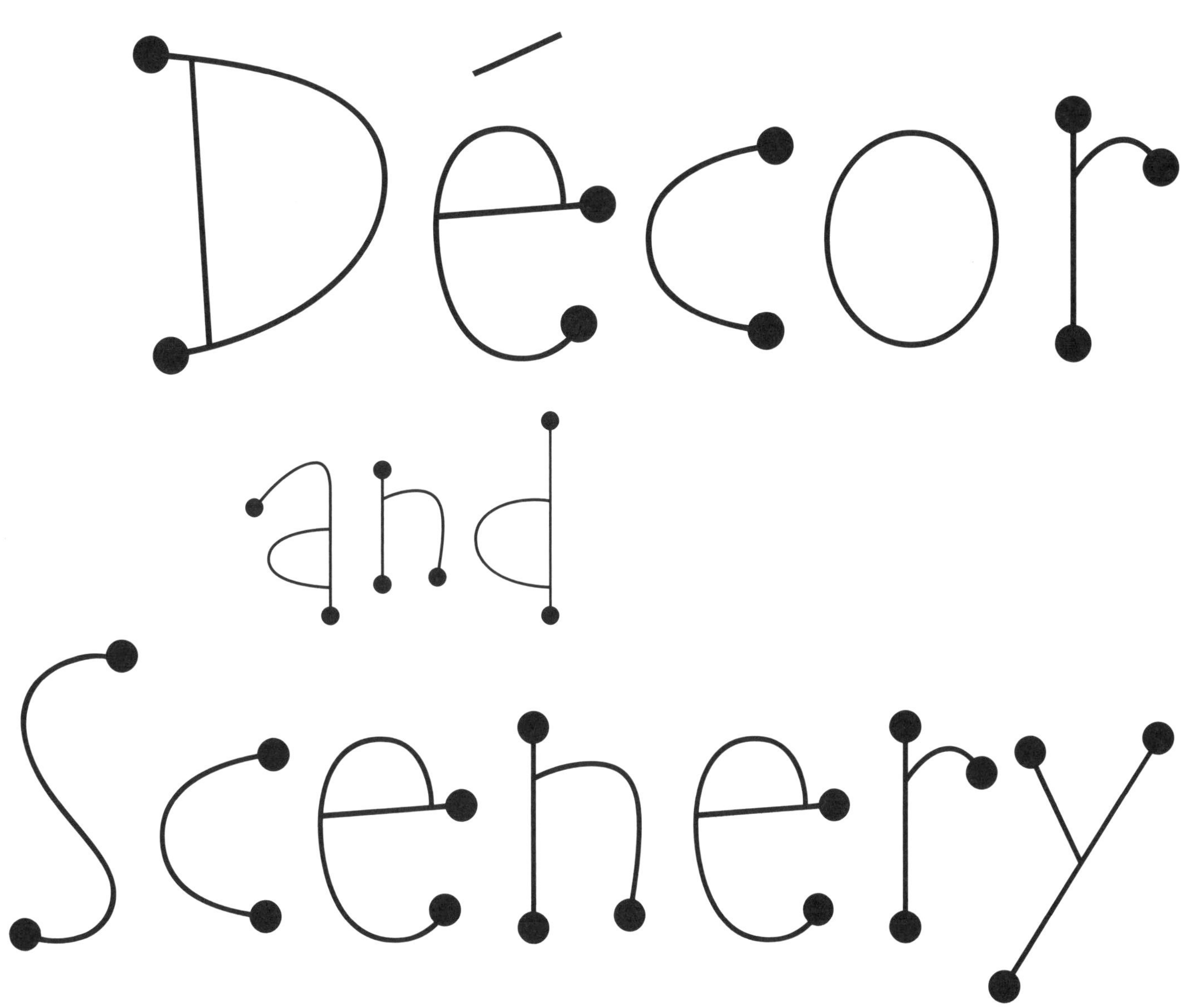

• *Bernard Girault, folded model for a set from* Jean-Baptiste Poquelin et son grand-père.

FOLDING TO LIVE, FOLDING AS AN ART OF LIVING!

"All the world's a stage, and all the men and women merely players. And one man in his time plays many parts"
William Shakespeare - Excerpt from *As you like it*, ca. 1599.

Scenery is the thing that symbolizes the world over the course of a performance. Scenery is typically associated with ornamentation. Making it generally involves projecting an image onto a support medium or screen. The support medium could be a bowl, a canvas in the background of a scene, a table set for a party celebration, and so on. Rejecting ornamentation and considering that a support medium (a place or object) reduced to its strictest minimalism produces a simple and functional beauty remains a unique aspect of scenery. So, in our world, no object from daily life or from a scene escapes our interpretation. To tell the truth, our interpretation of the world is based on representation: we capture information through the senses, and it is transmitted to the brain, which ultimately reconstructs a scene consistent with the observer's mental patterns. In a way, our everyday environment is also a form of scenery that we shape and that we use to imagine ourselves.
Scenery is an attempt to embrace the world (deployment) or a focusing on oneself in order to better concentrate attention on the subject.
And, looking a little closer, scenes from daily life are like successive "waves" or "folds." Let's take the example of a meal: initially, the table is set, napkins are folded… a bit like at the theatre, a foldout tells us about the various acts in which courses will be presented… Each scene linked to another through invisible "hinges" could be illustrated on the pages of a foldout…
Folding allows scenes from life to be arranged. It is still a very important feature of traditional cookery, because it allows food to be packaged or cloaked, making it pleasing to the eye.
The scenographer "folds" his or her story into the scenographic space and time (imbroglio), so that the viewer might be gradually "captivated."

• *Yoshinobu Miyamoto, folded display for Hermès, for the exhibition* Carte blanche *in Paris in 2014.*

Bernard Girault

FRANCE

• *Bernard Girault in his studio, 2015.*
• *Folded model for a set from Don Juan, 22 x 22 cm (8 11/16 x 8 11/16 in).*
• *Sketches.*

Faced with the need to easily communicate his research into scenic creations in three dimensions, Bernard Girault found in pop-up a clever way to bring his representations to life.
These props are truly folded poetry created by a man of great talent who has a keen eye and mastery of the particular constraints of the perspectives of theatre scenery.
"Bernard was born in 1923 in Pont-l'Évêque. He studied fine arts and architecture, which steered him towards the scenography profession. He pursued this career between the fifties and seventies, with paper as his material of choice for set design. Then, as part of the Atelier d'A (a structure for cultural events), he put into practice the principle of folding on different scales and in different materials for theatre and museum productions (with the agency Com et Graph).
For a few years, he passed on his knowledge to students at the graphic arts departments of art schools in Caen and Le Havre. The creation of an annual calendar in 1988 was what really led him to his first pieces of pop-up scenery. The rules were strict: no gluing, no tricks involving montage, and an exclusive use of folds to create space on a single sheet of paper.
He based his dozens of creations on themes that were dear to him: Norman architecture, theatre, boats, the sea and other inventive and subtle sources of amusement.
He is still folding today, creating his design studies on 170 g graph paper for his test models, the very essence of the creation. The definitive versions, meanwhile, are made with 300 g watercolour rag paper, which he washes in order to soften it and then dries so that the paper regains its rigidity at the desired time. The folds thereby stay in place and the work can be watercoloured. This gives his pop-up creations a unique picture-like look."

Remarks from Alain Chevalier, November 2014
(Alain Chevalier is a scenographer and a collaborator and friend of Bernard Girault.)

Cie Les anges au plafond

FRANCE

Le Cri quotidien, when folding becomes scenery

Camille Trouvé's hands transport us from scenery to scene... The Anges au plafond theatre troupe uses folds to create sets and props that produce surprise. Based on stories that are always simple, each performance is unique and deeply poetic. For example, a newspaper: through pop-up, the information will "get into the face" of Camille, who is both puppeteer and actress, with the character being "bombarded by information." It is therefore a scene with various characters: the hands (which create the rush) and the actress who plays the reader thrown off kilter. In some cases, the entire scenery is achieved through folding: a farm that turns into a village and then a city, or a wheat field that unfolds on stage. Of course, technically, there is a question of scale: the shift from folds of paper made using small-scale means (such as taping and scoring) to large folded scenery was a "battle with the material," says Camille, who designs and also makes the scenery. Folds are also aesthetic: the artist has sought to overcome technical constraints related to the weight and thickness of the life-size sets to preserve the impression of fragility of miniature paper scenery. What these folded scenes have in common is their being "something always in motion and under construction."

Remarks from Camille Trouvé, December 2014.

www.lesangesauplafond.net

• *Presentation of street scenery in* Le Cri quotidien, *a show created through folded and cut paper set to music.*
"We see paper men escape from words, cities and deserts unfolding and encroaching on the pages, and we hear the sound of a cello covering the key phrases."
Page and folding direction: Camille Trouvé and Brice Berthoud. A coproduction between Les Anges au plafond and Théâtre 71 Scène nationale de Malakoff.

• *The origamist in the field.*
• *A 3.50 m-high (98 in) pink flamingo for an exhibition in Les Ulis, Essonne.*
• *An interpretation of the t-rex at the Château de Boissy, Taverny (95).*

Julien Gritte

FRANCE

Julien Gritte is an origami-making entertainer. The speed with which he folds makes him a real magician. "I discovered origami when I was six through Gérard Ty Sovann. At the time, I began doing martial arts, and I discovered the magic of mathematics. These three disciplines have accompanied me for years. The day when I wanted to do clowning, and finally an artist, I understood that folding would be my main medium. Folding calms me, and also excites me and opens me up to another way to feel things. This is what I try to convey to people at shows and demonstrations.

Making giant origami is magical! It satisfies my inner child—and the puzzle-solving side of me as well. The field of possibilities opens before my eyes and so also before the eyes of others."

Julien's versatility has led him to create a flexible concept, where each performance is unique, and he constantly reinvents his art to respond precisely to each request. Whether it is giant origami that is over 5 m (197 in) high, shows, records to be beaten, TV programmes, workshops, or even exhibitions on paper folding, Julien makes use of his talents all over the world.

Very highly regarded in the show world because of his creativity, dexterity and talents as actor, Julien is a one-of-a-kind character!

He enjoys folding ever-larger sheets as quickly as possible within a given space, without support and without help, in order to give to the origami a scenic, spectacular dimension.

During shows, he "narrates" the concepts of geometry to the audience, while folding his giant sculptures. He tells stories, talks about all the practical uses of folding, and cheerfully encourages people to try it out.

For him, folding is a source of pleasure, calm and concentration. His credo is "make folds, not war!"

Remarks from Julien Gritte, October 2014.

✏ www.juliengritte.com

• Novel architecture, *giant pop-up book, line preparations, views of outside and inside. Design by Jie Qi, created in collaboration with Adrian Melia.*

USA

Giant book: folding takes us into history

Jie Qi learned origami from her mother at the age of three or four, and she started to create her own folded pieces for telling stories.

She trained as an engineer in robotics and uses this knowledge to "make electronics magical." For example, she uses simple activators such as nitinol wire (this nickel-titanium alloy has two very special properties: shape memory and super elasticity) to "make paper breathe": her interactive design projects always involve an ordinary object that she seeks to make magical.

For this giant book project, Jie Qi wanted to do something big: create a book of magical stories that would effectively be a room. Once open, it interacts with the reader and can surround him or her, and it can also serve as a separating screen.

The giant book was temporarily installed in a public place. When it was being exhibited, it became a sort of "unusual experience" that the public really enjoyed.

In line with this research, Jie Qi sought to create smaller animated books and concentrate on the message allowed by the expression of folds in movement. "A story is not magic because it is animated but because it touches our soul and drives us."

Remarks from Jie Qi, October 2014.

http://web.media.mit.edu/~bmayton/photos/novelarchitecture/
www.flickr.com/photos/jieq

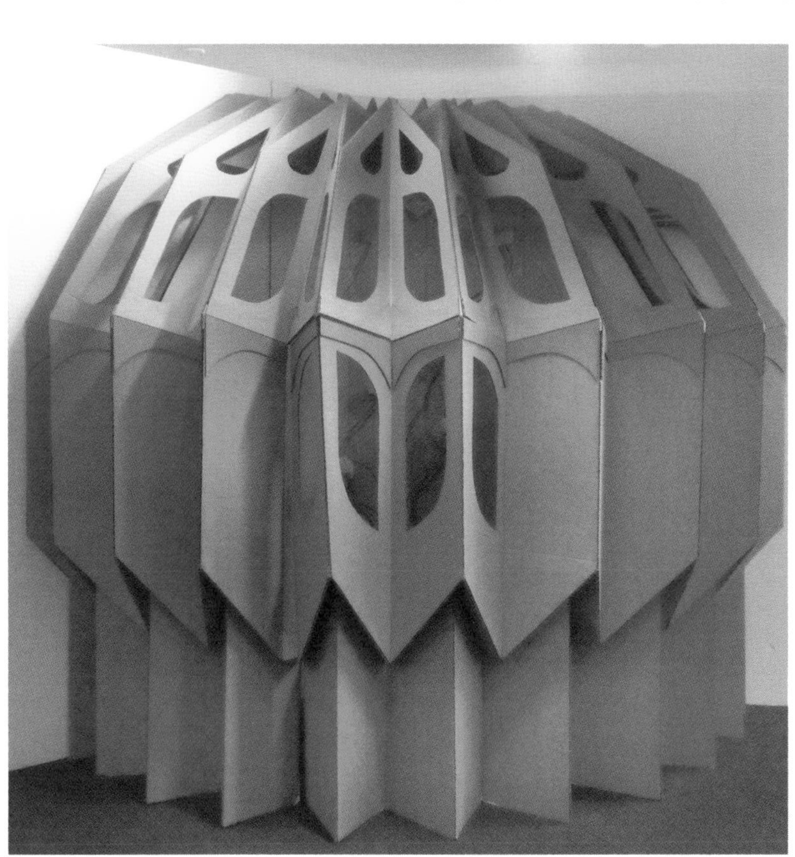

Delphine Huguet

CANADA

Delphine Huguet is a culinary designer and sculptural artist. "My first memory related to folding goes back to when I was eight years old, in the form of a book on origami for kids and my total inability to understand how to successfully make these splendid cranes that I was supposed to fold into the required shape without difficulty. At art school, I discovered the richness of transforming and using paper. I did all my studying at art schools, where there is an omnipresent relationship with paper.

It is a material whose areas of transformation are so vast that I have always found it exciting. For me, self-cultivation and self-nourishment are parallel actions: we can fill our belly or our spirit. Paper feeds the spirit, through its shaping or through the words that are printed on it. My approach to food is very cultural: in my work, dishes speak of stories and tastes. I had this fantasy of having an edible material that would allow me to get results as fine and as emotionally strong as creations made on paper and that moreover would incorporate tasting.

The only solution was to create an edible paper, which I managed after a lot of experimenting. I have put together a collection of recipes for creating my material based on the results desired (colour, flavour, texture and so on).

I also work on techniques for transforming this paper into an object that is eaten. My project received the support of the Institut français's Hors les murs programme, which allowed me to go to the Japan to visit traditional paper factories. This trip's goal was to adapt traditional paper-making techniques to food making. My transformational goals are really to experiment with the world of paper to create edible objects. Today, as I'm in a research phase, my transformation techniques are still very artisanal, but a semi-industrial adaptation is possible."

Remarks from Delphine Huguet, November 2014.

www.delphinehuguet.com

• Eat-it. *The form of things that we eat affects our tasting. Solids, voids, points: all these formal concepts supplement the experience of taste in a way that may or may not be pleasant.*
I tried to fold different sticky notes into different shapes—very simple and contemporary origami. My idea was to create a block of edible sticky notes that would be at hand on a desk when you feel a bit peckish or just want "a little something" to eat.
The Eat-it *is as practical for the person who uses it as any block of sticky notes in terms of its usage. It's a true work companion.*
• *Classic edible origami.*

Ofir Zucker and Ilan Garibi

ISRAEL

Ofir is an industrial designer and has worked extensively with concrete. Ilan, an artist and designer, is a university teacher of origami.
In the *Palmas* project, Ilan and Ofir were interested in "freezing" folded paper so as to capture its form in concrete.

Both posed one another many technical questions. "At the time," Ilan says, "I took a course in moulding. I realized that paper is one of the most unsuited materials for this work. When showing my collection of models to Ofir, I was sure that the *Diamonds* model was not appropriate. But that was the one he chose. It seemed impossible to do and I had to take on some unique challenges—transforming a flat model into a cylinder, finding a way to lock this form, holding the top and bottom edges of the folded sheet edges, perfectly pasting the inner layers, and so on."

"After choosing Ilan's model, I got home and was thinking: How can I pour concrete in that piece of paper? And it wasn't obvious. The paper could not support so much weight. It began to inflate like a balloon, got wet, lost its shape and finally collapsed. It took many folds and projects to find the proper technique so that a piece of folded paper could maintain more than 5 kg of liquid concrete, while also maintaining the accuracy of its folds. One night, I had a brainwave. The next morning, I called Ilan because I knew this was going to work. (…) I gently detached the paper from the dry concrete. The concrete object stood there with the exact lines of the paper model—crisp, precise and clean.
That was the moment when I started to design its form, proportions, finishes and edges, and to transform it into a 'folded' concrete vase."

Remarks from October 2014.

- www.ofirz.com
- www.garibiorigami.com
- Ilan Garibi; see also p. 63.

• *Ofir Zucker and Ilan Garibi,* Palmas *collection, vases made from concrete that was poured into moulds made from frozen paper.*
• *Ilan Garibi,* Single Star Tess Cake *mould.*

Charlène Fétiveau

FRANCE

"My folding story started in 2008 while I was studying at the art school in Angers. My encounter with Pietro Seminelli, a master folder, strengthened my interest in this art form. As a result, I made it my subject of study for my degree in interior design. Today I work in this area for an architecture firm in Nantes. Since then, I have shared my time between folding and architecture.

'The fold determines the form and makes it appear; it makes it into a form of expression.'

G. Deleuze*

Folding is a way to create a form and to go from a flat surface to a volume. It is the endeavour of a sculptor who, motivated by this promise, gets to work. The whole idea is to draw the folding pattern while imagining what volume it will become. It is a complex journey that demands a certain capacity for projection. This is the approach through which the *Folded cake* (in 2009) and the *Petits plats dans les plis* collection (in 2012) were born.

Folded cake

This is a prototype of some packaging containing a (ready-made) cake mix. With the snip of some scissors, it becomes a mould that is disposable after use. This project remained a model made out of baking paper. It required development of a new material capable of both preserving the food and being placed in the oven to be mass produced and sold commercially. To date, I have not found partners that can meet this demand.

Les petits plats dans les plis

This is a collection of porcelain table objects (tumbler, cup, cutting plate and so on). For this project, it was necessary to consider the process of developing folds as the hidden part of the working process, but it was important that they showed through the small details of the material. Each piece is therefore created through folding card stock, producing a model for shaping a unique plaster mould into which the porcelain 'slip' is poured (this fine ceramic is produced out of kaolin through firing at more than 1200 °C). The pieces of porcelain are then enamelled on the inside only. They remain biscuit on the outside—that is, rough, with the grain of the paper as well as the small bulges from folds noticeable to the eye and under the fingers. Everything is made in an artisanal way, in small series."

Remarks from Charlène Fétiveau, November 2014.

* Gilles Deleuze, *Le Pli, Leibniz et le Baroque*, Éditions de Minuit, 1988.

www.charlenefetiveau.blogspot.fr

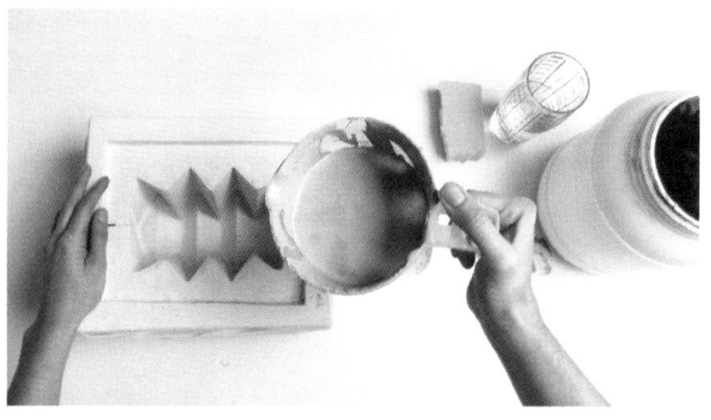

- *Collection of porcelain moulds.*
- *Creation of a model of card stock, followed by casting of the porcelain slip into a plaster mould.*
- Folded cake, *packaging containing a (ready-made) cake mix. With the snip of some scissors, it becomes a mould that is disposable after use.*

Pedro Núñez and Marc García-Durán Huet

SPAIN

Nenen is an attempt to mimic the movement of a sheet of paper with a new material, Corian®, which has been developed by DuPont™. It is composed of acrylic resin and minerals, and it can be thermoformed and worked with in a similar way to wood.

The genesis of the meeting between a plastic material and a catalyst (the architect) would be incomplete without a source of inspiration: folding. According to M. G. Huet, this adventure began with a meeting. In Spain, the Holcim Foundation was awarding a prize for the most exemplary constructions. Marc was requested by them to come up with a gift idea for contributors to this media event, and he had to represent the concept of sustainability. A piece of origami that he has seen in Madrid came to mind. He met Pedro Núñez, a sculptural artist who, before becoming his friend and collaborator, introduced him to becoming proficient in folding. An order for eight hundred pieces of the origami for the foundation followed.

One day, while Marc Huet's architecture firm was studying a project based on a Corian® facade, the French manufacturer DuPont suggested that the team participate in the Milan biennale. This was how Nenen was born. To date, the final version has not been made commercially available as a product range, but recently a design enthusiast made an order as a collector's piece!

Remarks from Marc García-Durán Huet, December 2014.

- Marc García-Durán Huet, architect: www.gdebarcelona.com
- Pedro Núñez Mardones, artist: www.pedronunez.com
- Mediodesign / Juan Pablo Quintero: www.mediodesign.com

• A mould was made using CNC milling, then a polyurethane countermould. The 2 mm (1/16 in) sheet of Corian® by DuPont de Nemours, is heat formed to obtain the finished plate and to optimally handle deformation issues, which become a problem once the folded material has a significant thickness. Design: Marc García-Durán Huet, artistic development: Pedro Nuñez Mardones, production: Mediodesign / Juan Pablo Quintero.

• *Opening sequence showing the self-locking packaging system and a presentation of nachos.*

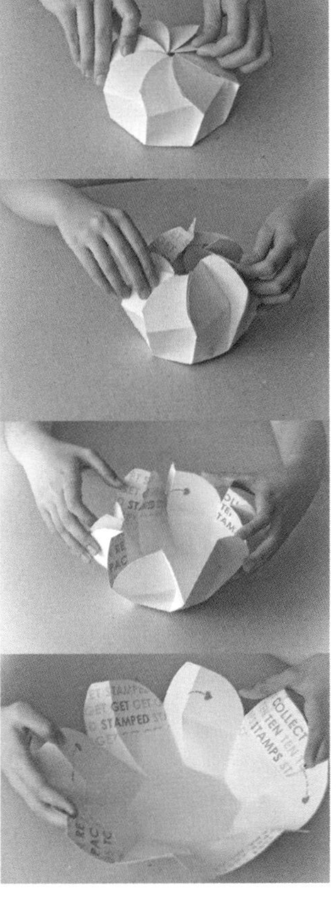

MEXICO

"*Guactruck* is a mobile restaurant that serves Filipino dishes in origami packaging. We have also created a packaging brand called Aphinitea. We believe that an experience for the senses begins with the way in which packaging is perceived. Our goal is to reinvent the ubiquitous square box by replacing it with a design inspired by origami that is made from a single sheet yet without sacrificing functionality. Aphinitea supports the idea that good things should be presented in beautiful packaging, giving that extra touch that creates a memorable experience.

Visually attractive, durable and ergonomic, the design uses origami techniques to create a 'bud' that opens into a flower and that has a self-locking mechanism that eliminates the need for glue. The bowl shape allows an easy grip and optimum comfort, even when the user is standing or walking."

Remarks from Michealle Renee Lee, February 2015.

www.guactruck.com
www.aphinitea.tictail.com

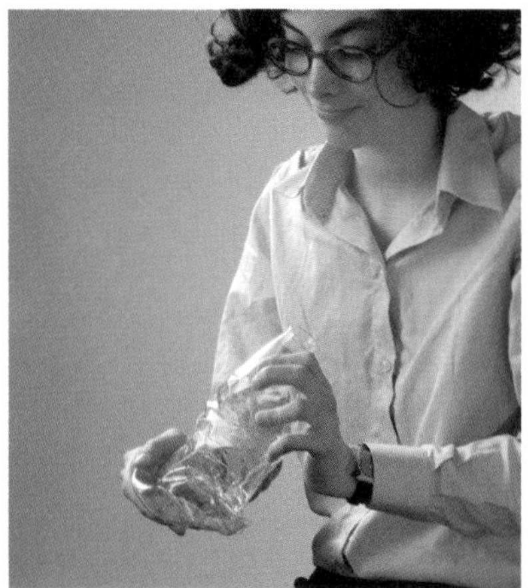

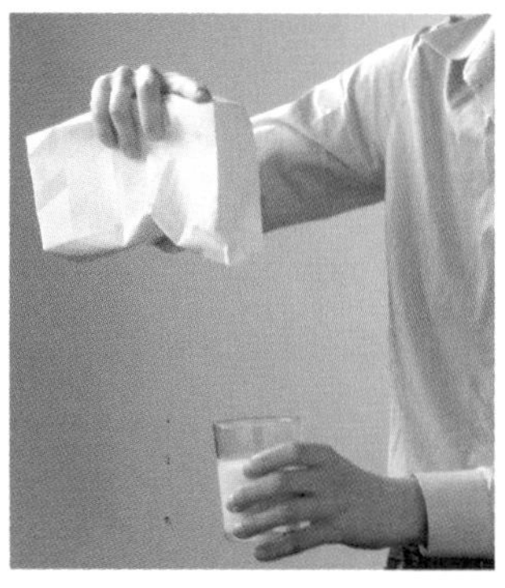

• *Test series of the* Brique *project and crushing.*

Lucie Dorel

FRANCE

The packaging that Lucie Dorel has worked on has its origins in a unique line of research into folding.

As part of her degree at the École nationale supérieure de création industrielle (ENSCI), this young designer created four packaging models based on a personal reflection on everyday objects and the end point in their lives.

Folding proved be a suitable language that has the property of making the processes of an object's creation and destruction possible. Lucie imagined packaging that could fold flat when empty, or even fold as it was used. The water bottle, for example, involves a design process that is the opposite of the classical method. It was first of all crushed, before then being unfolded; the network of folds created by this manipulation was then carefully reproduced through a resin casting. It took hundreds of compaction tests to find the right folded form. In compressed form, it is easier to recycle. The relief created by the folds reveals its deformation.

As for the milk carton, Lucie says, "I have always found it strange that you can never see how much is left inside. The box form of packaging is perfectly optimized, but in terms of use, the object could be more interesting." So she worked on the design of a carton that gradually deformed as it emptied as a result of a predefined framework of folds.

Through its folds, the tin can that she has created is durable and can also be compressed by hand. In this case, prestamping is envisaged for marking the folds, because tin cans undergo very significant pressure during filling, and their form in particular is what allows them to resist this. It is easy to imagine that the test versions were more difficult to produce in this case, as the folds marked into the final prototype were engraved by hand, and the compression tests required great force. Many tests using paper models were carried out to work out the distribution of the folds.

The fourth type of packaging that she designed is a little different. Its starting point was the following observation: "My grandmother had these huge egg boxes, and I always thought that it was a waste of space to keep boxes that soon became half-empty." So she designed an egg box made from a single sheet of folded paper. The folding covers and protects the fragile eggs, and the sheet opens flat once the box is open.

Folds' mechanics are an integral part of the use of these different objects.

Lucie's prior knowledge of the packaging industry allowed her to design these products so that they could eventually be manufactured through a classic industrial chain. This collaboration between method and material is an integral part of the profession of industrial designer. The desire to keep track of the process and to comprehend it is a strong conceptual principle that allows the production practices for objects to be reexamined. Here, the use of folds is as practical as it is philosophical.

Interview with and remarks from Lucie Dorel, December 2014.

www.ensci.com

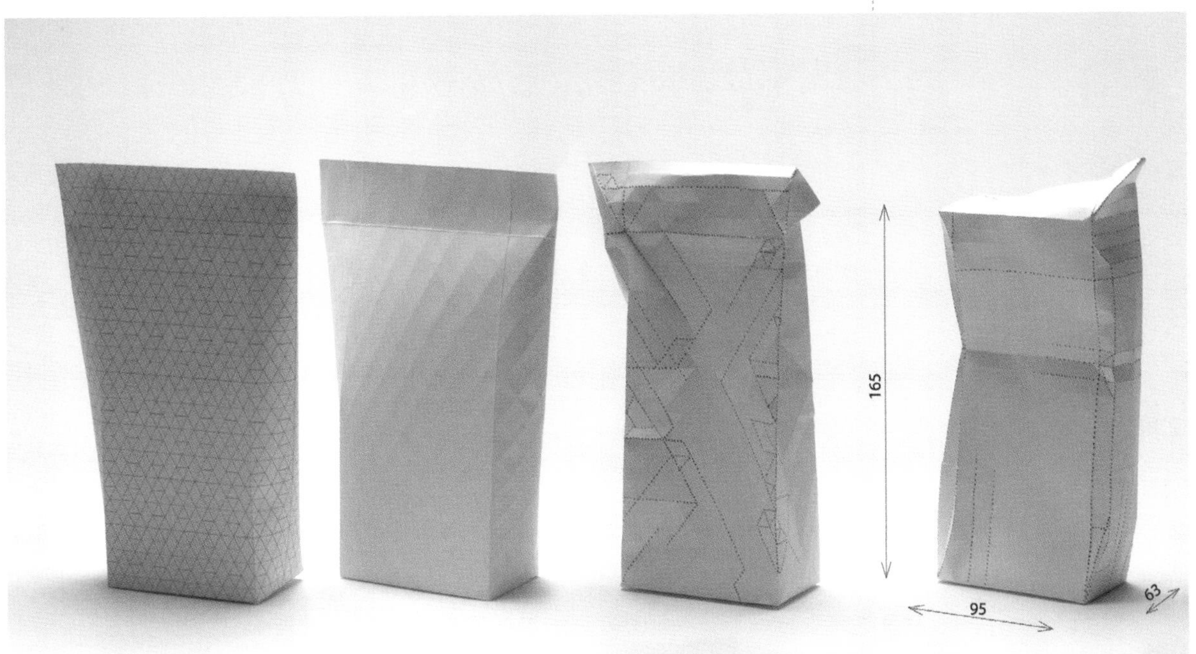

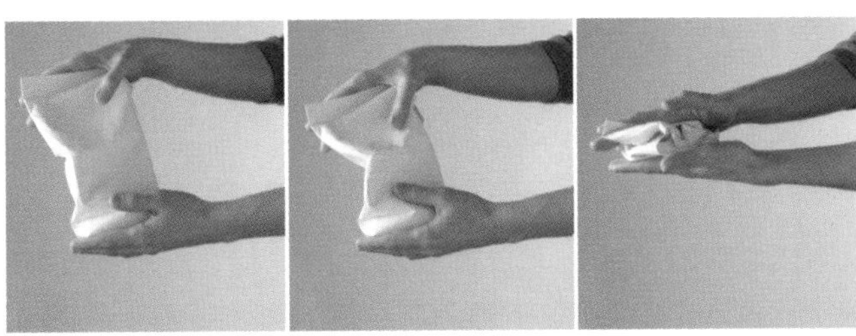

• *Test series of the* Conserves *project.*
• *Resin mould for the* Bouteille *project.*

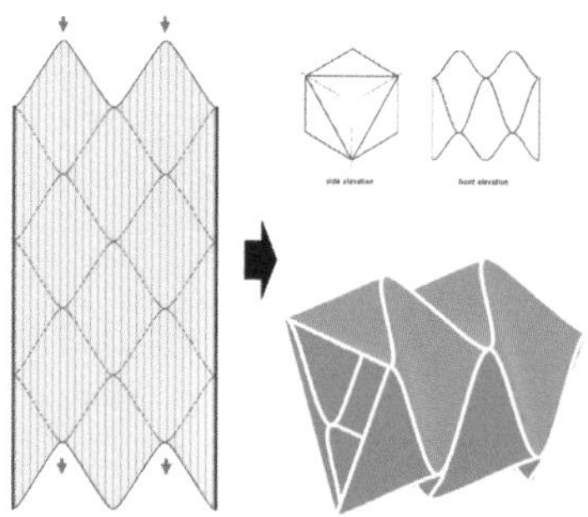

Otto Ng / LAAB

HONG KONG

Origami brick is a project based on the economy of matter. The basic idea is the design of a building component that can be made from wood, plastic or metal and that is created out of a fold.
Assembling the bricks allows a wall siding to be created. The wooden version, for example, represents a huge saving in material and work compared to a milled form that has been sculpted from a block. The challenge is to properly bend a thin sheet of wood, because the fibres (wood grain) give it a preferred curvature direction. For his test versions, Otto made his "origami bricks" in water. Doing so allowed him to soften the fibres, which otherwise would have broken.
This idea of modular tiling, which was in vogue in the 1970s, is fashionable again today owing to the new geometric possibilities that parametric 3D modelling allows.
The current forms are able to break free of the geometric models known since the times of Ancient Greece (regular polyhedra), which form the basis of this type of thinking on three-dimensional tessellations.

Remarks from Otto Ng, February 2015.

www.LAAB.pro
Otto Ng, see also p. 156.

- *Diagram of* Origami brick.
- Origami brick *made from a fine sheet of wood.*
- *Large wall tiling.*

Ilan Garibi / KAZA

ISRAEL / UNITED KINGDOM

Kaza Concrete manufactures and sells modular sidings made out of very fine concrete. These are the product of collaborations with designers and architects.
Ilan Garibi developed Quadilic tiling for Kaza. He has also created other wall tilings, including ones made from wood and folded metal.

www.garibiorigami.com
www.kazaconcrete.com

• Quadilic kazaconcrete *wall tiling and one of its modules.*

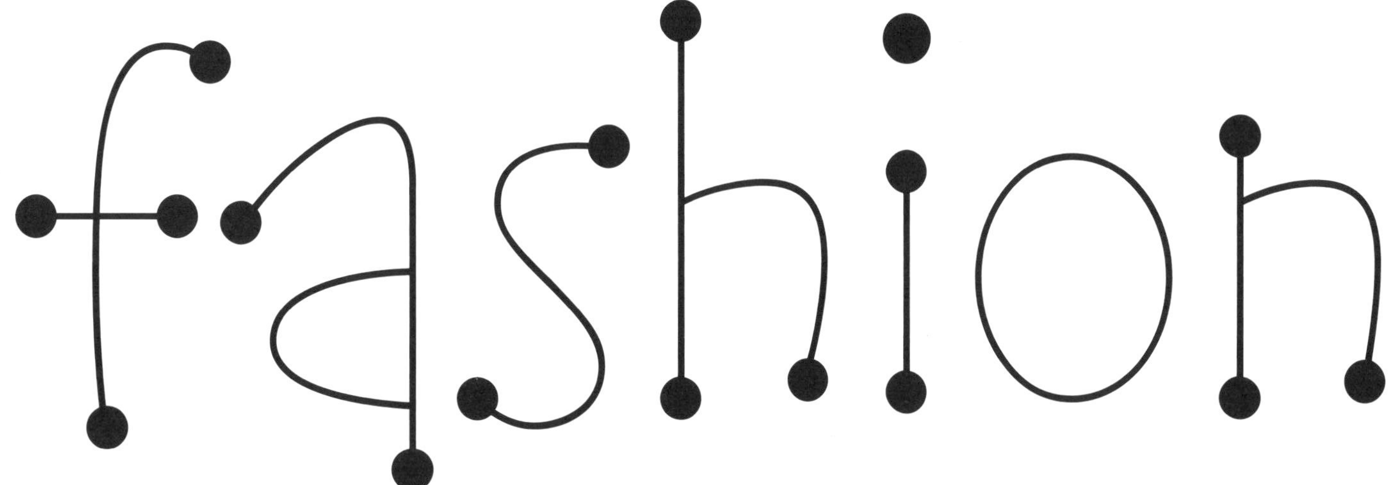

• Jule Waibel in London, a dress that changes shape on the basis of the movement of the body, and a bag and umbrella that can constrict and open out. The set is made using Tyvek®, a light synthetic paper that is resistant to water and tear.

FOLDING CHIC

Folding is the quintessential expression of sensuality. Its incessant interplay reveals the tension between what is visible and what is not. The folds of a veil instantly evoke the light flutter of a presence. Folding allows an interplay of shadow and light that gives relief to the forms: the whole meaning of a drape is related to suggestion.
It wraps the body and lets things be seen without revealing anything, and it gives rise to a form of eroticism.
Whether they are created through pleats or crumples, or whether they are a simple bending of the fabric, folds express a generosity. They awaken curiosity but never satisfy it.

Folding offers creators the possibility to give form to the material without the addition of extra elements. Once folded, the fabric expresses sensual nuances ranging from the misty to the crystalline.
Initially, folding fabric corresponded to a frequently used function: draping. The Roman toga, the kimono, the djellaba and the pareo all use a sophisticated folding technique on a generally rectangular piece of cloth (the product of a loom) to turn it into clothing. We might say in this case that folding is more a way to wear a garment than it is a garment in the sense that we understand the word today. It has many technical advantages in the creation of more elaborate clothing and finery.
In fashion—whether accessories or clothing—folds are constantly reinvented and rediscovered. From the constrictive frilled dresses of the beginning of the last century—with their multiple folds and puffs that produced an "overspill" of fabrics and lace—to Issaye Miyake's folds, which were conceived to release bodies from any impediment, folds have lent themselves to all interpretations of beauty.

• *Ilan Garibi,* Rounded Cubes in Metal, Forniron Jewellery, Diamond wood bracelet, *brass ring.*

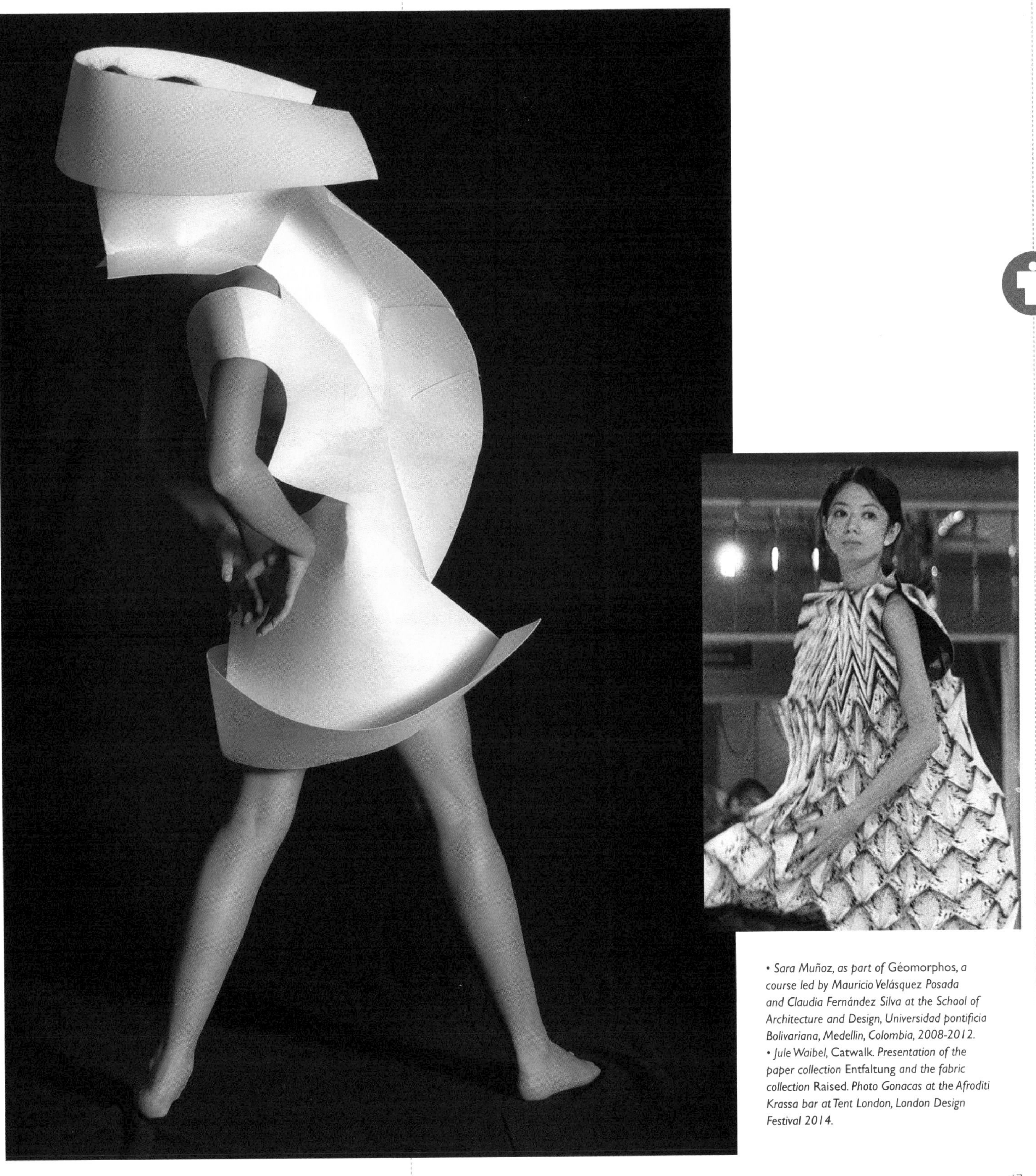

• *Sara Muñoz, as part of* Géomorphos, *a course led by Mauricio Velásquez Posada and Claudia Fernández Silva at the School of Architecture and Design, Universidad pontificia Bolivariana, Medellin, Colombia, 2008-2012.*
• *Jule Waibel,* Catwalk. *Presentation of the paper collection* Entfaltung *and the fabric collection* Raised. *Photo Gonacas at the Afroditi Krassa bar at Tent London, London Design Festival 2014.*

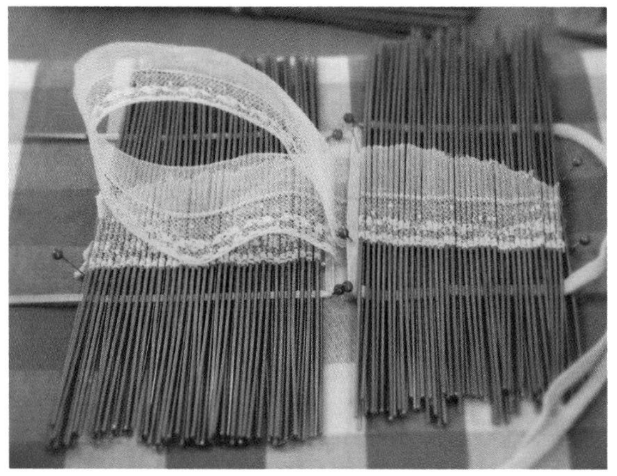

• Straw work on a headdress from the Saumur region. Collection of the Musée des Coiffes et des Traditions.
• Fluted cap from Saint-Mars-la-Jaille, 1860s. Collection of the Musée des Coiffes et des Traditions.

Museum of Headwear and Traditions

FRANCE

On the banks of the Loire, on Angers's doorstep, proudly sits a fifteenth-century dungeon. The last vestige of a summer residence of King René, Duke of Anjou, for more than forty years it has housed an unusual museum of headwear and traditions. Here, visitors will discover hundreds of caps and hats worn between 1820 and 1920 by women in all of France's provinces and in many countries, as well as the tools of embroiderers, lace makers and linen makers who made and maintained them.

It's important to be aware that in the past, a woman who left home with her hair uncovered was deemed to be of ill repute. To remain decent at all times, her outfits had to include many bonnets made of fine linen or cotton that she could make and maintain herself and one or two delicate and finely ornate items of headwear made to measure by a linen maker following the fashion of the village.

Expertly starched and ironed, and with varying degrees of size and showiness, the headwear was designed to highlight the woman's face on special occasions. Made from tulle, muslin cotton or fine lawn, and decorated with rich embroidery and precious lace, it represented a sign of wealth and belonging to a particular region for the woman who wore it and those who saw it.

Looking after the headwear, which required many hours of hard work, was entrusted to ironers who had learned the skill through three years of learning.

This special technique that involved many operations (taking apart, washing, stiffening, ironing, pleating, straw working or fluting and remaking) might have been completely lost without the passion of a few collectors.

The last linen makers were interviewed, and as a result their techniques and formulas have been preserved. These are now passed on to collectors and lovers of fine linens through training courses organized by the friends of the Museum of Headwear and Traditions.

Their book *Coiffes de l'Anjou* also gives an overview of these techniques, which require specific tools for their implementation and the acquisition of the ironers' famous dexterity.

Excerpts from the book Coiffes de l'Anjou, *Editions AMC, Association des amis du château-musée des Coiffes et des Traditions.*

www.amisdumuseedescoiffes.com/musee-des-coiffes

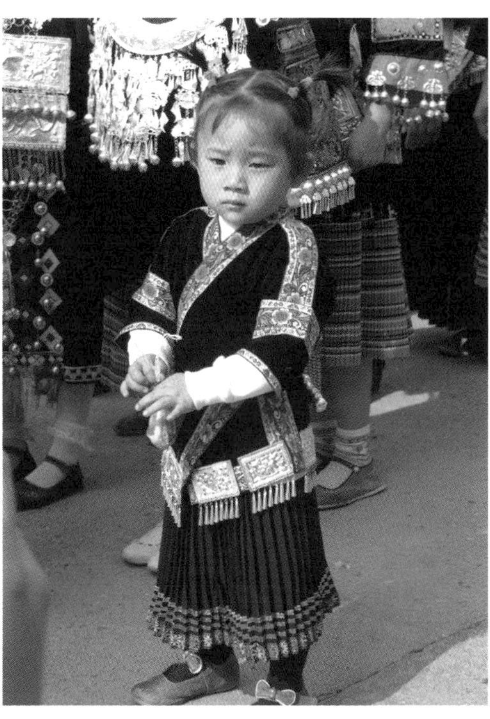

- *Drying of previously pleated textile.*
- *Miao child wearing the traditional pleated dress.*
- *Detail of pleated, dyed and embroidered textile.*

Traditional Miao clothing

CHINA

Susan Weitzman Conway lives in Atlanta, but she has spent many years travelling through China with Jessy (Yingbo) Zhang. She is a person who likes to meet people and discover the world.

Since her childhood, she has been interested in the habits and customs of the world, and especially those of Asian cultures. She collects objects that reflect the necessities of daily life (food, clothing, shelter). The antiquities in her collection can be seen on her website. They tell us about people's daily lives and their tremendous creativity. She is interested in China's ancient tradition of pleated textiles.

Although pleated robes are made and worn by many ethnic minorities in China, they are particularly widely worn by the Miao, who live in the region of QiaoGang, LeiShan.

Twenty-three varieties of pleated robes can be distinguished, and these can be placed into five characteristic types.

These beautiful robes, which are mainly worn by women, are difficult to make.

The textile is first flattened on a board and sprayed with a rice-based adhesive liquid.

Folds are then formed by hand with great precision and needle sewn. Regularly spraying the liquid on the fabric allows the folds' shaping to be preserved.

Depending on the region, the fabric is then stuck between boards or on a curved form for drying, which lasts several days. Colour is then added by successive dyeing and washing. The dyeing process goes on for a month.

Embroidery and ribbons may be added as distinctive signs in accordance with tribes and regions.

Remarks from Susan Weitzman Conway, January 2015.

www.asianethnicartifacts.com/
www.rugrabbit.com/profile/4682

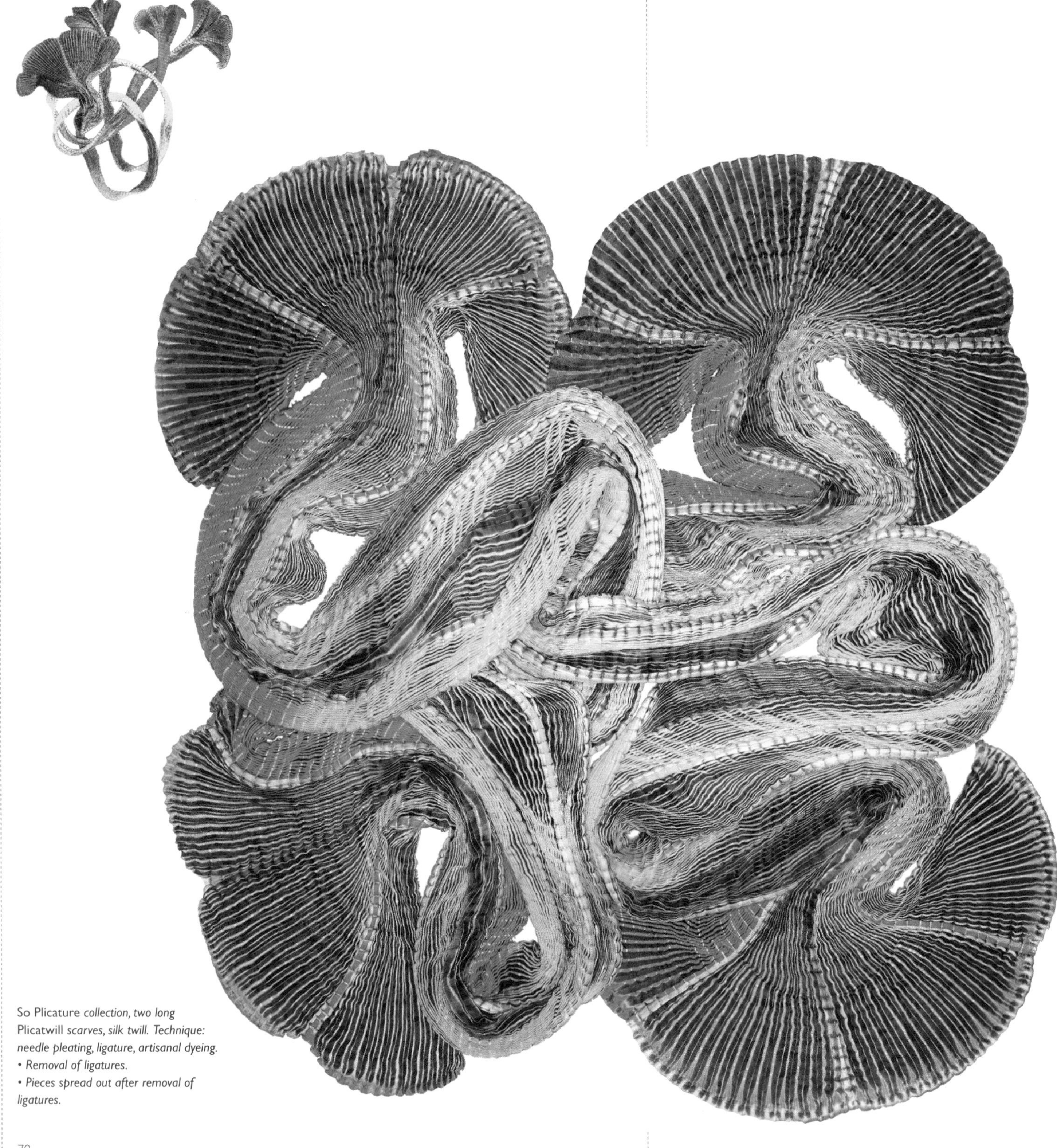

So Plicature *collection, two long* Plicatwill *scarves, silk twill. Technique: needle pleating, ligature, artisanal dyeing.*
- *Removal of ligatures.*
- *Pieces spread out after removal of ligatures.*

Atelier Sophie Guyot

FRANCE

Sophie Guyot has developed her approach as a textile designer through exploring the relationship between material, colour and function. She gained her know-how at the Lycée Diderot in Lyon, at Winchester University in the UK, and then through working with Mauritanian dyers. She received training in natural fermented dyeing from master dyer Anne Rieger. Since 2001, Sophie has taught at the Lycée La Martinière-Diderot and leads research workshops. She won the young designer competition at the Ateliers d'art de France 2004.

In her studio-boutique in Lyon, this designer comes up with artisanal textile objects, silks and trimmings that have a contemporary feel.

Inspired by the traditional techniques that she has revisited, she created a line of accessories called *So Plicature*. The transformation work is carried out in her studio, and each piece is unique. The folding techniques employed to transform white or ecru silk allow the accessory to be given its form and colour. For dyeing, she uses *Itajime Shibori* (reserve dyeing), a Japanese technique in which the fabric is enclosed to create a reserve in the dye bath (similar to the technique employed in a different context by the painter Simon Hantaï).

To create the folds, she uses a needle pleating technique, making a regular fold using a needle and thread. She then rolls the piece and forms a ligature to expose only certain parts of the fabric to the dye, which creates the patterns (according to the fibres used and the number of bathings, various renderings are possible). She designs the object, cuts it and sews it, but the folding comes about at the very end of the process. The result differs depending on the fabrics (for example, jersey, organza and chiffon), in terms of impact, volume, dye and so on. Silk pleating continues to be a painstaking process for exceptional works. It is a sophisticated piece of artisanal knowledge that has emerged out of the encounter between tradition and contemporary research.

Interview with Sophie Guyot, February 2015.

www.sophieguyot.com

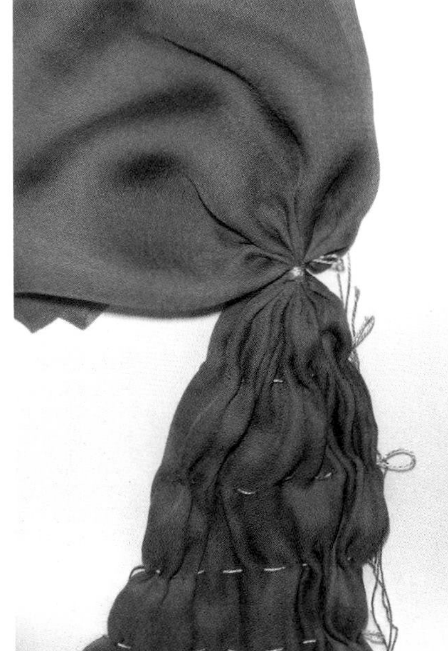

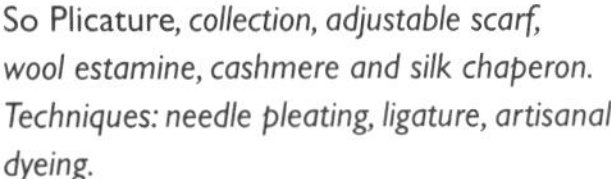

So Plicature, *collection, adjustable scarf, wool estamine, cashmere and silk chaperon. Techniques: needle pleating, ligature, artisanal dyeing.*
- *Completed piece worn as a chaperon.*
- *Completed piece spread on the shoulders and knotted at the back.*
- *Pleating in process on silk muslin.*

Julie Bénédicte Lambert

CANADA

Julie Bénédicte Lambert studied studio art at Concordia University (2000) and textile processing techniques at the Montreal Centre for Contemporary Textiles (2013). She divides her time between her artistic practice and her work as a technician in the department of Fibre Arts and Material Practices of Concordia University.
This designer weaves paper sculptures, and with great attention to detail she shapes the rigid and malleable surface created out of weaving. In her view, the structure of fabric is both concrete—the intertwining of threads—and abstract—spoken language. Textile and text share the same etymological root; working with paper as a material merges fabric and language. Much more than a movement, weaving is an allegory of our system of thought. "To weave my work, I mainly use threads of paper from different sources: wood cellulose, bamboo and flax paper. And metal threads (steel or stainless steel) are incorporated. It turned out that my first 100% paper samples were too vulnerable to atmospheric change. The addition of a few threads of metal in a chain or weave solves the problem and can be invisible. Humidity is both an enemy and an ally. Once woven, the parts are typically steamed to facilitate folding. They dry while keeping their shape. The main difficulties encountered are primarily on the loom. Paper threads have no elasticity. Tension equal to warping (*) is fundamental for a good result on the loom. A constant rate of humidity is also desirable in the studio. Up to four warp beams (**) are sometimes needed to weave complex parts. Obtaining sufficient rigidity and perfect finishes has also required a lot of research."

Remarks from Julie Bénédicte Lambert, February 2014.

(*) preparatory weaving work.
(**) large loom spool.

www.papiertextile.com

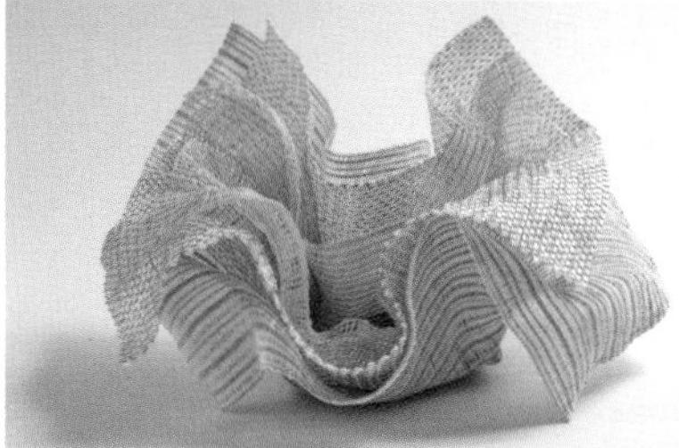

• Variation sur deux plans IV. *Paper (wood cellulose and bamboo), steel, nylon stainless steel, linen. Double weave. 2013.*
• *From the series:* Les dires. Entre les paroles et les mots II. *Paper (wood cellulose and flax), stainless steel, silk, steel. Weave of multiple thicknesses. 2013.*
• *Jacket. Paper (wood cellulose), cotton and rayon. produced from a handmade weave. Pattern and assembly by the artist. 2011. Model: Christelle Trottier Gallant.*

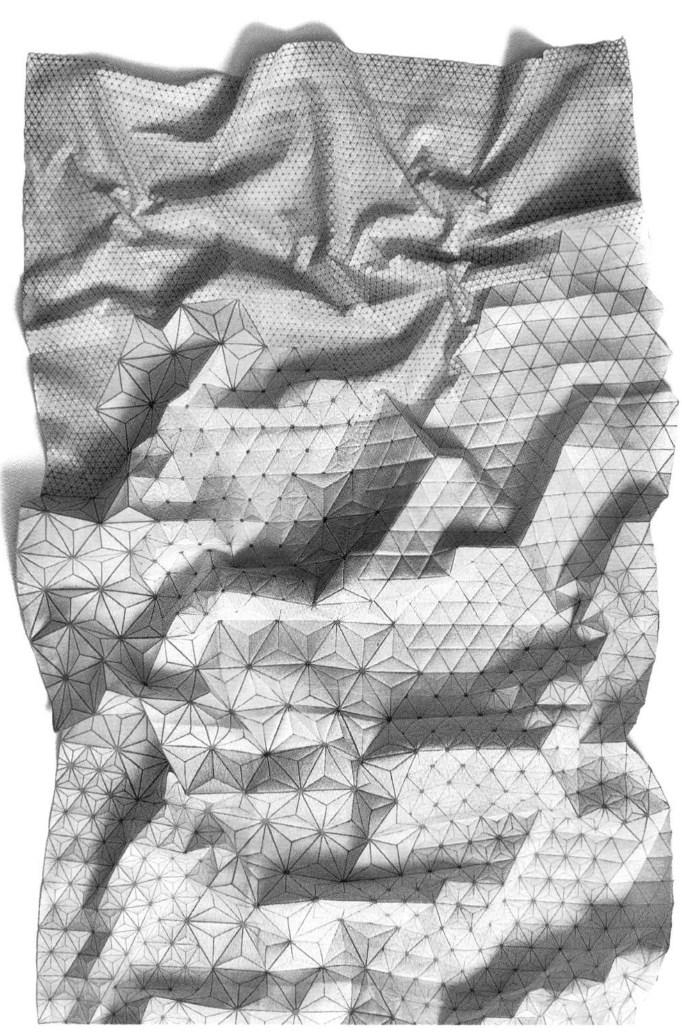

Mikabarr

ISRAEL

Mika Barr is a textile designer. She develops and creates innovative 3D textiles based on particular printing techniques. Her fabrics are inspired by folded paper models that she produces.
She begins by observing, painting and folding different forms. She uses the screen printing technique, with certain adaptations and different patterns that she transfers onto the fabric. A pattern that is very geometric truly structures the fabric: the printed and more rigid faces behave like origami faces, while the nonprinted fabric between faces, which is more flexible, works in a way similar to a hinge. When the pattern is more organic—in the shape of leaves, for example—the folding is more delicate. Mika creates the prototypes in her studio, and she then produces her collections in collaboration with local artisans, for printing and sewing.

www.mikabarr.com

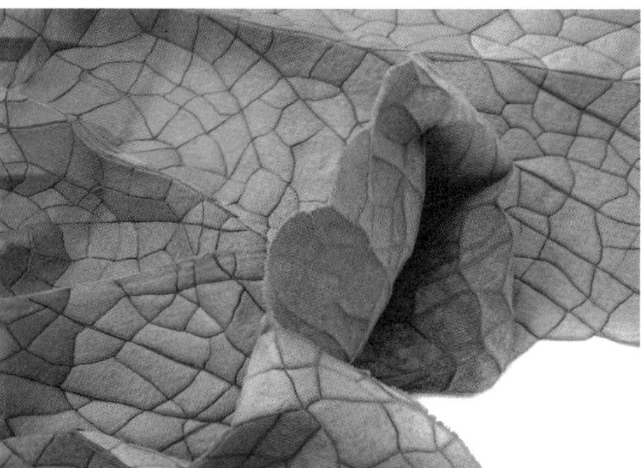

• *Untitled*, from woven consciousness, *Eretz Israel Museum exhibition, Tel Aviv.*
• Leaf like fabric, *detail of fabric inspired by a leaf.*
• Flowers.

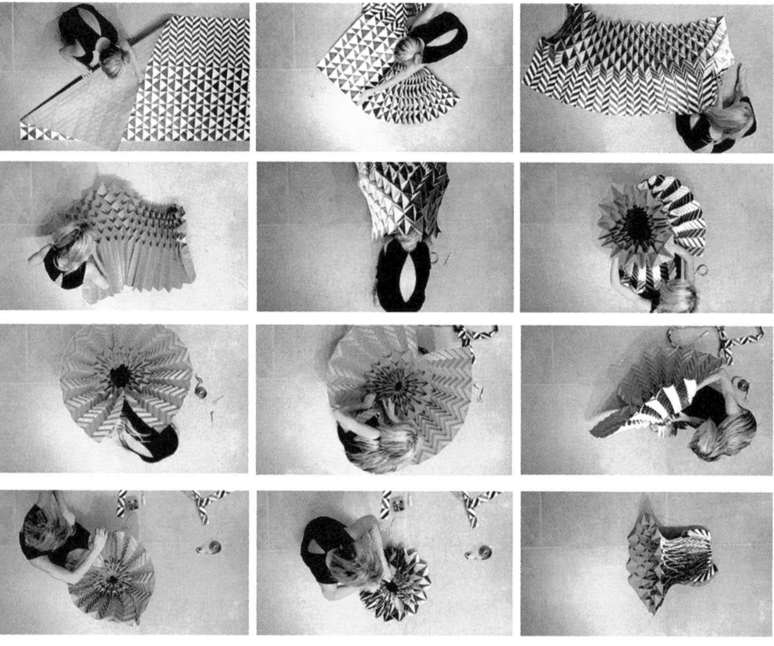

• *Folding of a dress for an exhibition with Bershka, 25 dresses for 25 cities. Barcelona, January 2014.*
• *Jule Waibel in her workshop in London.*

Jule Waibel

GERMANY - ENGLAND

Jule Waibel's folded work is entertaining, surprising or simply beautiful to look at. And it always has a touch of humour and a little sparkle.

"I always want something unexpected to happen—something that inspires people—otherwise it would be boring," says the 28-year-old German designer who has a studio in London, where she lives and works. After graduating with a bachelor's degree in industrial design from the Hochschule für Gestaltung, she decided to study product design at the Royal College of Art in London, to "express/unfold herself"—something that she has done in a literal way.

With a rather impatient nature, this artist forgets everything around her when it comes to folding card and paper. She questions the reaction of various materials to folding and queries how three-dimensional objects that change shape and volume can be made based on folds. In her view, there is nothing more exciting than unfolded structures. The technique is an old one, though its implementation is still contemporary and surprising.

This year, her work has been praised by the international design press. Her beautiful paper creations were exhibited in the leading department stores around the world in cities such as London, Paris, Istanbul, Osaka and Mexico. For Design Week in London in 2013, she came up with an unusual show where dancers from the English National Ballet wore her transforming paper and fabric clothes. She is currently working on a collection of folded seats. Their folds are similar to those of her dresses (they involve a steaming technique), though they are made from a completely different material: folded felt.

Remarks from Jule Waibel, November 2014.

www.julewaibel.com

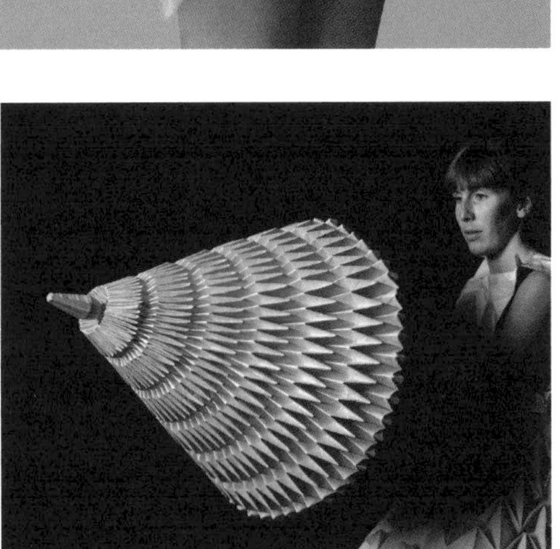

- Pleated dreams pt.2, *Germany.*
- *Detail of Tyvek® umbrella that can contract and open out, London.*
- *Folded dress for an exhibition with Bershka, 25 dresses for 25 cities, Barcelona, January, 2014.*
- *Details of a dress that changes shape depending on body movements and of a Tyvek® bag that can contract and open out, London.*

HOID

GERMANY

Hande Akcayli and Murat Kocyigit are the cofounders of Berlin's HOID design studio. HOID is a merger of their former design studio, Mashallah, and the research project *The T/Shirt Issue*. Along with Rozi Rexhepim, they are continuing their production of ready-to-wear fashion and art installations based on 3D.

"We came from different backgrounds such as product design and experimental fashion design. Our field of interest has expanded and we started to push the boundaries of building 3D models, which is at the heart of our research.

Our work is based on 3D applications that are intended for video-game animation design. We use various techniques to create 3D pieces that range from everyday clothing to pieces of art. Geometric polygonal structures, the foundation of these types of software application, are essential for displaying 3D geometry, and they give us artistic freedom. After sculpting these pieces, we use the software program Pepakura to unfold the geometries. The last step is to digitally adjust the paper patterns and turn them into sewing patterns for our cotton T-shirts.

After converting the 3D data into 2D sewing patterns, we laser cut each piece of fabric and the internal interfaces, and then we sew the pieces together. The creative process depends on the conceptual idea of the piece that we are working on. Sometimes we digitize 3D objects and bodies, assimilating them into the 3D model in the digital design process. This is a new and highly intuitive way of creating in three dimensions. At other times, we sculpt out of nothing, without references.

In 2008, we had the goal of changing that most fundamental of garments: the T-shirt. The idea was a simple one: customize a T-shirt without using printing. Through the *Melt* project, we sought to make a garment that seemed fluid, while also reducing the amount of polygons.

During our six-month stay at the Victoria & Albert Museum, we created *Dream-Land*, a sculptural installation inspired by the Edgar Allan Poe poem from 1844.

From the beginning, our work has generally been motivated by the idea of digital democracy. Technology opens up a wide field of possibilities for designers. Today, with CNC machines, transferring data from the virtual world to the real one has never been easier."

www.hoid.co

• Melt 1, 2, 3 and 4. *Each polygon represents a different facet of the person.*

• Muybridge N°2, *a work on movement.*
• Dream-Land, N°903: Christ on an Ass (A.1030-1910) & The Frog Princess.
• Dream-Land, N°895: The Crouching Venus (A.5-2012) & Golden Eagle (Cast Court).

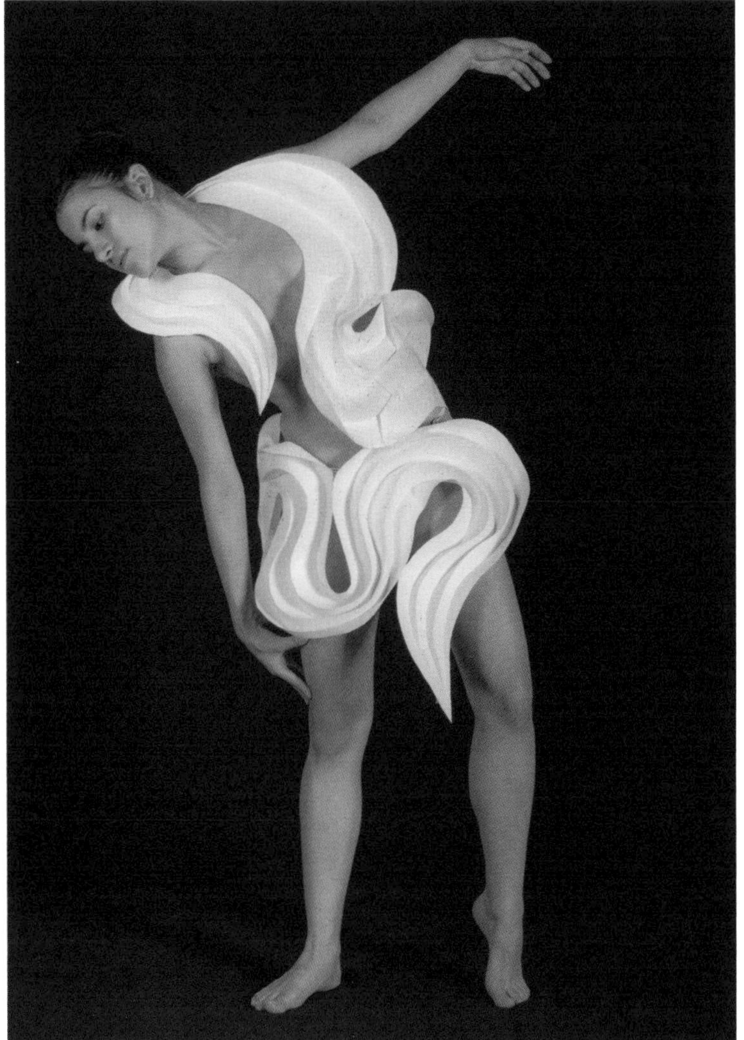

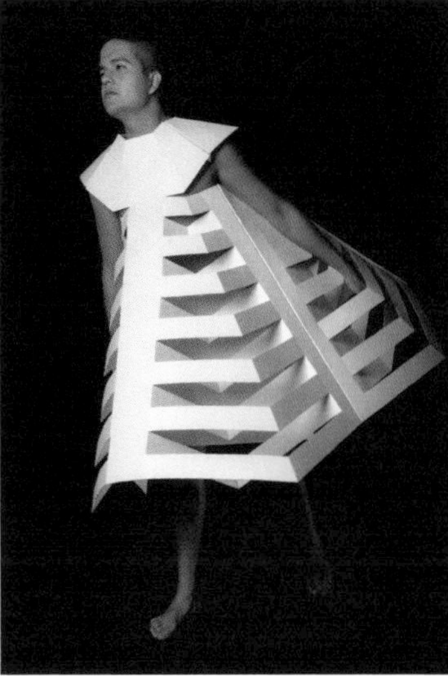

• *Catalina Valencia,* Geomorphos.
• *Sara Muñoz Gil,* Geomorphos, *School of architecture and design, Universidad Pontificia Bolivariana, Medellin, Colombia. 2008-2012.*

Mauricio Velásquez Posada and Claudia Fernández Silva

COLOMBIA

Geomorphos, *Strange and folded bodies*

As teachers and researchers, we are constantly thinking about certain issues that we consider fundamental to the study of the clothed body: volume, space and structure. The clothes that we wear on a given occasion are determined by these three aspects, which we wanted to highlight and explore through this project.
In addition, *Geomorphos* involves research to find an alternative response to traditional ways of thinking about the design of clothing, steering it away from fashion as a paradigm that dominates the creation process, production and understanding of clothing practices in our culture.
Geomorphos has become about the interplay between forms and surfaces—paper and geometry—that comes from a creative process oriented towards experimentation with the body in the creation of unimaginable clothing ideas.
This year, we decided to take a step forward by merging *Geomorphos* with movement. The result is *Animorphos*, in which the categories of movement are combined with form, structure and space.

Remarks from February 2015.

www.expacios.wordpress.com
www.youtube.com/watch?v=w9gsqqwJkwo
www.youtube.com/watch?v=7bBtMA2miHc

Amila Hrustić

BOSNIA-HERZEGOVINA

The Plato, collection, or the fold as metaphor for the female body

Amila Hrustić hails from Bosnia-Herzegovina. She is a product designer who currently works as an art director for a communications agency in Prague. Her training has given her a way of seeing things that interacts with an artist's sensibilities.

She is not a clothes designer by training. The *Plato* collection (2010), whose lines derive from Platonic solids that are folded and sewn, was an experiment on her part. Amila simply wanted to create theatrical costumes. These pieces and their cubist lines were not intended to be worn as clothing, because they were fragile. the *Plato* collection was exhibited in many places. These dresses' abstract contours tell us about the contemporary history of fashion: a search for abstraction and bodily sublimation.

The work of this young designer is the result of conceptual research, the theme of which was the female body and its deconstruction based on geometric shapes. She was inspired by origami and *Paper Art,* as well as a "simultaneous simplicity and complexity," to make solid forms from paper. For this costume designer, this was a work of patience and perseverance, motivated by conceptual research: What dresses and shapes the female body? To turn her folding ideas into real forms, Amila sought to recreate the crystalline forms of regular polyhedra (Platonic solids) in a garment that was fluid and elegant when worn.

What is moving about this project is that it works: rough shapes disappear and give way to the sensual expression of movement.

Remarks from February 2015.

www.dezeen.com/2010/11/23/platos-collection-by-amila-hrustic

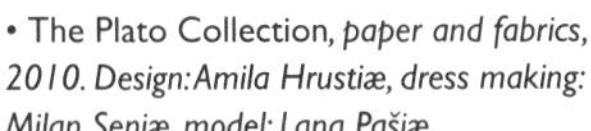

• The Plato Collection, *paper and fabrics, 2010. Design: Amila Hrustiæ, dress making: Milan Seniæ, model: Lana Pašiæ.*

• *Dress with flounces. Inspired by the Bauhaus style, this dress is uniquely made from a single piece of rectangular fabric that has been pressed in certain places. The geometric pattern is formed by folding and light, through the superimposition of translucent materials.*

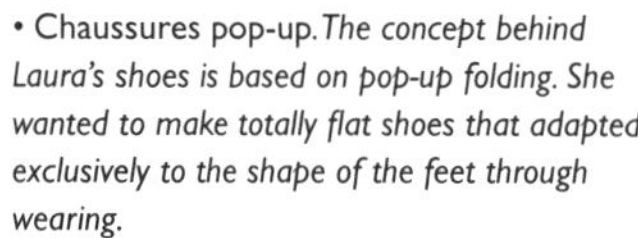

• Chaussures pop-up. *The concept behind Laura's shoes is based on pop-up folding. She wanted to make totally flat shoes that adapted exclusively to the shape of the feet through wearing.*

Laura Papp

HUNGARY

Specializing in the design of accessories, bags and shoes, in most of her work, Laura Papp explores the concepts of transparency and shaping out of a single piece of material based on techniques inspired by origami. The material used depends on the function of the object. She uses different materials such as leather for shoes and bags or textiles (linen and polyamide) with the appearance of paper. "For the *Layered Dress*," she explains, "the choice of fabric was determined by the objective of producing strong folds. I also took advantage of the fabric's transparency. As a result, the technique of folding not only shapes the garment but also allows the appearance of a form of pattern."

www.laurapapp.com

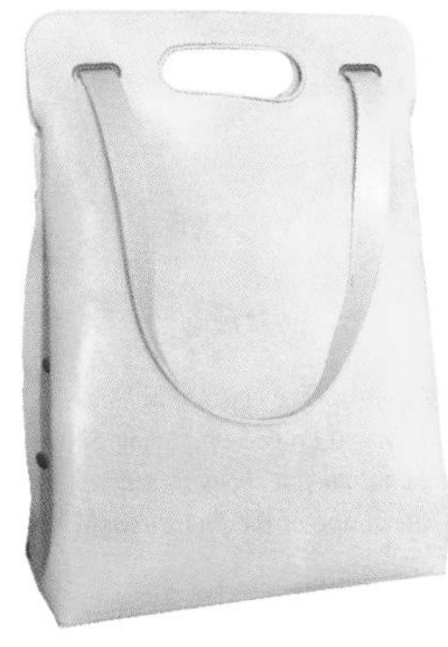

FFIL

FRANCE

When folds revitalize

During her studies in applied arts, Claire was fascinated by transformable objects. So she set about studying all kinds of folds deriving from pop-up. The problem she addressed was the following: How could you make a one-piece fashion accessory based on a shaped template (a single piece of paper)? The first test models were mittens.

Claire wanted to produce her pieces in France. She went back to her native region, Maine-et-Loire. A small proportion of the pool of textile know-how and tools that the region once boasted remains. There are also plentiful stocks of raw materials, with surpluses of leather and textiles.

In 2007, Claire decided to participate in the Maison et Objet fair in Paris to present her ideas. With the application of folds and pressure to the model, people can make their own bag, which is both entertaining for the customer and economical in terms of manufacturing (no stitching is required) and transport (the parcel delivered is flat). This concept became what guides the company Deux filles en fil (FFIL).

Leather folds well. The object's form is created either through shaping (bags), or folds marked by grooves (suitcase cubes): a machine is used to thin out the leather. The material passes through rollers and a blade "bites" into it, allowing folds to be marked out and sharper geometric lines to be created.

It is a beautiful project, because of its social and environmental engagement on the one hand, and the choice of simple lines dictated by the material and the folding technique on the other. And the end result is "a leather bag for everyone"—made in France!

Interview remarks from Claire Batardière, October 2014.

www.deuxfillesenfil.fr

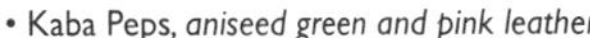
• Kaba Peps, *aniseed green and pink leather.*

Maori Kimura

JAPAN

Maori Kimura is a textile designer who has created bags manufactured from textiles that fold based on what is printed on the fabric. This was her degree project, and for Maori working on origami also means giving fold lines and shadows a beautiful hue through the use of many colours.

"We suggested a fabric that folds along the outline of a pattern, based on foam printing stiffening the fabric. Generally speaking, when you use foam printing, the printed part of the fabric becomes stiff. Inspired by the work of Ron Resch* and original patterns, we produced three-dimensional designs that seem to come out of the fabric.

Most bags are made from a rectangular pattern, and the shape of the bag is itself obtained by folding. These backpack and handbag models also have interesting stretching and shock absorbency properties. And, depending on the angle that they are viewed from, their colours change. If the mountain and valley folds are reversed, the appearance changes once again. For the bottom of the backpack, the folds naturally define the shape of the bag itself, based on the distortions that appear on the bottom."

* Ron Resch (Ronald Dale Resch), an artist and computer scientist to whom we are indebted for, among other things, his substantial research on tessellations.

Remarks from Maori Kimura, January 2015.

www.flickr.com/people/maori_k

- *Bags.*
- *Hexagonal textures.*

• Maori Kimura, Barnacle.

Quinoa Paris

FRANCE

Sasha and Stéphanie, the cofounders of Quinoa Paris, are fashion and design enthusiasts.
"While working on an interior decoration project, we were looking for leather storage baskets that could be easily folded and stored in order to be switched with one another, and that could also be turned into a bag at the same time as keeping an elegant appearance. Of course, we didn't find any, and so we had to make them ourselves!"
The Quinoa Paris bags are made of a single piece of leather and are put together using an intelligent folding system. Alongside this use of folding, the fact that they are not sewn makes them more durable. In addition, they are made in France out of tanned plant leather (without the use of any toxic products at all), meaning that they are high-quality and exceptionally durable bags.

Remarks from Quinoa, December 2012.

www.quinoa-paris.com

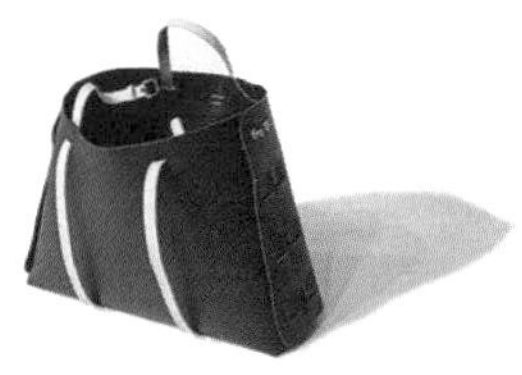

• Margot *Bags*.

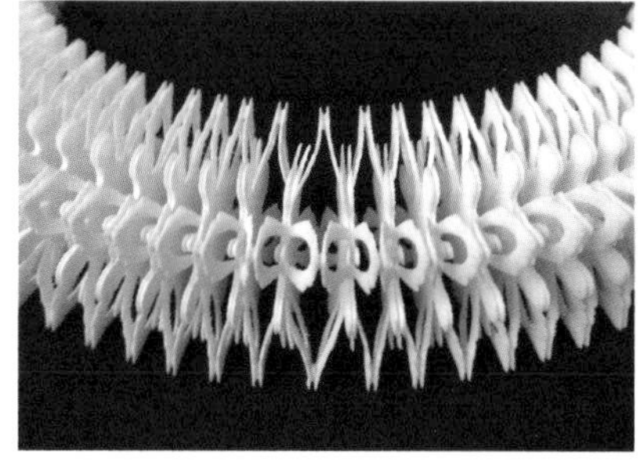

Studio OOOMS

THE NETHERLANDS

This Dutch design studio founded by Guido Ooms and Karin van Lieshout designs functional and unique objects and organizes creative workshops.
"The use of folding in this design comes from the fact that at the time when it was created, 3D printing was still fairly expensive. We studied products and foldable objects, and we were inspired by the holiday garlands that you usually see. These paper garlands are approximately 1 cm (3/8 in) thick when you buy them, but when you decorate the room, they can extend more than 5 m (197 in)."
The necklace is made using a 3D printer. The plastic material is a powder that is melted with a laser to create a three-dimensional shape. The use of this technique allows the necklace to be produced with a very thin material and a lot of details.

Remarks from Studio OOOMS, October 2014.

www.oooms.nl

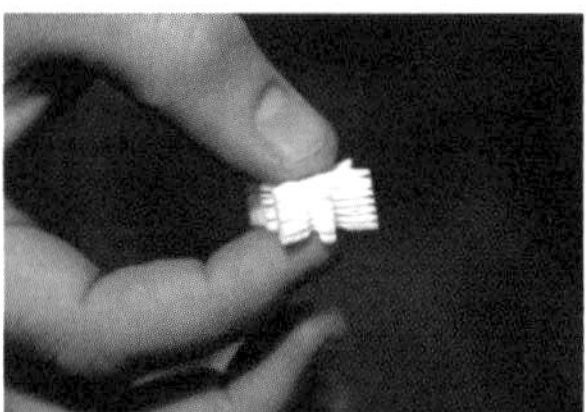

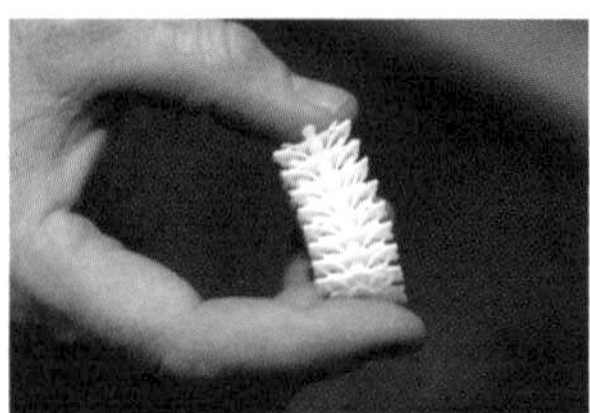

• Necklace made with rapid prototyping Dimensions: 25 cm (9 13/16 in in), diameter: 2 cm (13/16 in in).

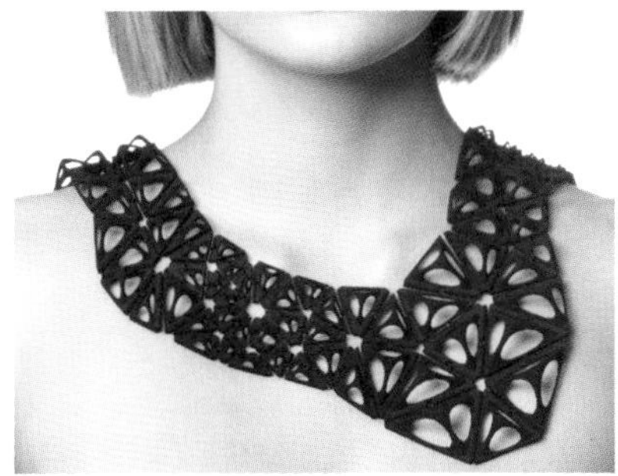

Nervous System

USA

Nervous System is a design studio that works at the intersection between science, art and technology. Inspired by natural phenomena, its members write computer programs based on imitating patterns found in nature, and they then use these programs to make objects and jewellery using CNC machines. Each piece of *Kinematics* jewellery is a complex assembly of hinges and triangular pieces that behaves like a continuous folded piece of fabric, adapting to the body of the person wearing it.
The parts are manufactured layer by layer from a sturdy but gently flexible nylon plastic, using the technique of laser sintering, a type of 3D printing. The hinges are built during the printing process so that each piece of jewellery leaves the printer fully assembled. The pieces are then polished, but they retain a delicate texture from the printing process. The jewellery uses magnets as a fastening mechanism.

www.n-e-r-v-o-u-s.com

- *First experiments with 3D printing.*
- Kinematics *necklace.*
- *3D-printed bodice.*

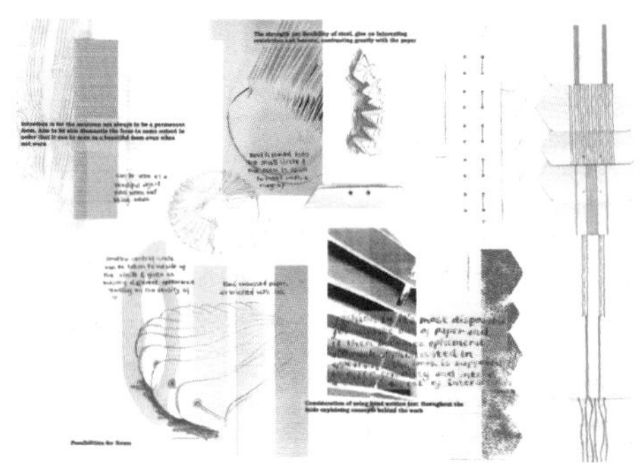

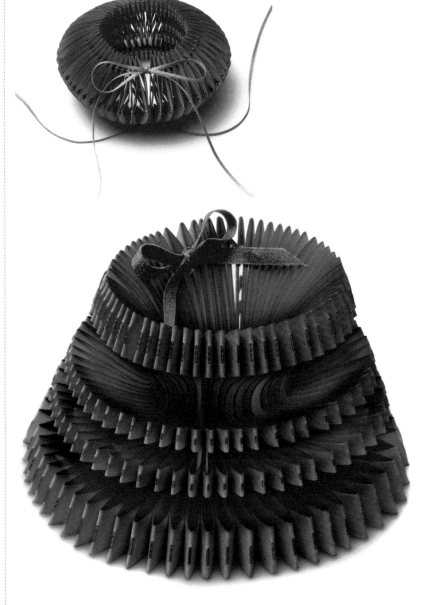

Sarah Kelly-Saloukee

ENGLAND

Having used paper to design models of jewellery pieces that were then made out of conventional materials such as metal, Sarah Kelly started to use folded paper in her final jewellery productions, a technique that offered her greater freedom. She uses thick and embossed paper, on which she applies a lacquer to protect it over time. After successfully making a suitable hand-folded model, she draws the diagram in 2D using design software. This then allows her to laser cut the paper with a very high level of accuracy. She then folds each piece by hand with the help of a folding tool, and she assembles them with rivets. The final jewellery piece stretches and shrinks, adapting to the wearer.

www.saloukee.com

Sarah Kelly has published a book on folding techniques for jewellery making, *Paper Jewellery*, Design and make, A&C Blake, 2012.

- *Project development notebook.*
- Solitary Bracelet *black.*
- Obverse Collar *black.*
- Obverse Bracelet *grey.*

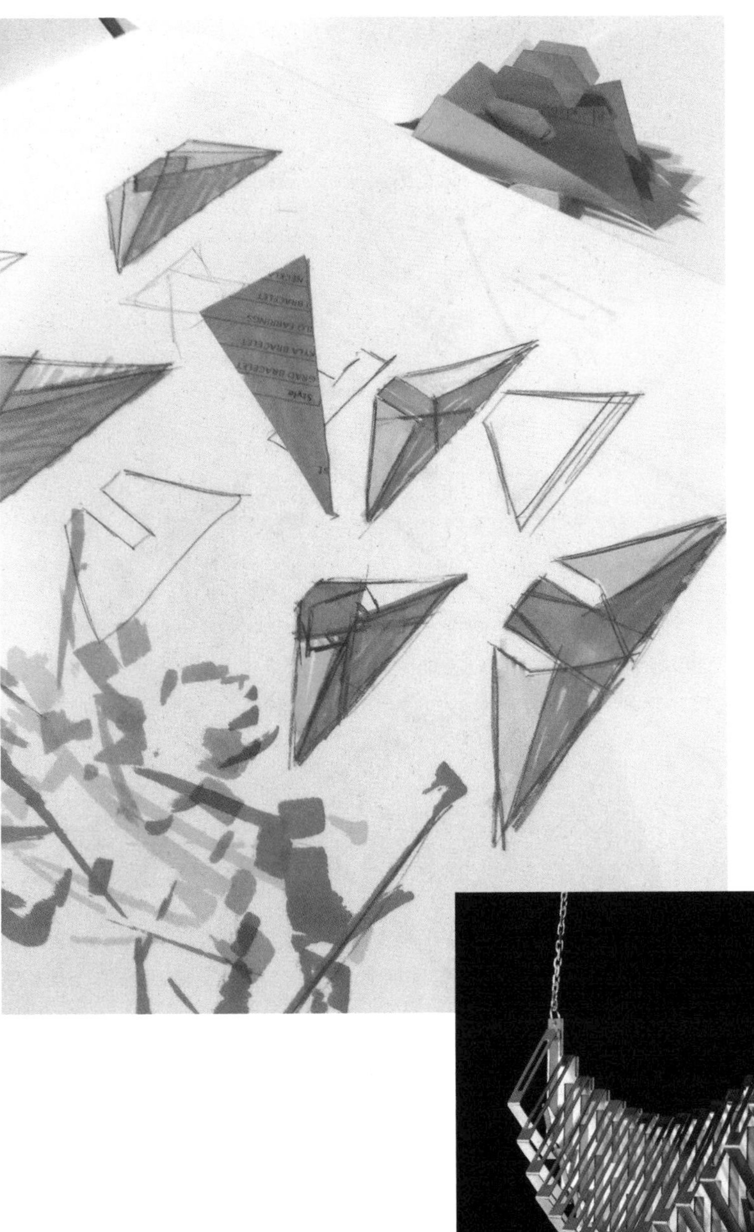

Sarah Angold Studio

ENGLAND

Sarah Angold Studio is a multidisciplinary design house that creates products and installations by combining cutting-edge digital processes, innovative applications of materials and crafts.
They use folding for experimenting with structures and patterns, and also for their finished metal or paper pieces. For example, the undulation of the surface of the "Trufelo" necklace (designed in collaboration with Studio Prod Designs), was developed using folded paper, which was scanned and printed in 3D with grey metal powder. Conversely, their Rondot and Prisere lighting pieces are each made of two pieces of folded cardboard, with the cardboard receiving an ultra gloss lacquer for a metal effect. Each piece of jewellery is manufactured as a custom limited edition and hand made in London, "I like the encounter between hypermodernity and crafts," Sarah says. While in residence at the Design Museum in London, Sarah created lighting installations for the exhibitions, which subsequently inspired her in her jewellery creations.

www.sarahangold.com

- *Research board.*
- Lyrio Red *necklace.*
- Tansigna Suza *necklace.*

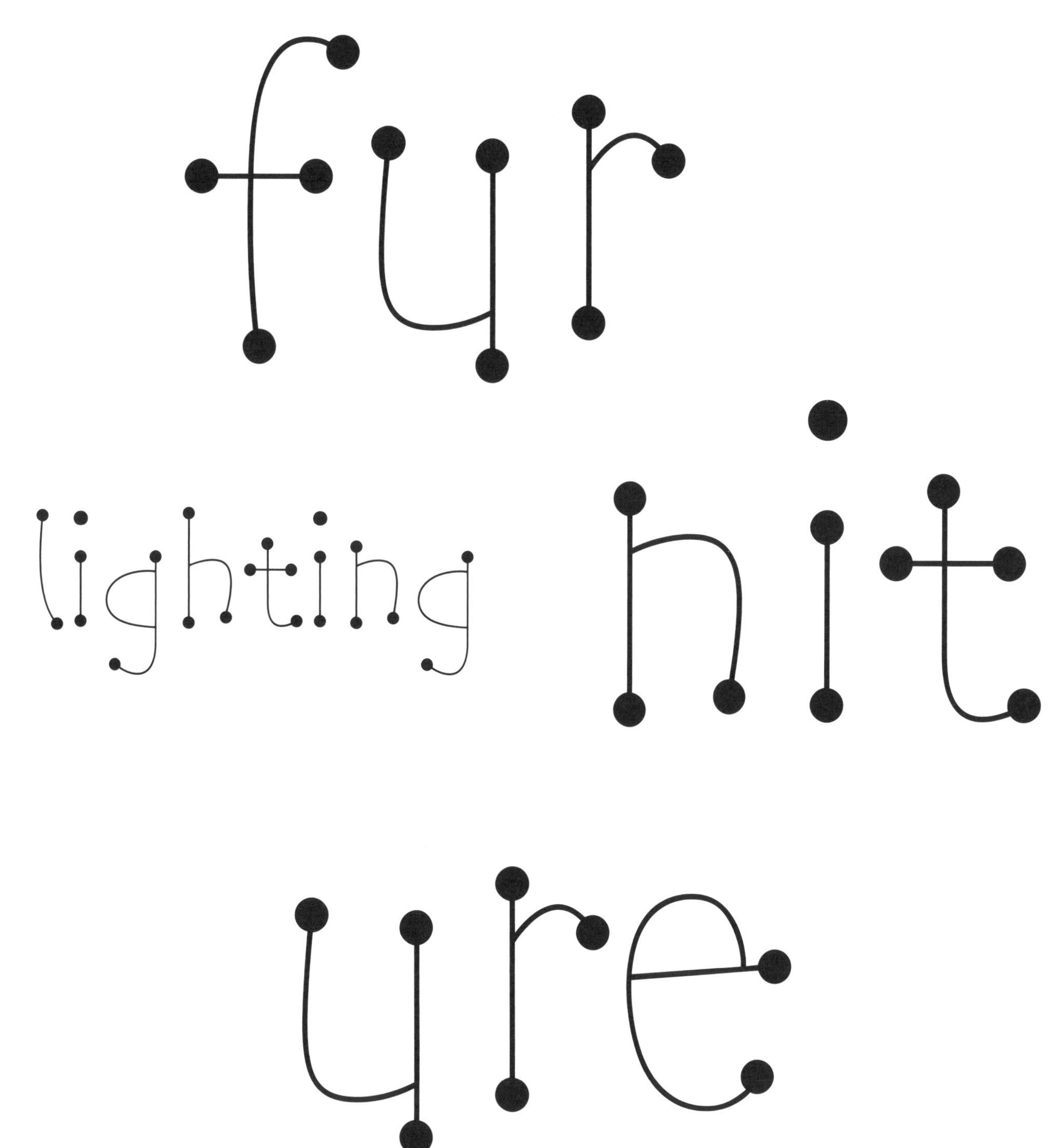

Daimonds Pučko,
Contving, Grand - Fire Pit, *3 mm (1/8 in) steel.*

COMFORTABLE FOLDS

Design is a discipline that stems from the applied arts. It encompasses many skills and trades such as furniture design, interior layouts, graphic arts and so on.
Design as an expression of beauty transcends the functional first dimension of common objects.
As a body of work, it is the culmination of an initial experimentation that has successfully become know-how. Folds can fulfil many functions and can become a kind of vocabulary that brings coherence to forms.
So, during the modelling phase of a furniture project, folds can first of all be a mode of design (for example, a folded model). From the idea to the studio, folds can then contribute to the shaping of the final object (for example, a folded mould for the formwork of a casting). They can also be used for structural purposes (rigidity, as in the case of a metal bracket) or for articulation (mobility, as in the case of a hinge of a notebook or the bellows of a bus). During the manufacturing process, in terms of technical advantages, folding may meet implementation requirements or facilitate the transport and implementation of prefabricated elements.
One can only be amazed at the variety of expressions that folds allow and at the diversity of creators and their approaches to the question of folding.
The designer of a piece of furniture must achieve a mode of production that is consistent with commercial objectives, and for this reason he or she will make strategic choices (technical materials, costs, environmental and social footprint and so on).
It is rare for designers to manufacture and distribute their products themselves. They usually need partners to access a distribution network. As a fashion phenomenon, design contributes to the mass-consumption and production society. It satisfies a demand for objects that are more beautiful, more functional and lighter than those of the past. But everyone must consider the life of objects, the origin of the resources used to produce them, the conditions for the workers who have manufactured them, their environmental impact at the end of their life and so on. Folding can help to save on materials through the form factor—here it suggests a way to reduce the environmental footprint of tomorrow's objects.

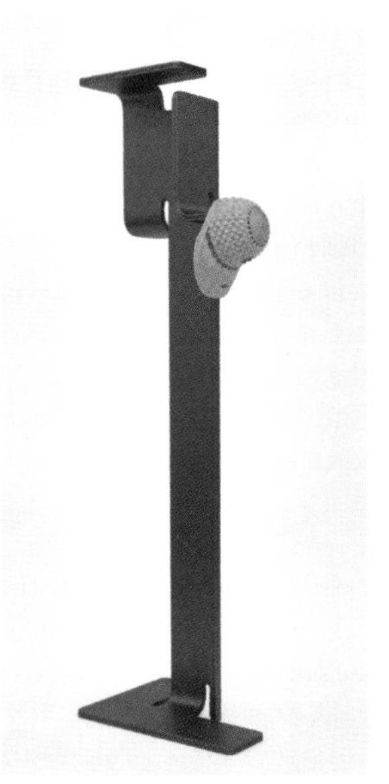

• *Claudio Colucci and Dominique Serrell, coat rack,* Génération *project, created with the support of Pierre Staudenmeyer, founder of the Mouvements Modernes gallery.*

Claudio Colucci

FRANCE

• *Preliminary models,* Génération *project.*
• *Console table,* Génération *project.*

A "generation" of folded objects from the association between designer Claudio Colucci and Dominique Serrell

We have chosen to present *Génération* to you. It was created for the contemporary furniture gallery Mouvements Modernes, and in more than one respect it is an avant-garde project. Firstly, as its name suggests, the original concept expressed, in the context of the eighties, the intuition of what design in the twenty-first century would become: an exploration of new generations of forms and the eclipse, thanks to computer technology, of some of the canons of the past.

This particular project is above all a manifesto: it is a limited series—and destined to remain that way—that was developed with complete freedom. *Génération* inspires the visionary idea that objects belong to "families" that have their own "genetic code" and that can be "cross-bred" with varying degrees of success, just as living beings or components of a formula in chemistry can.

Initially, the intention was for the project to use several materials, which was consistent with the idea of clear research. In the end, the formula retained used a single material, moulded wood, and consisted of several different parts: thirteen families of "generations" have been produced.

The folds are made with a mould and a countermould to "press" the form: thin and flexible wooden plates are glued together to achieve the desired thickness. This technique is also found in frame work with glulam. Carpenters have had to resolve stability issues related to material flexibility. These interchangeable and modular wood pieces, intended for use as a coffee table, sideboard, wardrobe and so on, were covered with a stretched fabric with a "sunken" invisible seam: a bit of a technical feat to achieve.

Génération speaks, in short, of all generations of objects and the mystery of function.

Remarks from Claudio Colucci and Dominique Serrell, March 2015.

www.colucci-design.com
www.mouvementsmodernes.com
www.terresnuages.com

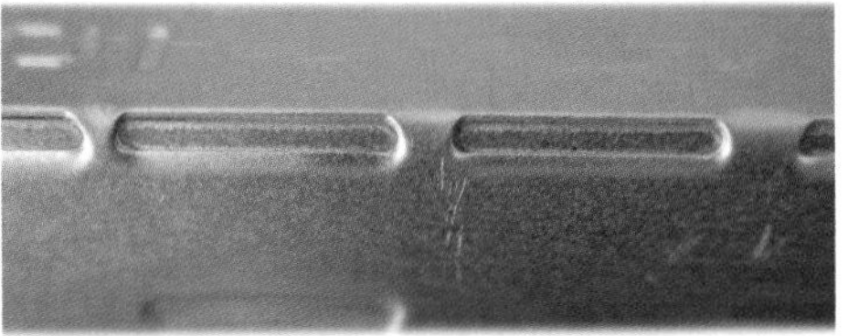

Industrial Origami

USA

Industrial Origami® is a company based in Cleveland, USA. It holds many patents, including ones related to industrial applications of folding.
The technical advantage sought is to reduce the thickness required for the strength of the object, to allow more rapid assembly, or even to minimize assembly.
The optimization of the given requirements of the folding allows the customers of Industrial Origami® to design folded parts in complex forms that are optimized for industry.
Folds are made with little effort thanks to a consideration of geometry that takes into account material deformation. They can be marked by stamping or laser cutting. The folding of the final object can, depending on what is needed, be achieved with simple hand tools (for example, laser cutting), with automated pneumatic folding, or with a production chain that uses robotic arms.
Folding is a language that we can use to create new generations of objects!

www.industrialorigami.com

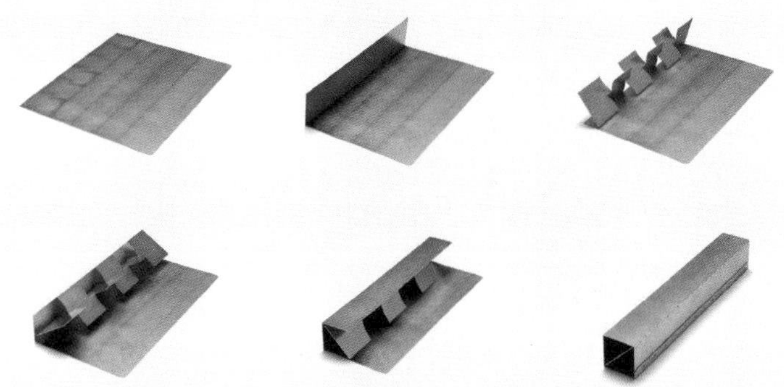

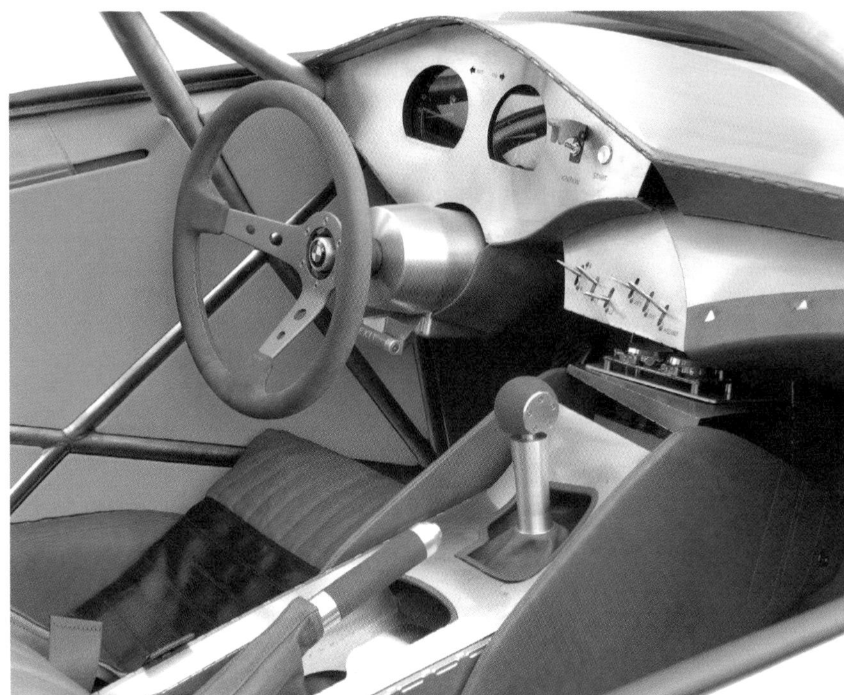

- IOI Lances.
- Lasered Beam.
- BMW Concept Car IOI dash.

Daimonds Pučko / Pioes Sia

LATVIA

Contving Fire pit and *Sidostool*

This company, based in Riga, Latvia, combines craftsmanship and high-precision machines such as laser cutters and hydraulic presses.
Folding and new technologies allow the costs of industrial production to be reduced and manufacturing to be simplified. An economy of materials can contribute to the emergence of a production of objects and components in small, flexible units near the place of order.
These new ways to organize production could contribute to reducing the energy footprint of objects and also allow more direct access to the development of technology for the greatest number and for anywhere in the world.

www.contving.com
www.red-dot-21.com/products/contving-fire-pit-potrable-fire-pit-22242

- Contving, Grand - Fire Pit, *3 mm (1/8 in) steel.*
- Wody - Firewood basket, *3 mm (1/8 in) steel.*
- *Detail of the folds in* Sidostool.

Bakery Design Studio, Ran Amitai and Gilli Kuchik

ISRAEL

NOM is a series of lightweight stackable furniture. Each object is folded out of a laser-cut aluminium sheet, which is then folded to the final form using a bending mould.
The concept of the project is to combine origami with straight folds and more natural curved ones. This is achieved through folding, which has the side effect of causing stretching and bending in the material. In other words, by folding the legs of the objects, the surface reacts naturally. This interaction between strict and natural folds creates a form that is both regular and soft.
Nature of Material, the prototype of the *NOM* series, was presented at the 2010 Design Week in Milan. The project was put into production by Cappellini.

http://bakery-design.com
http://cappellini.it

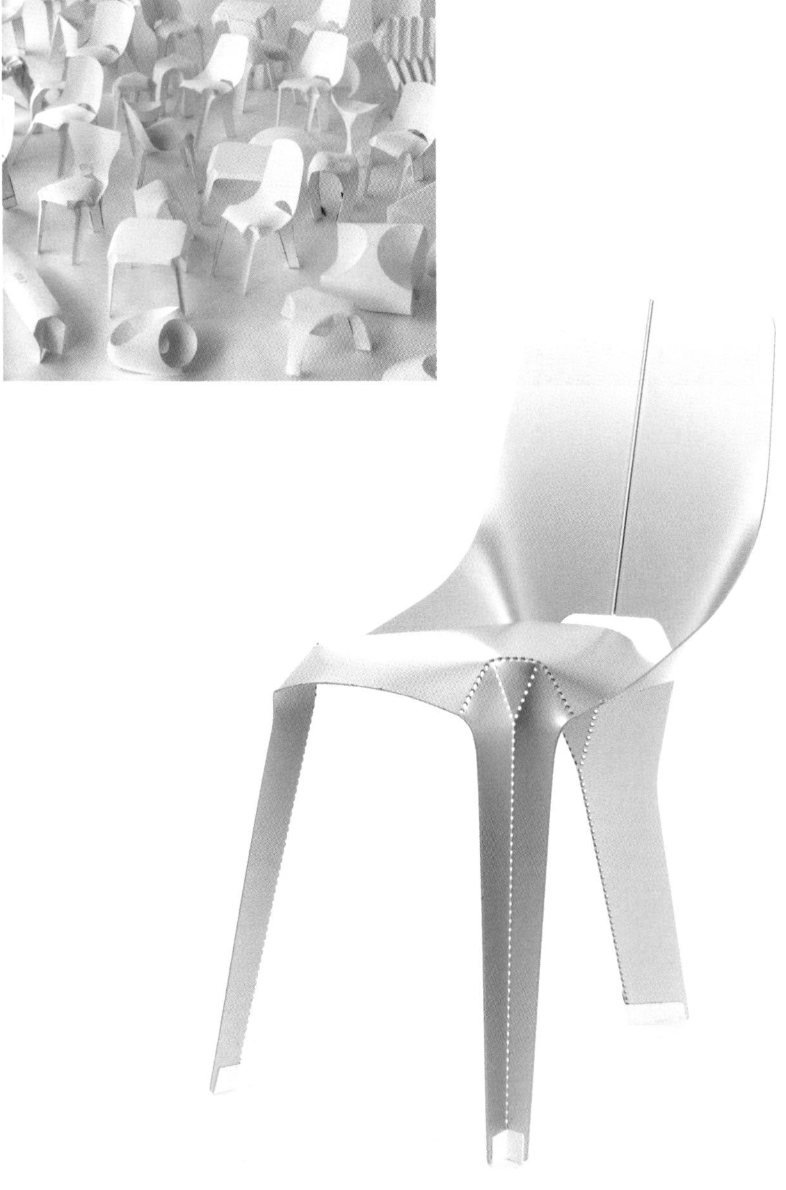

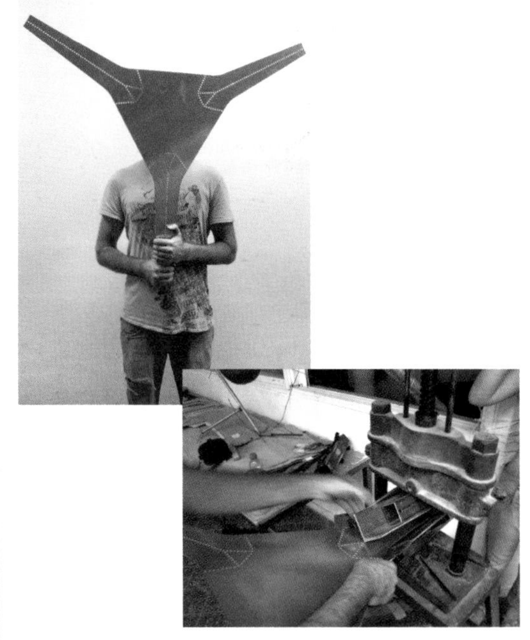

• *Study models, paper.*
• Nature of material *collection, chair and stool.*
• *Stool before folding and folded.*

Tobias Labarque

BELGIUM

Tobias Labarque is an architect and designer. "Adapting mathematical forms to ergonomic uses is something that I see as a challenge. I love the contrast between the apparent discomfort of a chair, and the comfort that one feels when one actually sits on it. The technique of folding, origami, brings limits to design. You must follow certain geometric rules. I consider design to be an invitation to explore the limits of what is possible.

I love the design of this chair, which expresses the way in which it was made. Manufacturing techniques matter as much to me as the final result. Unlike other projects that can be designed and manufactured in two to three months, this chair required much more working time from me. It is made of 6 mm (1/4 in) thick aluminium, and to avoid the resulting weight, I made the choice of using perforated aluminium. The use of a perforated plate led to the development of a unique production process with triangular wooden panels that sandwich the aluminium plate. The use of chains and tensioners to fold the material is a fun way of manufacturing: it's low-tech and brutal. Anyone could make the chair in their basement!"

Remarks from Tobias Labarque, December 2014.

www.tobiaslabarque.wordpress.com

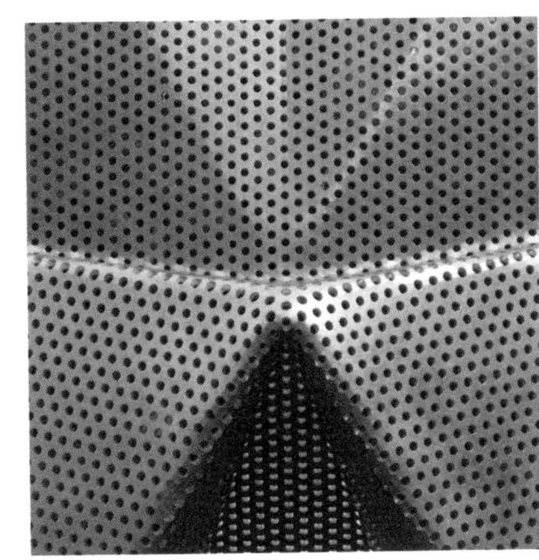

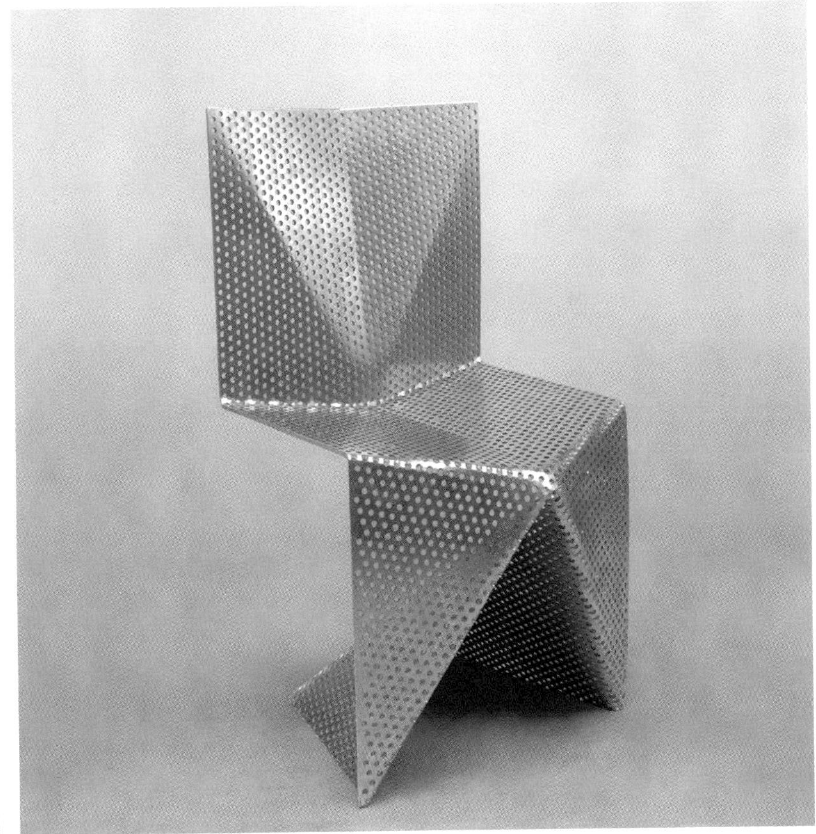

• tlf03 *chair, aluminium.*
• *Folding articulated wooden template.*

Normal Studio

FRANCE

Folded sheet-metal furniture

"Normal Studio is an industrial design agency that was founded in 2006 by Jean-François Dingjian and Eloi Chafaï. These observers of the technical and customary processes of technology transfers focus on everyday forms through simple and precise design that glorifies functional qualities. They are equally interested in product design and space or scenography."

The agency's furniture projects made from folded sheet metal are the perfect expression of the potential of folding in terms of economy of material and lightness. They are a body of work that in our view fits in with the tradition of the great modern pioneers of metal folding such as Jean Prouvé. In postwar France, the modernist movement sought to explore new forms of objects and buildings in relation to industry. Jean Prouvé's ideas influenced many of his contemporaries, and in his studios he produced numerous light facade, furniture and structural pieces using a revolutionary modern folding machine, a device of technical inspiration that serves an aesthetic of action.

The Y trestles created by Normal Studio and manufactured by Tolix in 2009 are based on the principle of forms that can be developed from flat and folded to form rigid elements. Here, four folded legs are assembled with a "beam" comprising a "U" shape. This overall setup has the advantage of being stackable through the legs' being folded into "L" shapes.

Excerpts from the Normal Studio website.

www.normalstudio.fr
www.tolix.fr

• Y/Tolix *trestles. Stackable trestles. The four legs are assembled on a U that create[s] a rigid and stable beam. Painted steel sheet, 2009. Pa[rt] of the Fond national d'art contemporain collection and the permanent collection of the Musée des Arts Décorati[fs] Paris.*

• *4 x 4 chair, prototype 1, August 2012.*
• *Coffee table, prototype 2, November 2011.*

Different+Different

FRANCE

"Above all, I use folding for technical reasons: it requires no investment in tools, and it can be used for both small and very large series, which is very important when launching a brand. And folding allows very complex pieces. It offers a fluctuation between hardness and flexibility. I love to see a sheet of metal be pressed with more than 100 tonnes in a die, or liquid metal flowing like water into a sand casting mould.

In designing the 4 x 4 chair, I was looking for the simplest and most obvious folding that would produce a seat from a sheet of metal. As is often the case, when I design using folded metal, I work alongside sketches and Bristol paper that I cut and fold. We were very careful when it came to the corners because having no foam to cover the seat meant that the product had to be very ergonomic. The final version has a 6° tilt in order to distribute the weight, and the angle between the back and the seat is 100° in order to have a comfortable active position for working, eating or having a drink.

Tabasse was the first project to be produced. I had previously designed three objects based on the same leitmotiv of perspective: *Tabasse* for a different flow, *Blibli* in order to sculpt space, and *String* for the obviousness of the seat and suspension! The goal was that once together, the whole would completely change the piece's perspective and perception, making it much more dynamic by creating imaginary vanishing points. *Tabasse* was designed with a sense and a dynamic that are the starting point.

This product was the most difficult to put into production because of its form and its number of folds. The top is directly cut from sheet metal, which means there is no play between the assembled parts, with the paint taking up the cutting thickness."

Remarks from Adrien Camp, December 2014.

www.differentanddifferent.com

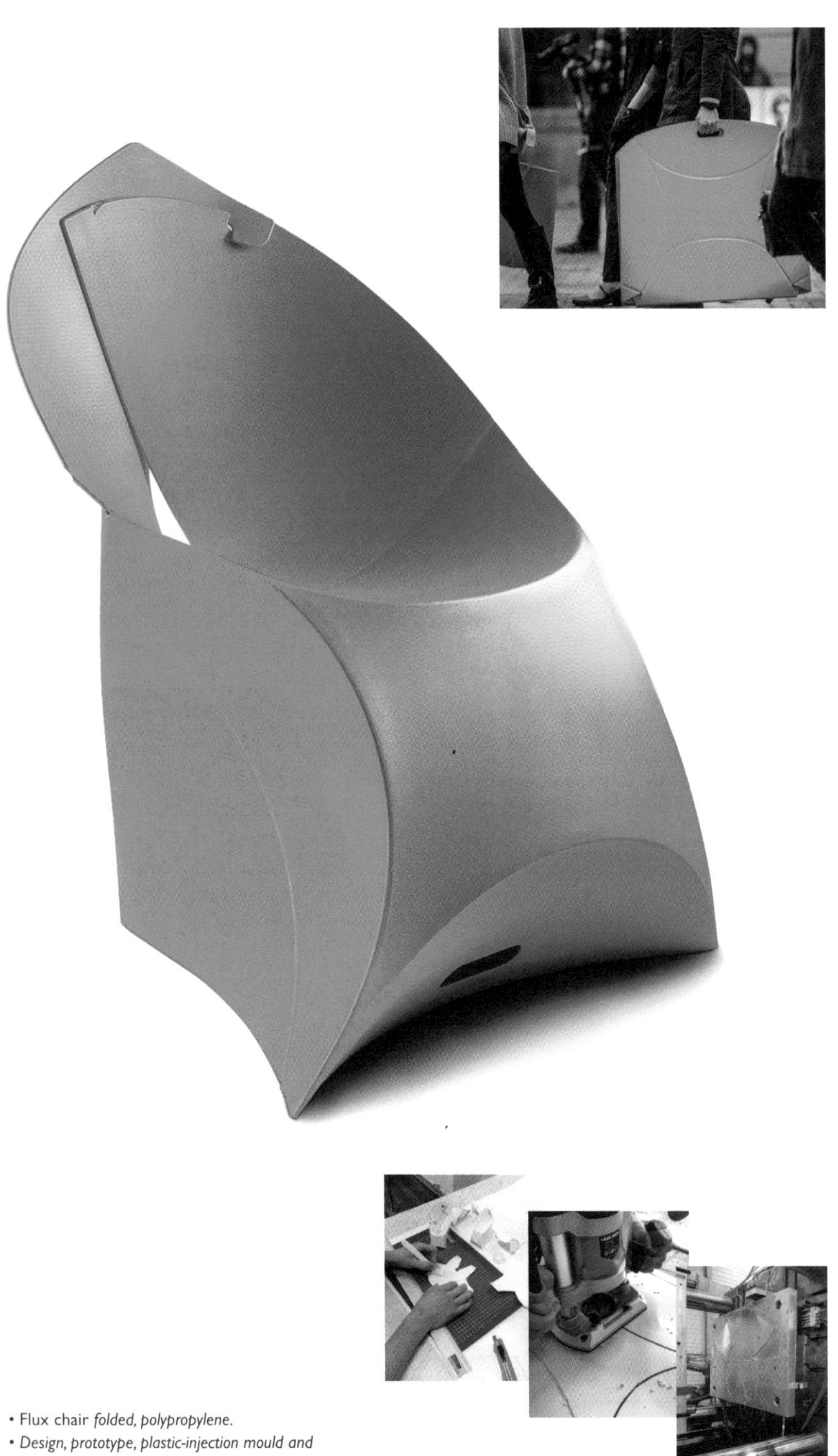

• Flux chair *folded, polypropylene.*
• *Design, prototype, plastic-injection mould and unfolded chair.*

Flux Furniture

THE NETHERLANDS

In 2008, Douwe Jacobs began to work on the concept of the *Flux Chair*: a folded and folding seat made from a single sheet. It was his degree project. The starting point for the folding scheme was four curved folds forming the seat. Then a back made of two raised and crossed portions of the sheet and rear support for rigidity are added.
After graduating, Douwe met Tom Schouten at the Technical University of Delft Faculty of Industrial Design Engineering.
In 2009, they founded their company. They then won many awards, which made production of the first prototypes possible. The first tests and models allowed them to establish that it was better to retain the principle of making the chair out of a single material—a thick polypropylene—and to incorporate all of the required fasteners into it. Material was removed through scoring at the place of the folds using a CNC machine. However, this type of manufacturing is still too costly for wide dissemination. The two partners then chose plastic injection, a technique that allows more than 10,000 pieces to be rapidly produced—though the cost of the mould is very high.
In 2010, they managed to acquire the funds to invest in the manufacturing of the mould, which would weigh 12 t!
However, its development turned out to be more complex than expected. There were issues with temperature, pressure and the material. The plastic struggled to fill the folds with the required thinness of 3 mm (1/8 in). It took more than a year for the mould to be ready. The first series was produced in early 2012. Another difficulty was to combine strength and flexibility, as the chair needs to be able to be folded and unfolded hundreds of times. This first experiment allowed them to go on to design and produce other pieces of foldable furniture, principally for use in events. These pieces are manufactured with a CNC machine in smaller series, offering the advantage of being easily customizable.

Remarks from Douwe Jacobs and Tom Schouten, November 2014.

www.fluxfurniture.com

Studio Nuy Van Noort

THE NETHERLANDS

Studio Nuy van Noort is an Amsterdam-based interdisciplinary team of architects, urban planners and product designers and researchers. Its first model, the *VW01*, is from 2009. The studio wanted to develop a flexible, useful and accessible product. Innovation in the use of materials and in waste reduction are the project's founding values. These principles inspired the creation of a foldable cardboard chair. The team received the Thonet Mart Stam prize for this innovative project.
The process began with models and sketches by hand, and then full-scale tests. The chair had to pack flat and be easy to carry, and for this reason folding was required. Cardboard is a material that offers a little-known level of potential. The chair's outline is a reflection of the geometric distribution of forces, which allows thickness of the material to be optimized. The studio then turned to a manufacturer that produced in-store displays. It had a CNC cutter that could produce three chairs in a sheet of Re-board®.
The designers and their partner had to find a new element for folding this honeycomb cardboard. In 2010, they began to explore alternatives with different materials and considered if a more luxurious version of the chair was possible. As a result, the *WW02* was born.

Remarks from Studio Nuy Van Noort, November 2014.

www.vouwwow.nl

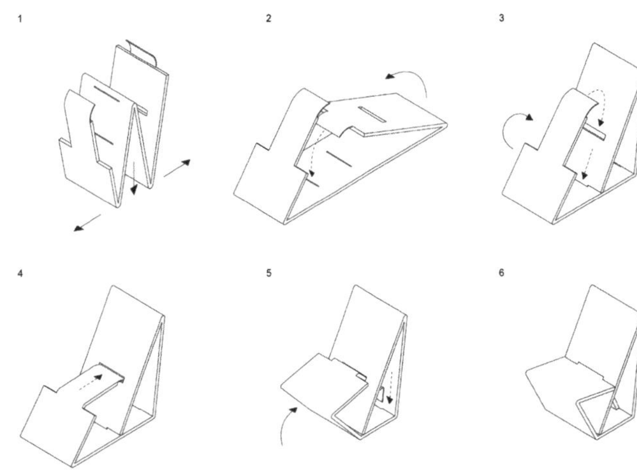

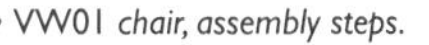

• *VW01 chair, assembly steps.*
• *The VW02 is made out of six pieces of plywood that are covered in PET-felt, a plastic made from recycled bottles. It provides a tactile and coloured finish and acts as a hinge, while the plywood plays a structural role.*
A piece of Velcro® keeps together the chair, which is delivered flat. The cardboard is recyclable and biodegradable, and it therefore contributes to reducing the impact of furniture production on the environment.

CartonLab

SPAIN

Folding to create the event

CartonLab is a laboratory for ecological design that was founded in 2009 by the architecture firm Moho. It is a team of ten people whose design work focuses on stands for fairs and congresses and on ephemeral architecture for exhibitions and interior design, as well as on furniture, decorative items and creative products for children. All their design projects are light, durable, functional and easy to carry and store, and they are assembled without adhesives or additional connectors. As a result of their knowledge of cardboard and the local partnerships that they have established with manufacturers, they are able to directly provide their customers with custom parts that are recyclable, reusable and produced in Spain with FSC-certified materials. Their cardboard furniture pieces are interesting because they are the perfect expression of the material. The form produced is adapted to the function, and this balance produces beauty and accuracy. The firm's stand projects reflect this same ability to give a purpose to design, in this case with folding being one of the keys to this formative and functional expressiveness.

The *Stand Origami* project, produced in Barcelona in 2011 (in collaboration with Ability Diseño Gráfico and Graphispag BCN), illustrates the great creativity of the CartonLab team, and it caters to the representation needs of large companies at events. The use of three-dimensional triangular tiling based on folded cardboard allowed all the technical interfaces necessary for exhibiting (electric wiring and audiovisual equipment) to be integrated into the cavities of the elements.

Interview with Nacho Bautista Ruiz, October 2014.

www.cartonlab.com

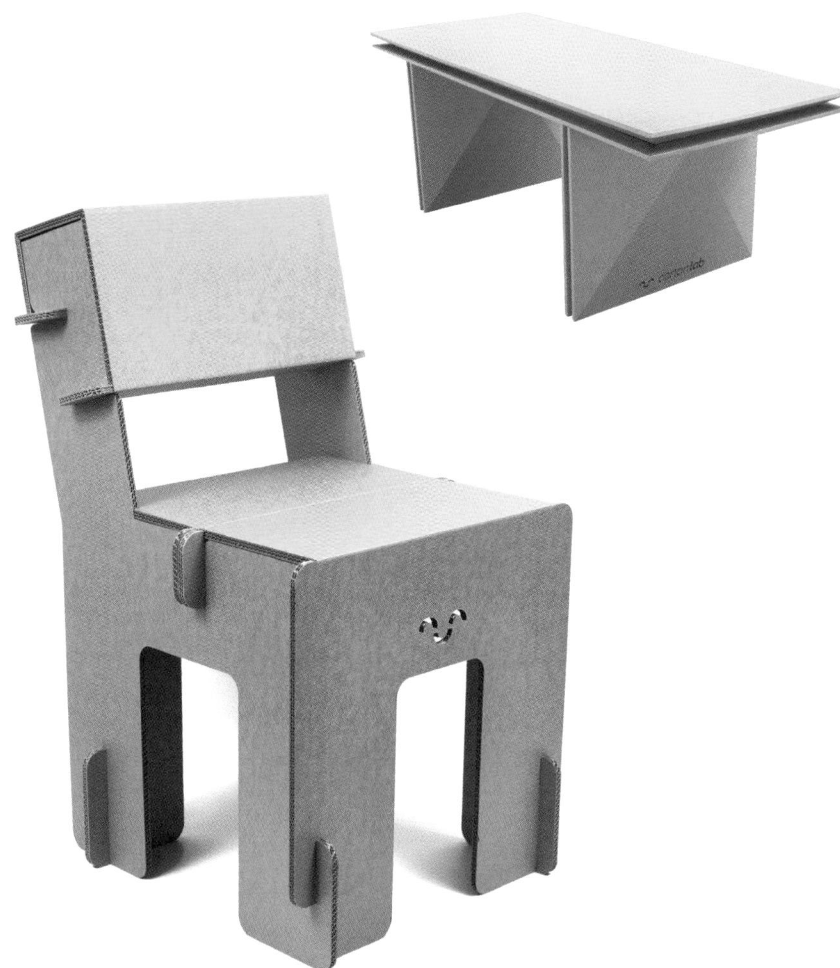

- Meeting table, *corrugated cardboard.*
- Taray *chair, corrugated cardboard.*
- Origami stand.

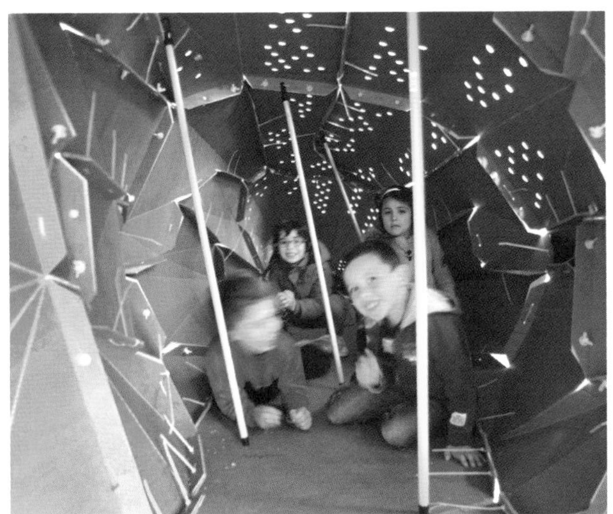

• *The project* Play day Bilbao: Mobydick *(cocreators: Onyon + Peopleing / Ayuntamiento de Bilbao) is an ephemeral installation created using a cardboard structure in the shape of a whale. Specially designed to encourage children to play and get involved, this piece was designed to promote art and creative freedom in urban spaces. The animal's body was made from more than fifty different pieces of cardboard. They were assembled using electric self-tightening plastic clamps. It was assembled on site in two hours, and the total weight of the piece was about 60 kg.*

• *benchwall + cloud softlight at Orgatec 2014.*
• *Installation sequence for* softseating.
• *White textile* softblock *plus LED.*

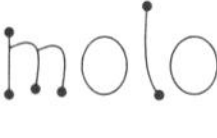

CANADA

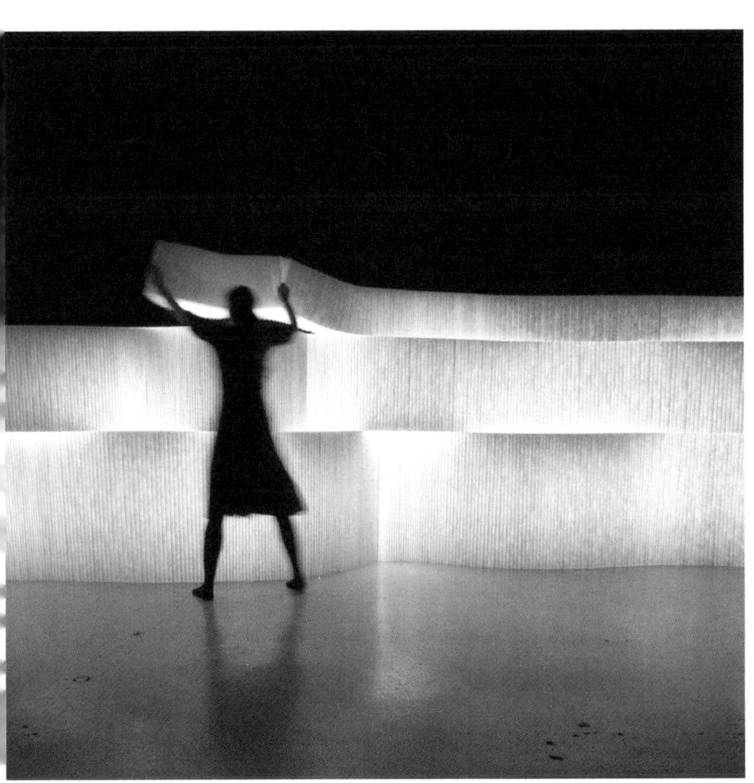

Based in Vancouver, molo is a collaborative design and production studio. It is led by founders Stephanie Forsythe and Todd MacAllen, who are both architects by training.

Inspired by the idea that tactile objects have real potential with regard to the physical experience of space, molo creates objects that define temporary private spaces.

softwall and *softblock* are modular and flexible partition systems that are made from paper or textile (nonwoven spun polyethylene). *softwall* is flexible in length, expanding from 50 mm (2 in) compressed to a full 4.5 m (177 in). Its honeycomb structure creates hexagonal cells that give it more resistance than simple accordion-folded paper. Magnetic end panels allow several *softwall* or *softblock* modules to connect together.

Two years of work were required to design and develop machines capable of producing these unique honeycomb forms on an unprecedented scale.

The process of creating a *softwall* begins with a very large roll of material—paper or textile—which is rewound by hand, cut to feasible lengths and rewound again on smaller rolls. The starting, stopping and tension of the rolls are continual features of the process, and everything has to be done by hand to ensure that the tension level is correct. The rolls are placed in a machine that unrolls and glues the sheets, thus producing the honeycomb cell structure. This results in large and roughly cut honeycomb units. These move on to a cutter, which cuts them to their final form and size. Holes are then made perpendicular to the honeycomb (these holes are used for hanging and or the integration of LED lighting strips).

Remarks from October 2014.

www.molodesign.com

ARCA Steven Leprizé and Erick Demeyer

FRANCE

Airwood: *from folded wood to inflatable wood*

Steven is a cabinetmaker, and although he "grew up with wood," he managed to forget the techniques and took a step back from the material to focus on creating from a different angle, combining ancestral techniques and innovation. His studio output is given new life by a spirit of exploration and continuous improvement. This teacher communicates his passion and creative sense to students at the École Boulle. Folding is part of his research into giving wood form and plasticity. In designing his projects, he initially seeks to forget any technical constraints and combines 2D design by hand with 3D modelling. He creates models to prefigure production and makes test samples prior to manufacturing.
For example, he uses moulded plywood to create a fixed movement on wood with different forms. Inflatable wood, which he developed with Erick Demeyer, is a sophisticated process reserved for exceptional applications. It has not yet been used on a large industrial scale. It offers something that wood cannot normally do: create a "surprise." Inflatable wood brings out a pattern on a veneered panel, with the inflation causing folding made possible by fine scales. The panel is composed of an elastic sealed membrane on which wooden or cork marquetry is affixed; an inflation system distorts this grid and prints a movement on it. The result is beautiful and disturbing: the wood seems animated by it, almost as though it were alive.

Remarks from Steven Leprizé, October 2014.

www.arca-home.com

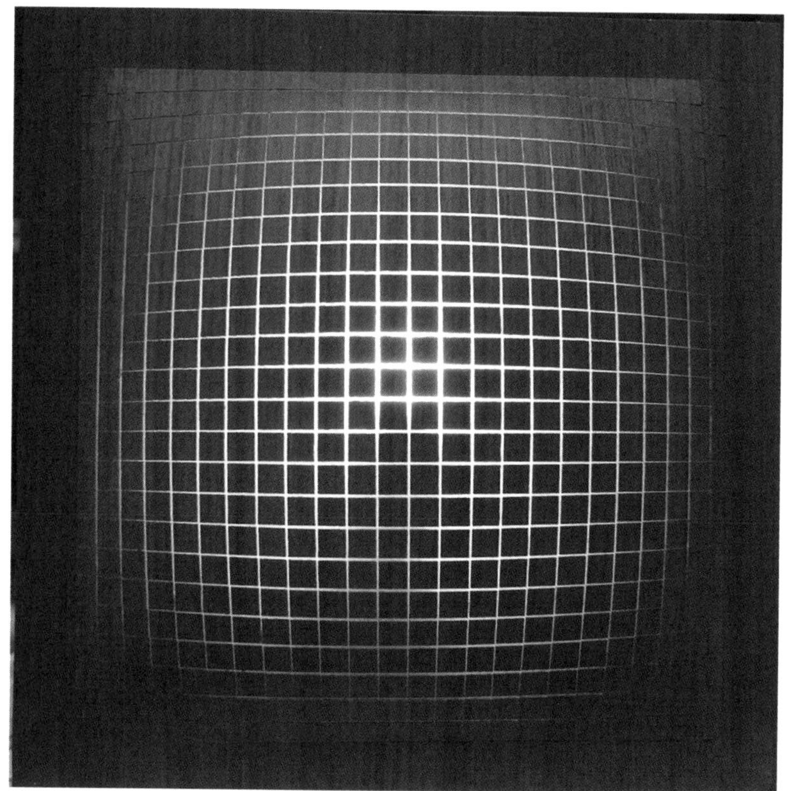

• *Inflatable wood.*
• *Project on the theme of movement.*
• *Trombone.*

• *Cutting.*

• *Caoutchouc wood.*
• *Inflatable wood.*

• *Inflatable wood.*

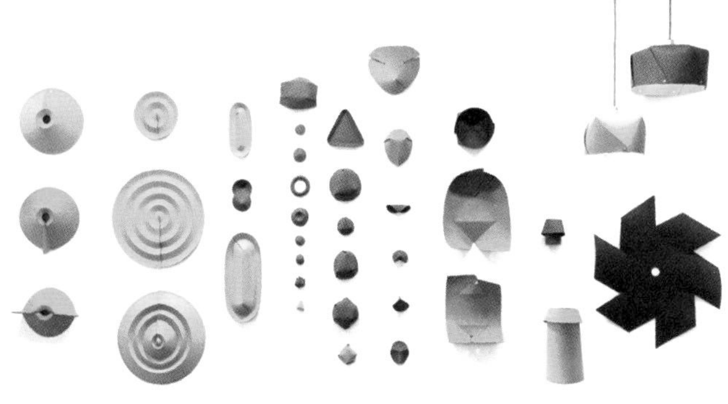

• *Research.*
• Capas *seat and its components.*
• *Series for Tolix.*

Sébastien Cordoleani

FRANCE

"I am an industrial designer, and I spent many years at the Ateliers Saint-Sabin of the École nationale supérieure de création Industrielle (ENSCI), where I developed the habit of challenging my ideas through models. The first step toward reality often involves a paper model, and I think that an appetite to directly create form with a very accessible, simple material that can be complex and very rich from a formal viewpoint is what led me to consider supple materials such as leather, cork, paper, thin sheet steel and sheet aluminium. These materials that come flat can be shaped with a few folds.
Being able to produce directly with little investment in tools by going through a template is a way of doing things that I like. It lets me achieve results that are similar enough to that of serial production, with patterns, punches and so on.
My stay in Japan at the Villa Kujoyama led me to origami and in a much simpler way to designing lamps with sheets and battens, followed by *Alcôve*, a free-standing lamp. After one release, Objekten called me to develop the project, but another firm, Moustache, was going to include it in its catalogue. We decided to start another project from saltpetre and recycled leather. I have designed small office items such as lamps and baskets.
My work with leather continued with the *Capas* wooden chair, which became the leather and oak *Strates*. The goal was to produce a seat that was as comfortable as a moulded shell but with a simple piece of leather wrapped around a wooden skeleton. Strictly speaking, there is no folding, no edge between one plane and another, but rather big curves because of the nature of the material—kinds of macrofolds."

Remarks from Sébastien Cordoleani, December 2014.

www.sebastiencordoleani.com

Sascha Akkermann

GERMANY

Sascha Akkermann is a master carpenter and has been a freelance designer since 2002.
For him, "Form 100% follows function; things are as they should be." Sascha seeks expression through perfect and minimal form, the only possible solution to a technical problem. He is attracted to folding because it allows him to make transformable objects. A project originally given the name *Poisson mobile* and then rechristened *KOII, foldable deckchair*, is a lounger inspired by the ones used on transatlantic liners. It consists of a reinforced PVC membrane (similar to that used for truck tarpaulins), onto which mitre-cut slats are affixed. Great precision in the angles of the cuts (which are all different) allows the correct fold. Only one manufacturer among the many available rose to such a technical challenge. The form and effectiveness of this easy to ship and store design are what have made it successful.

Remarks from Sascha Akkermann, February 2015.

www.sascha-akkermann.de
www.ackermanngmbh.de

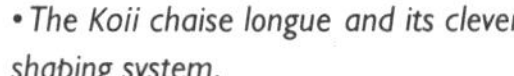

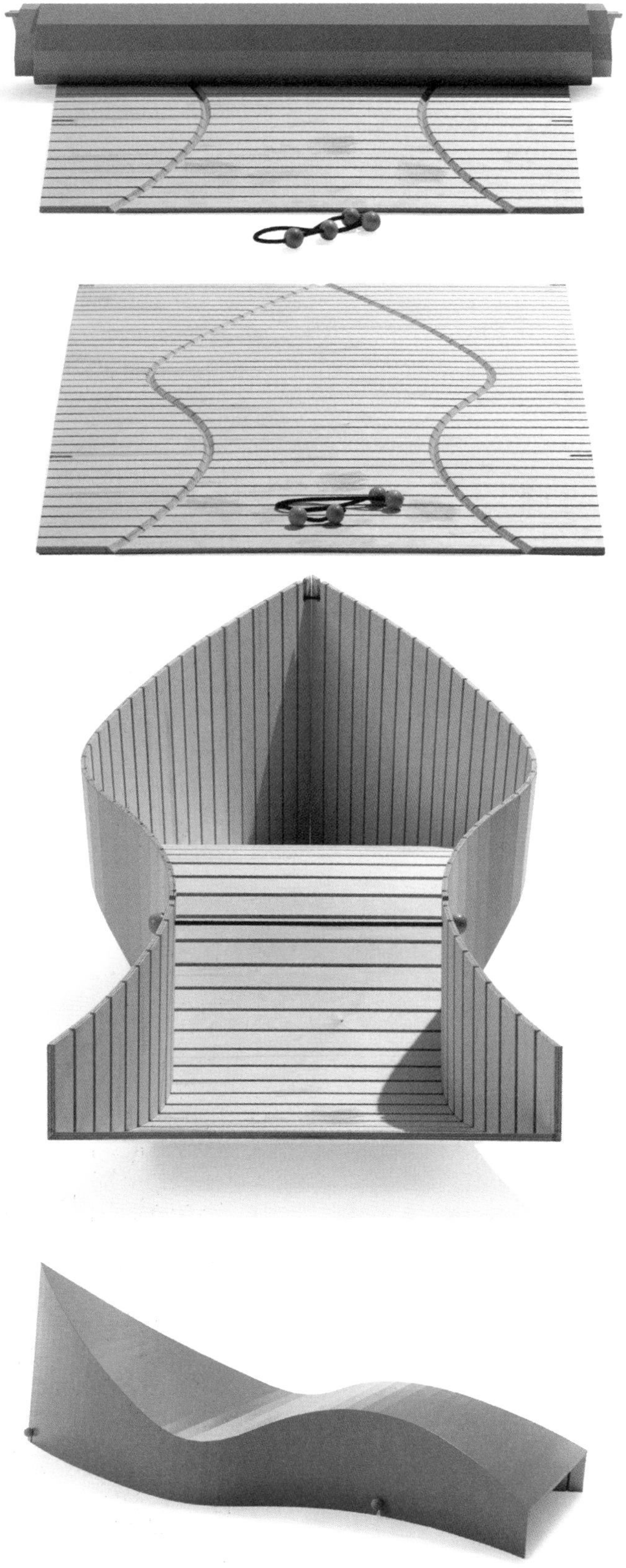

• *The Koii chaise longue and its clever shaping system.*

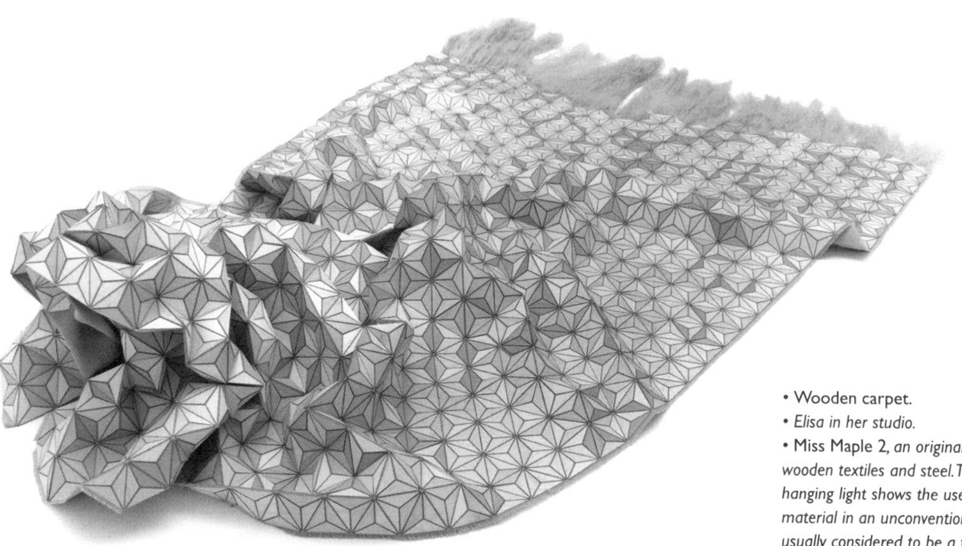

• Wooden carpet.
• *Elisa in her studio.*
• Miss Maple 2, *an original lamp made from wooden textiles and steel. The* Miss Maple *hanging light shows the use of a familiar material in an unconventional way. Wood is usually considered to be a flat surface, but here it is broken down into a grid of triangles, allowing this hanging light to manually take its shape and become a true sculpture.*

Elisa Strozyk

GERMANY

Wooden Textiles offer a new tactile experience. We are used to experiencing wood as a hard material; we are familiar with the feeling of walking on floors, touching a table or feeling the bark of a tree. But we usually don't get to experience a surface made of wood that can be manipulated by touching it.
Elisa Strozyk is a textile designer who seeks out ways to give wood the properties of textiles. The result is a material that is half wood and half textile. It is neither hard nor soft, and it calls into question what we might expect from a category of material.
It looks familiar, but it leaves a strange feeling, because it is able to move and take on shapes in an unexpected way.
Laser-cut pieces of wood are glued by hand onto a piece of fabric. Depending on its weight and rigidity, each surface behaves differently. Different objects such as rugs and tablecloths have been created using this process.

Remarks from Elisa Strozyk; excerpts from her website in November 2014.

www.elisastrozyk.de

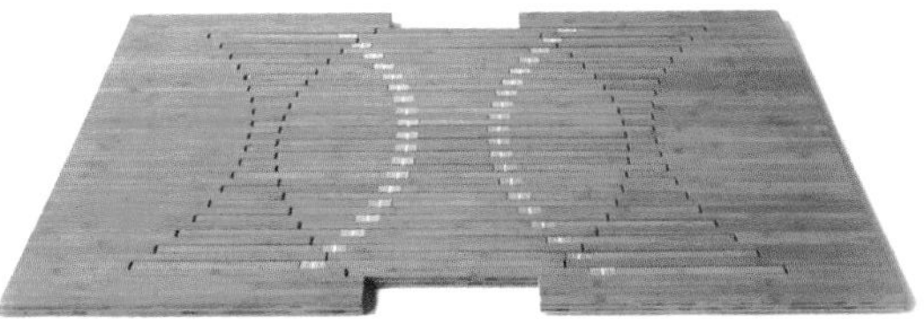

• Rising Table.
• Rising Chair.

Robert van Embricqs

THE NETHERLANDS

Robert van Embricqs finds his inspiration in nature's forms such as bone structures and the life and movement of plants. One of the important aspects of his design process is the marriage of functionality and aesthetics.
Functional, flexible and foldable furniture does not have to be banal and predictable.
The starting point of this folding furniture is a flat surface incised in several places and then pushed and pulled to create the volume.
The pieces in his *Rising Furniture* series are constructed using an innovative hinge system, which ensures a light weight and ease of manipulation, without loss of the furniture's almost sculptural aesthetic qualities. All the furniture in the series can return to its original state: a flat panel.

Remarks from October 2014.

www.robertvanembricqs.com

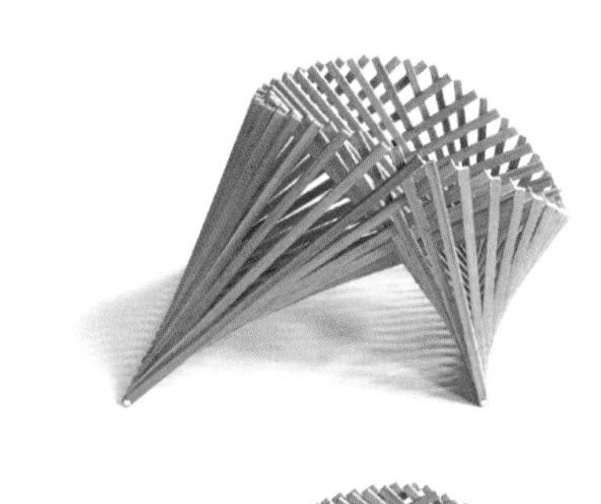

Christy Oates

USA

Hanging on the wall, the *Wallpaper chair* is a piece of perfectly flat marquetry. Once taken down and unfolded, it turns into a fully functional chair. Christy Oates began making pieces such as this one of while she was a student in fine arts at San Diego State University in California. In her small apartment, the issue of the place occupied by the furniture was a crucial one. It was from here that the idea of creating furniture that hung on the wall emerged. She began to fold paper models. Although the first prototypes were made entirely by hand, she currently works with a laser cutting machine controlled by a computer, allowing her to produce the extremely thin and precise parts of the marquetry.

One of the crucial details in creating these folding works is making the hinges, which must be both discreet and solid for the furniture to be functional. The invisible hinges of these furniture-tableau pieces are made from tensioners inserted into the bevelled panels and screwed internally. Christy is currently researching other types of hinges that provide greater stability. Her artwork/furniture is sold in galleries, and she also makes laser-cut marquetry kits.

Remarks from November 2014.

www.cargocollective.com/christyoates

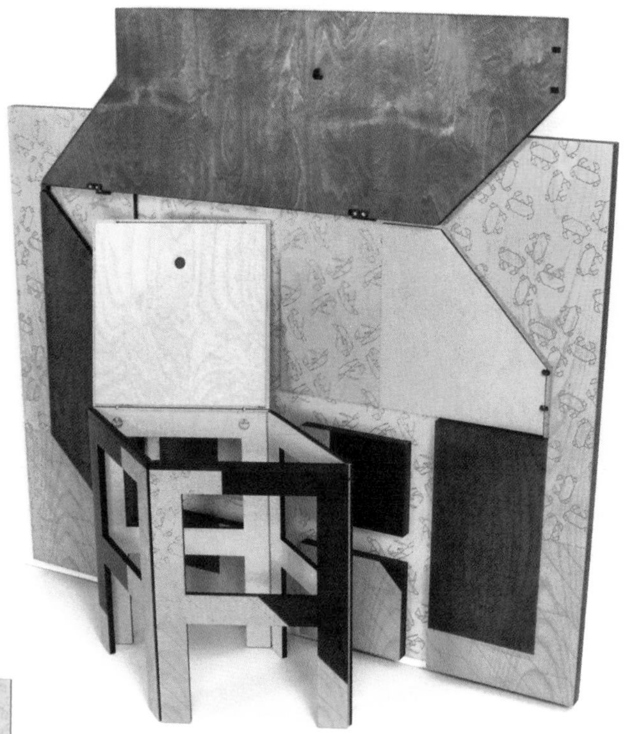

- Wallpaper chair.
- Skyline.
- Crab Desk.

Alexander Rehn Designstudio

GERMANY

Alexander Rehn is a designer and specialist in interior architecture. He also teaches at the Academy of Fine Arts in Munich. *Cay Sofa* was released by the French company Structure.me. It is a variable geometry seat whose folds are motorized. "After an exhausting day, there's nothing better than coming home to relax in front of the fireplace or TV or with a good book. *Cay Sofa*, a 'folded landscape' for your living room, will meet these needs. The user is its protagonist. His or her movements change the shape of the furniture, and he or she is free to choose if to sit, lie down or relax with someone else."

Remarks from October 2014.

www.structures.me
www.alexanderrehn.com

• *Prototypes of the convertible* Cay Sofa.

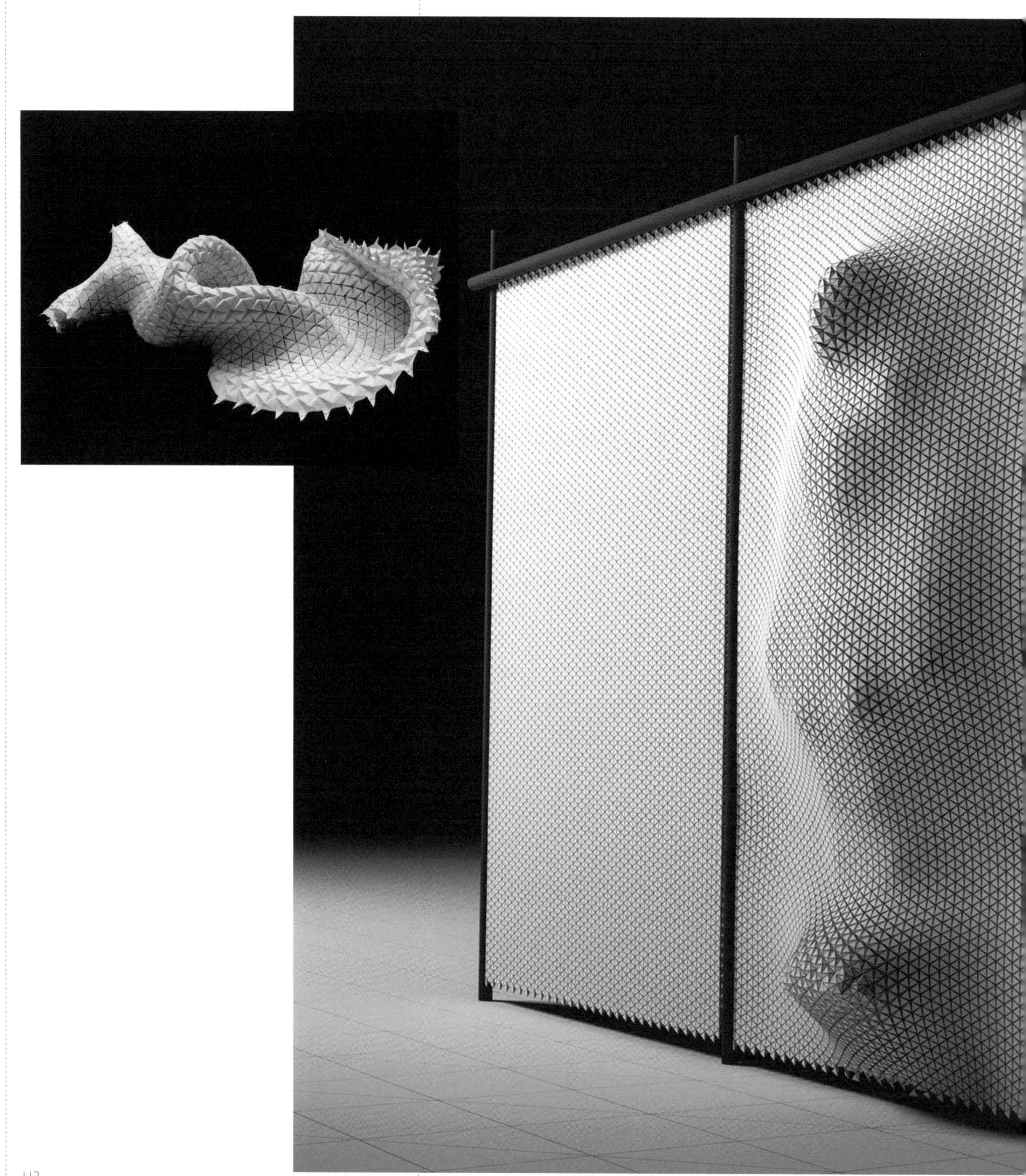

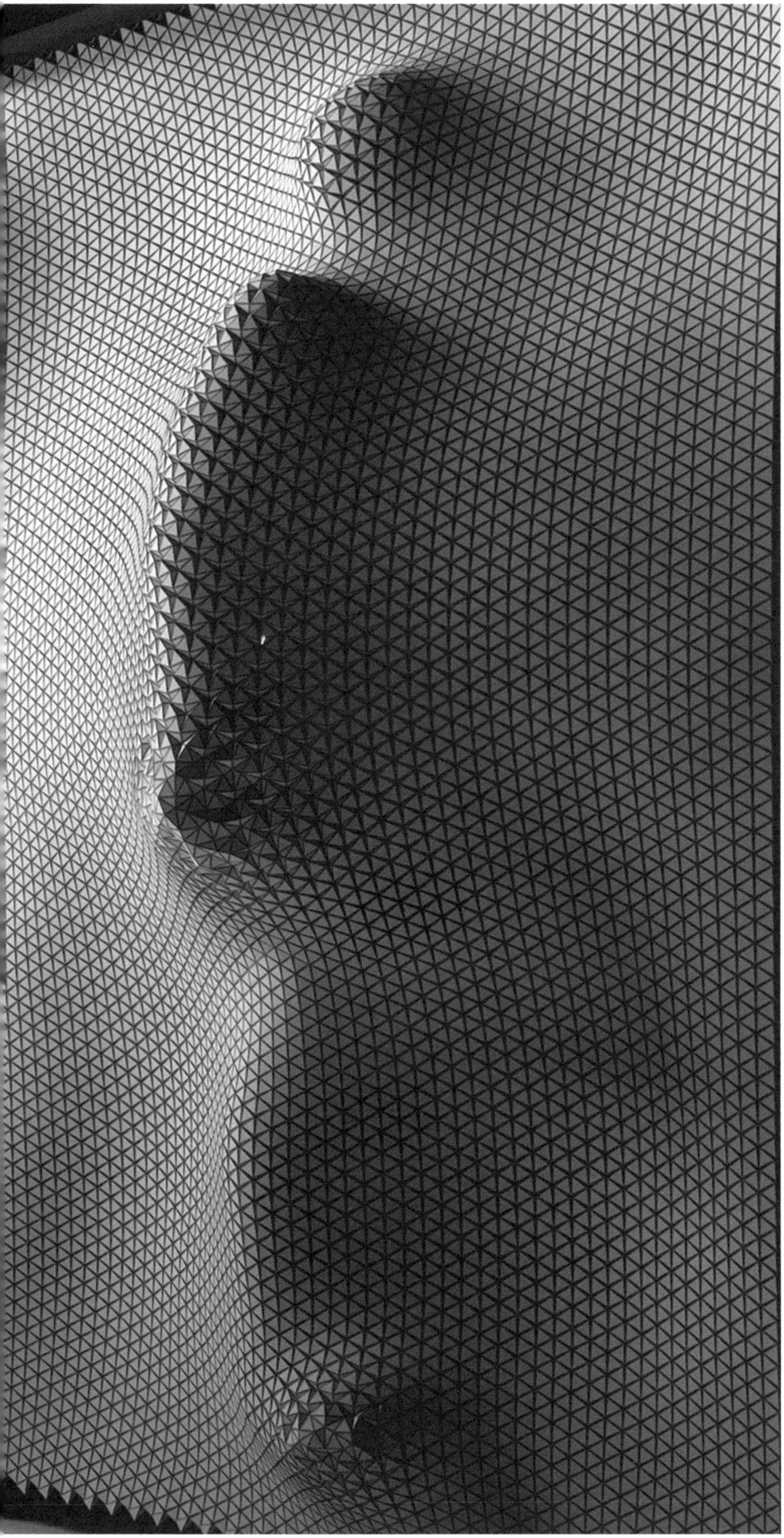

Thomas Diewald

AUSTRIA

As an architecture student, Thomas worked on the project "Like costumes: Invent a form that wraps around your body," as part of his studies in the 2009/2010 school year. The idea was to create a textile layer that hugged the shape of the body. After folding many paper models, he chose a tessellating pattern (***Triangle Twist***), which was particularly flexible, to be made into a full-scale prototype. So that it retains its shape, the folding of the fabric was carried out using tweezers and a heat gun. 3D simulations then helped to define an overall shape for the installation.

Remarks from October 2014.

thomasdiewald.com

Freyja Sewell

ENGLAND

Hush & Smush, a felted bubble

Through creating an enclosed space, *Hush* provides a personal retreat, a luxurious escape in a dark, cozy, natural space in the middle of a busy hotel, an airport, an office or a library. *Hush* offers a quiet space in an age when the population is growing exponentially and when privacy is an increasingly precious commodity. The body of *Hush* is cut from a single piece of 10 mm (3/8 in) thick wool felt. The interior is made of wool fibres that have been recycled from the English carpet industry.
Smush is a *Hush* that has been squashed! This more social version offers a more traditional open seat that is large enough for several people.
Hush is made in Durham by trained craftspeople at Ness Furniture as part of an effort to revitalize local crafts.

Press release excerpts.

www.freyjasewell.co.uk

- Smush *and bonding.*
- Hush *and sleeping beauty.*
- Ness furniture, *Clare, David and Freyja,* Hush manufacture.

• A clever folding mechanism for a door-opening movement, creating a kinetic work.
© avincze_torggler.

Klemens Torggler

AUSTRIA

EvolutionDoor 2013, an open door

The *EvolutionDoor* project developed by Klemens Torggler, an artist inspired by movement, is a fantastic example of the potential of using folding to create new mechanisms. Can something as ordinary as a door still be moving? The answer is yes! A dynamic object by nature, this movement may itself be the result of a special level of attention. Thanks to its patented system, it is possible to move the door to the side without the use of rails.

The "triangle" door of this series is made from wood and metal, consisting of two panels that are folded down the middle into two triangles and articulated by a central pivot. In its operation, it opens with the elegance of a butterfly spreading its wings. Klemens's artistic works are more than mere objects of utilitarian design; they open the doors of a creative universe in motion.

Remarks from March 2014.

www.torggler.co.at
© avincze_torggler

Issey Miyake / Éditions Artemide

JAPAN–FRANCE

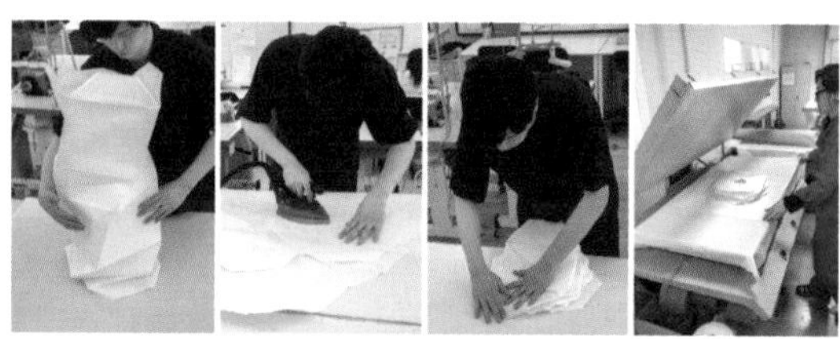

"In Japanese, *IN-EI* means shadow, darkness, shade. The art of lighting owes part of its design heritage to the Miyake Design Studio, and in particular to Issey Miyake and his research and development team Reality Lab, which, in 2010, presented *132 5. ISSEY MIYAKE.*"

This new process was developed using a mathematical program developed from mathematician Jun Mitani's principles of three-dimensional geometry. This project, a product of the alliance between creativity and mathematics, has given birth to a garment that can be completely folded flat and redeployed in surprising three-dimensional forms, using a single piece of fabric. Reality Lab explored the potential of *132 5. ISSEY MIYAKE* in the creation of clothing and accessories, and then extended its application to lighting products, a natural objective for this research process.

IN-EI ISSEY MIYAKE lamps came about through an encounter with Artemide in a uniting of experience of technological excellence in the lighting sector with the innovative approach of Reality Lab in terms of design and use of materials.

The structure made from recycled material with a supplementary surface treatment allows these lighting pieces to perfectly keep their shape without the need for an internal frame and to be kept flat once more if need be. These lamps can therefore be easily stored when not in use.

Text excerpt © Artemide.

www.artemide.com

• *Unfolding of the* MENDORI *lamp and manufacturing sequences of the* MOGURA *lamp.*

Opposite page:
• KATATSUMURI *(left) and* TATSUNO-OTOSHIGO *hanging lights (right) and the* MINOMUSHI TERRA *floor lamp.*

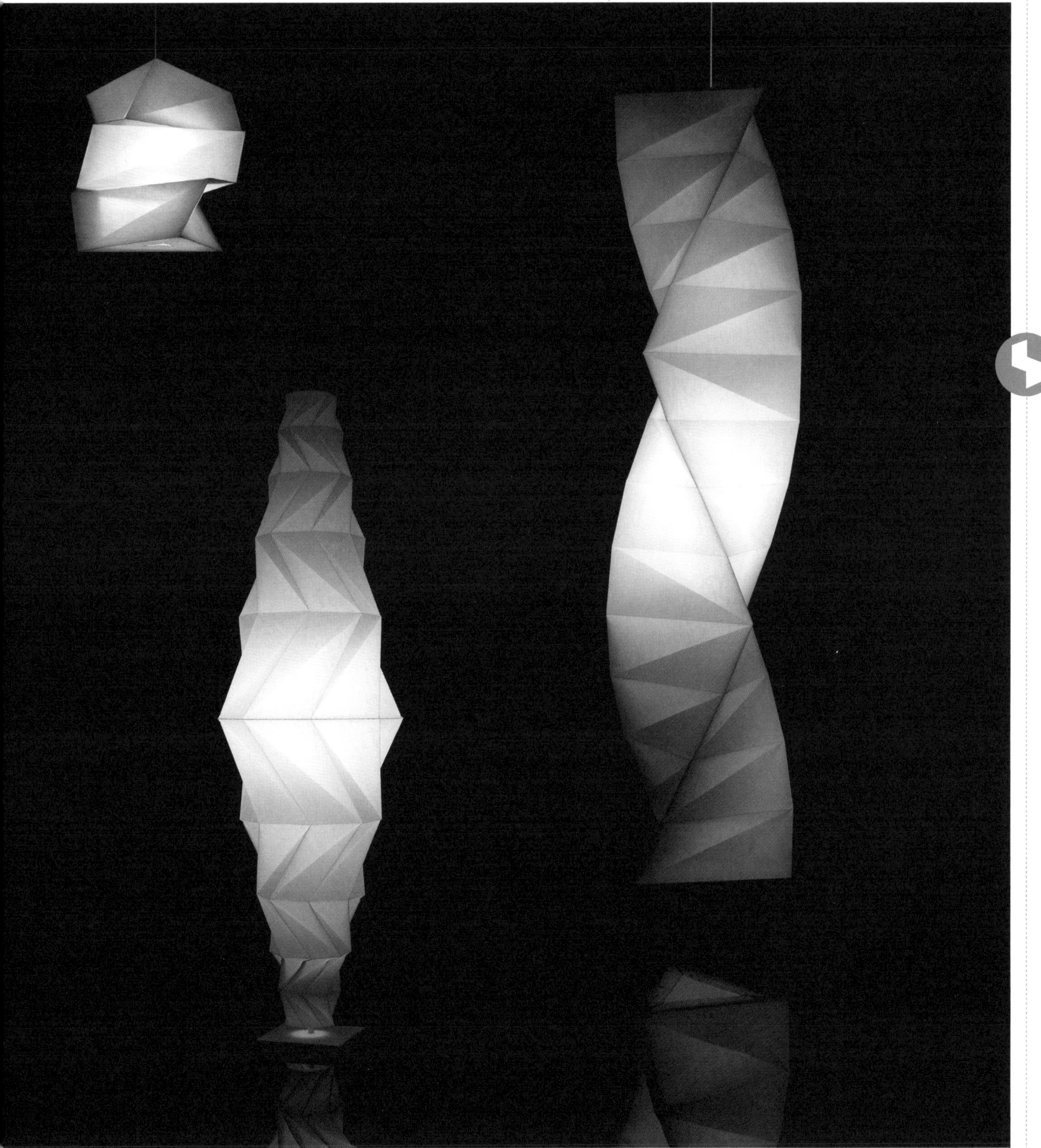

Formosis / Aki Hiltunen

FINLAND

As an architect, Aki Hiltunen has always been interested in the fluidity of space and shapes. To fold is to represent the fluidity of a material and the continuity of a line or a plane, which can be used to create a consistent design. There is also an economic idea behind folding: the entire surface is used to create the form. During his studies, Aki designed various projects based on fold patterns. Although he has never been able to experiment with folds in his architecture, he has been able to use them in his design work via the *Step* lamp.

The folding is done in such a way that the lamp has a very different appearance depending on where it is viewed from.

The acrylic sheet is laser cut. From there, the rest of the work is essentially done by hand and involves creating the form. The fold lines are heated for one to two minutes, and then the sheet is folded and cooled for two to five minutes. Different types of acrylic panels are employed. These are translucent to varying degrees, which produces different lighting effects.

The *Step* lamp is one of three products that Formosis™ Helsinki launched in September 2013 at the Habitare design show.

Remarks from November 2014.

www.formosis.com

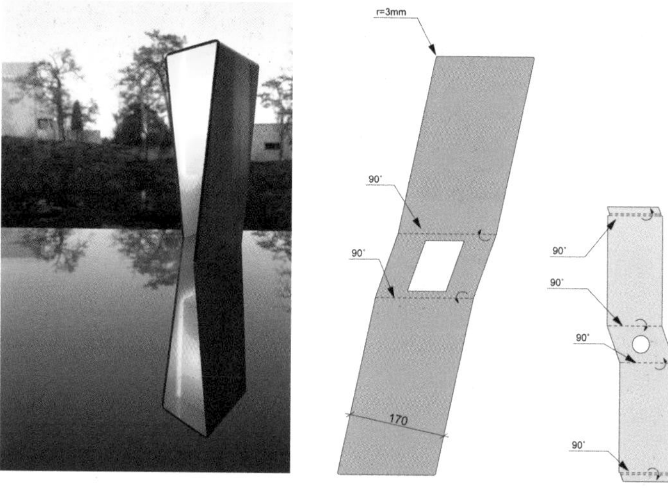

• Step *lamp.*

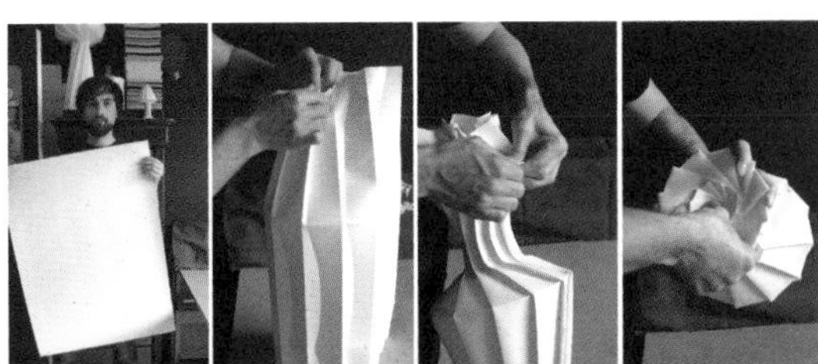

Arturass

FRANCE

Arturas Sargaitis designs and manufactures origami-inspired lighting pieces in his studio in the Paris region. The light brings out the material's superpositions.

"I've been folding for over twenty years. I started with small things, and then I became interested in tessellations. Later, I started working with the idea of creating functional objects like lights. I work with materials that are inexpensive but ennobled by the quality and perfection of the folding work."

Creating a model for a light starts with producing prototypes. Most of the time, the folds are done on paper and by hand.

The folds are then modelled on a computer because doing so allows a very high accuracy. The shape and dimensions are adjusted, and the scale may completely change the balance of the folds and the result.

The folding pattern is then created on a polypropylene sheet using a plotter. The folds are marked on the sheet with a tip. Arturas then forms the folds on the support, which is often a laborious step, and he then assembles the piece. When several folded pieces are assembled, he uses stitching, lending an elegant and discreet detail. Polypropylene is a very difficult material to glue, and the glue would possibly be visible with light. In addition to polypropylene, he is currently experimenting with moulded folds in concrete.

"With concrete, there is more freedom in terms of finishes and colours, and this is what I'd like to explore. But casting folded forms is complex. The material has to be distributed evenly, and it is quite difficult to achieve neat folds."

Porcelain is finer than concrete. Before his studies in applied arts, Arturas studied ceramics at an art school in Lithuania, his home country. He is currently working on a porcelain vase project that draws on the folds from one of his lights, *Astroid Wave*.

Remarks from Arturas Sargaitis, November 2014.

www.arturass.com

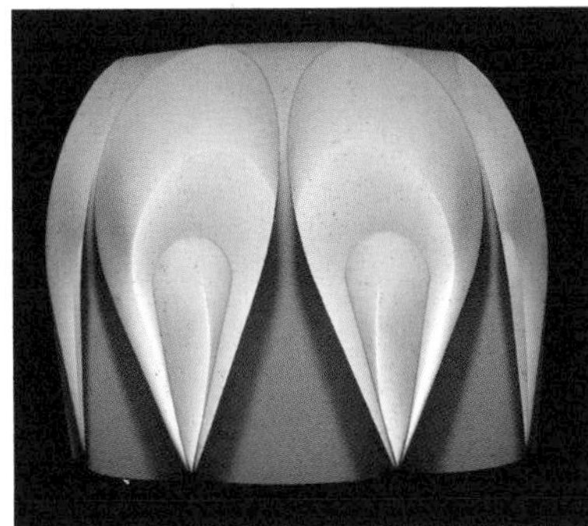

• *A few of the manufacturing steps in the studio.*
• Astroid Wave.
• Ama.
• Water Bomb.

Luisa Robinson

PHILIPPINES

As a designer, Luisa Robinson manipulates materials and their applications before even knowing where she would like to use them. Living in the Philippines gives her the opportunity to work with many local natural materials. The folding technique used for the *Dragon's Tail* is based on a simple game of questions and answers produced with the folded paper that she played with when she was a child. "The shape was interesting and I wanted to make something bigger out of it. I made the series with different sizes, fastening them together at different angles. When the piece became very large, I decided it would be better to organize according to a certain rhythm rather than putting things together at random." After several tests with other materials, Luisa finally returned to paper to create this lamp.

Remarks from November 2014.

www.luisarobinson.com
www.designbyhive.com

• *A set of* Dragon's Tail *hanging lights by Hive.*

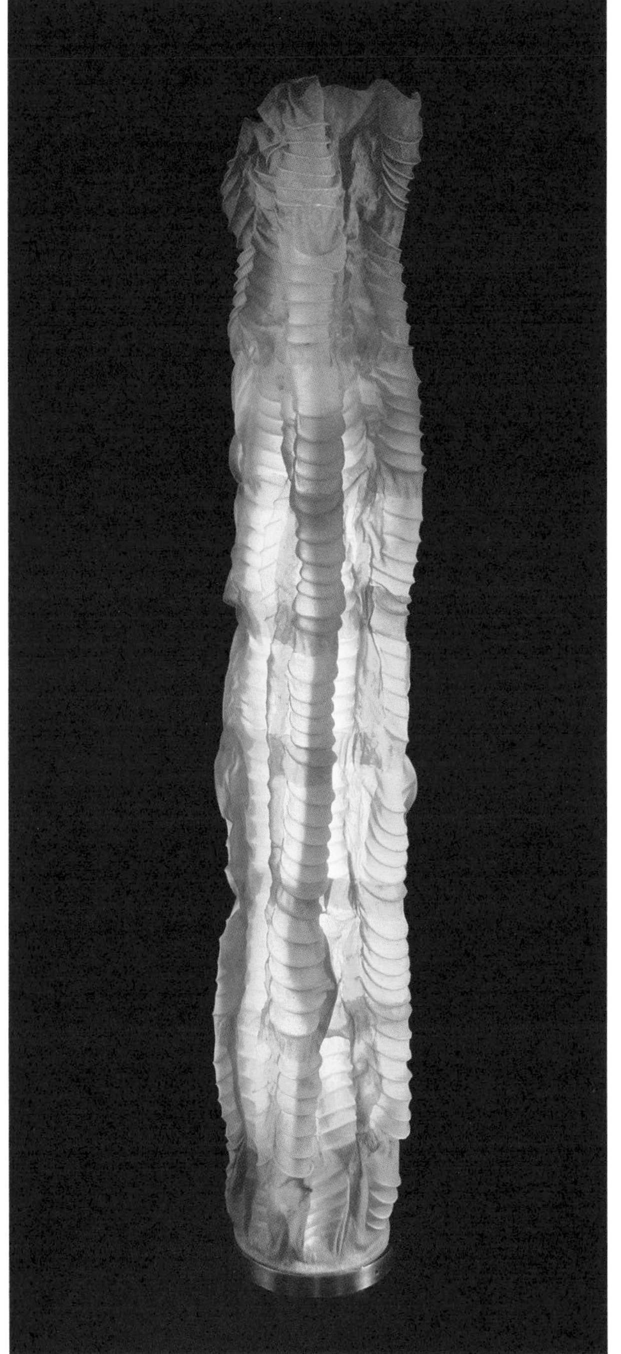

• Colonne *and* Cloud.

Studio-glow

USA

Years of experimentation led Riki Moss and her husband Robert Ostermeyer (Studio-glow) to use abaca, a paper made from the fibres of bananas from the Philippines. It has some great qualities, including strength, significant shrinkage upon drying and translucency.

The sheets of paper are first ground for more than seven hours, the time needed to cut the small fibres to produce optimal shrinkage later on. The pulp is then poured into a large container, in which the moulds are immersed and then drained. The sheets are then laid on felt. At this point, different materials are integrated and another sheet of wet paper is layered on. The whole thing is then pressed. Once the sheets can be manipulated, they are suspended and fastened together around a template—between thirty and one hundred of them—according to the size and shape of the sculpture to be created. When the paper is being dried, the way in which it interacts with the framework as it shrinks completes the process of creating the form.

Remarks from November 2014.

www.studio-glow.com

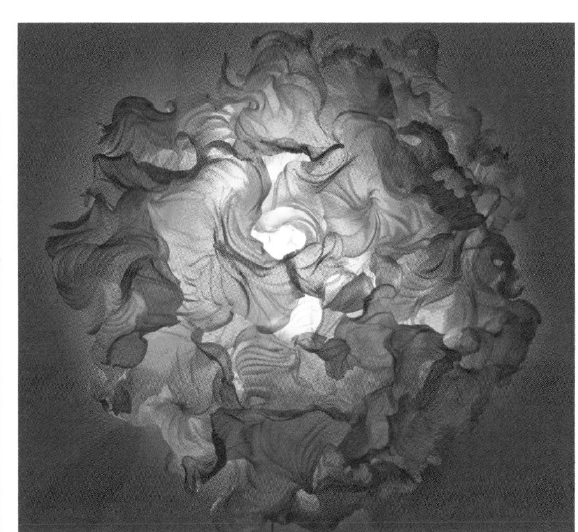

Charlot et Compagnie

FRANCE

Charles Macaire, a graduate of the Higher School of Optics, was a researcher at the CNRS, France's national centre of scientific research. Although he knew nothing about folding, his discovery of crimping at CRIMP (Centre de recherche international de modélisation par le pli) ten years ago brought him into a completely new world: he completely abandoned research and astronomy to focus exclusively on this new passion.

Behind this seemingly simple principle of crimping sheets of paper lurks a world of endless variations: "There are many things to discover: enough to fill a whole lifetime! That's what made me want to go down this path."

Charles Macaire applies procedures developed by CRIMP for his own creations of sculpture-lights. The network of folds creates an interplay of shadows that are revealed by the light.

These sculptures with organic forms seem to emerge from the material itself. To begin with, there is a sheet of paper in a basic geometric shape (a square, triangle or octagon, for example). This is then folded in a way similar to conventional origami, in order to produce a repetitive geometric pattern. This sequence of folds gives the sheet a structure once it is unfolded. The sheet is then lightly crimped with the help of a water mister. Many crimping patterns are available. The base pattern is a sun pleat with radiating folds.

"You never know what you'll find when you begin. After crimping, form is what inspires me, making me think of a sheet or a fish. I make many variations based on this form until I find one that I like.

So this is a way to combine folding of the starting geometric shape with a type of crimping that brings out this or that form. You can find the same form by repeating the same process as many times as you want."

Remarks from Charles Macaire, October 2014.

www.charloecie.fr

www.le-crimp.org

• The light sculptures that make up the Aquatiques series were created in 2009 and 2010. They evoke the animals of the seabed though without imitating them, which gives these creations their poetic dimension. The form is not the result of a lengthy work of design; it is born of its own accord during the manufacturing process.

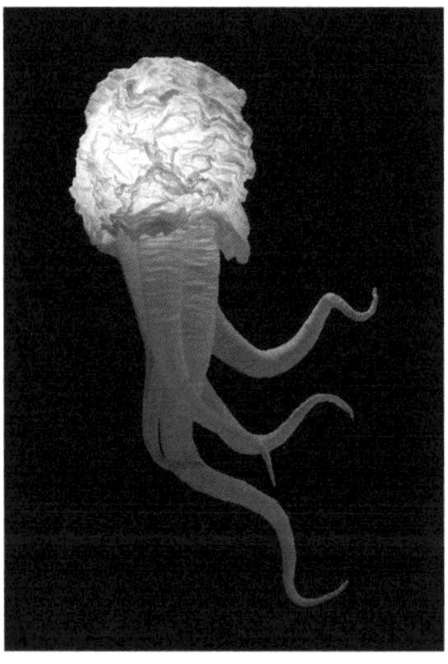

Si Studio Verónica Posada

CHILE

Hunter origami hangers and lamps, a folded menagerie

Si Studio was born in Milan in 2009 and moved to Chile in 2011. The team, led by industrial designer Veronica Posada, aims to recycle everyday situations and objects and reformulate them based on new perspectives. They seek to produce emotion, a source of real added value for the user. Their emphasis is therefore on ethics in the modes of production. For Si Studio, relevance must take precedence over the industrial viability of the objects produced.

Origamis Hunter is a series of wall lights that are an abstract representation of hunters' trophy walls. Origami helped in achieving this abstraction of rhino, deer and ibex heads. The folded parts forming shades are produced from a heat-resistant laminated paper and then attached to a metal base on which the light hangs.

Migration is a ceiling lamp inspired by migrating birds' formation of a V as they fly together. This formation is known for its aerodynamic properties connected to synchronization between the group of birds. In a similar vein, this is an economical creation in terms of energy thanks to a specific LED light built into the translucent acrylic birds, which are made using origami techniques.

Remarks from December 2014.

www.sistudio.cl

• *Veronica during folding of the* Origamis Hunter *series.*
• *The manufacturing process of* Origamis Hunter, *made from laminated paper that is resistant to high temperatures, first of all involves marking out the cuts and the folds of the lines with a mould of the segment. Each head consists of three parts that are folded by hand and rolled together using a special adhesive tape.*
• Migration *lamp.*

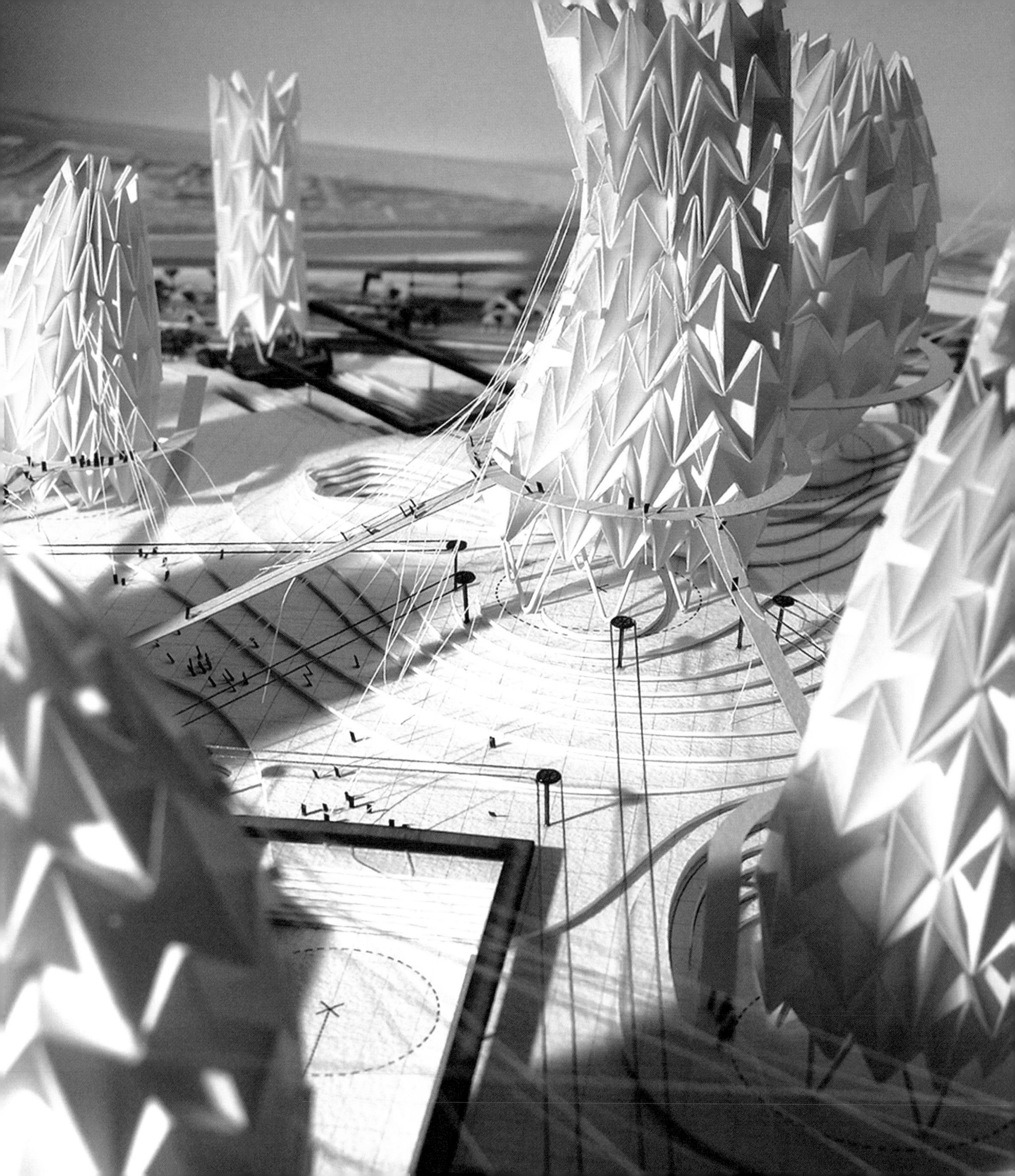

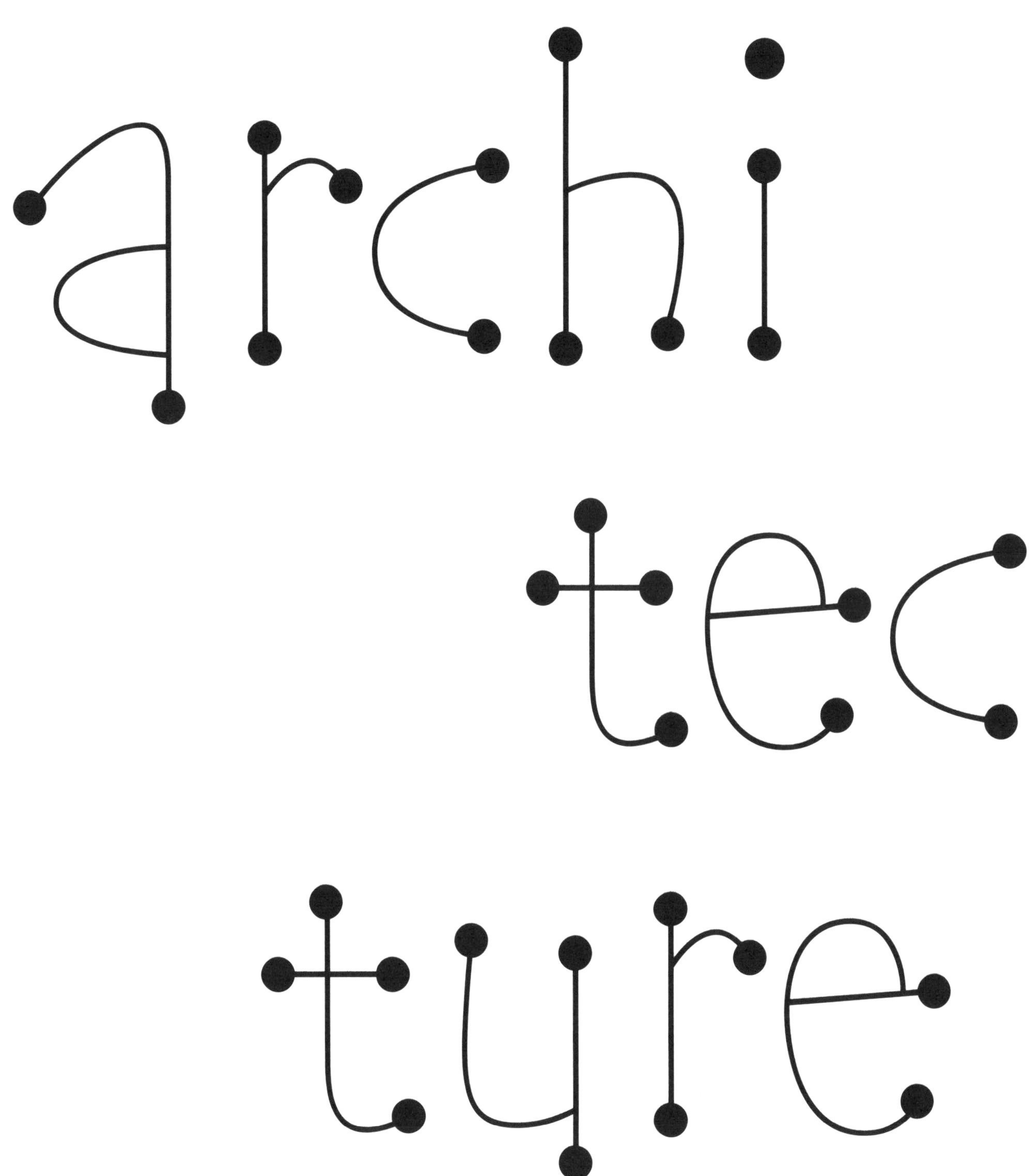

Thomas Hillier, The Emperor's origami lungs, *project model.*

FOLDS AS AN IMPETUS FOR ARCHITECTURAL SKETCHES

The requirements and initial information related to a building project are mapped out and then arranged in a system that is consistent with the project's spatial organization. The fold is a set of logical relationships whose genesis can be compared to the birth of a building. Again, folding may become an organizational factor, an aesthetic slant or a recurring type of form within the project. Architects naturally integrate folding into a polymorphic vocabulary as one of the "phonemes" that can lead to a coherent overall design.

In architecture, folding has as many functions—organizing, covering, deploying—as it does in nature. It can be used as support for the spatial organization of functions, based on a given site and programme. It is therefore an interesting compositional principle in that it allows the space with its various functions to be organized more smoothly: folding entails a degree of continuity, even between fragmented spaces. It is sometimes used directly owing to its sculptural qualities: because of the way in which shadows fall on a folded surface, it can transform spatial perceptions. But folding can also optimize a structure so that minimal materials are used. Or it can introduce movement, allowing mobile architecture that adapts to changing situations.

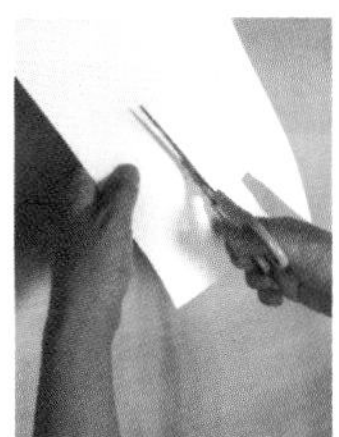

• *3 Gatti Architecture Studio, design process involving a paper model for the Automobile Museum project in Nanjing.*
• *Yoshinobu Miyamoto* The Tower of Babel.

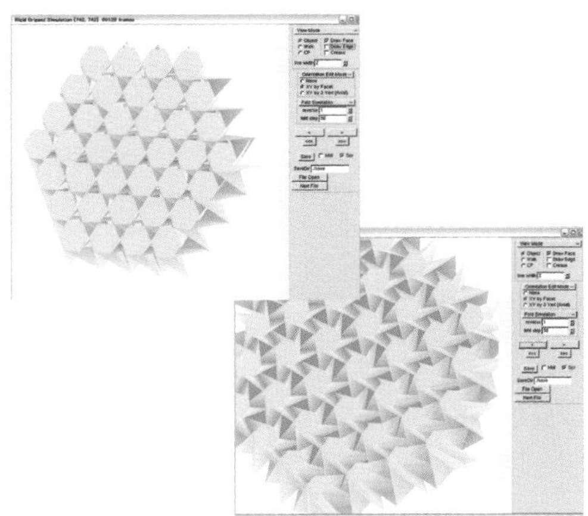

Yoshinobu Miyamoto

JAPAN

Yoshinobu Miyamoto is an architect and professor of architecture at the Aichi Institute of Technology (AIT) in Japan.

"The art of folding brings beauty under the constraints of materials. Today, 3D printer technology allows us to produce any free form without too many constraints. But these formal appearances would not have an effect on us if there was no reason for them. All forms in nature follow the laws of physics, and our sense of beauty has evolved through observing nature. The art of folding is a natural and universal strategy of the genesis of forms. I offer the concept of extended origami, which incorporates origami and kirigami in a systematic way."

Remarks from Yoshinobu Miyamoto, January 2015.

www.flickr.com/photos/yoshinobu_miyamoto
Kawasaki theorem in Origami Mathematics: www.mathworld.wolfram.com/KawasakisTheorem.html

• *Tessellations based on hexagons,* Kagome Pattern, *with flat top and concave surface in the process of unfolding, 3D model generated with* Oripa *and* Rigid Origami Simulator.
• *Vertical deployment sequences.*
• Dodecahedron Paradigma, *paper modular sphere inspired by* Kusudama Origami Paradigma *by Ekaterina Lukasheva, valley fold crossed joints, a sheet of A3 paper for 4 strips of 3 pentagons.*
• Octagon star.
• *3 x 3 square cells.*

FOLDING FOR FUNCTIONAL ORGANIZATION OF SPACE

Folding is sometimes used by architects when they are working with sketches, early in the design of a building project.

For some architects. it is a tool that allows the functions of the programme to be organized while maintaining significant continuity. Making a folded paper model is similar to making a quick pencil sketch, only in three dimensions. When the essence of a project can be expressed in a few folds, with limited resources, it is often the result of the challenging task of producing a synthesis.

Thomas Hillier

ENGLAND

The Emperor's Castle: *when architecture becomes a narrative*

Thomas Hillier is an architect and teacher, but he is also a "narrator of spaces." His talents as a designer and illustrator are, combined with a vivid imagination, the key to the success of his agency. Fleafollyarchitects explores architectural ideas that are implemented in the light of literary works.

The *Emperor's Castle* project was inspired by a traditional fairy tale whose characters have been converted into architectural metaphors, brought to life in the parvis of the imperial palace in central Tokyo. The project lasted eight months and was based on a trip to Japan. Initially, the Thomas worked on a sketch book, and he then used folded paper to produce scenes that evoke the contrast between technology and traditional arts. The work questions modern Japanese society and culture. The viewer/reader is captivated by the magic of the folding, which allows them to discover architecture in the form of a legend.

www.thomashillier.co.uk

• The Emperor's Castle, *collage*

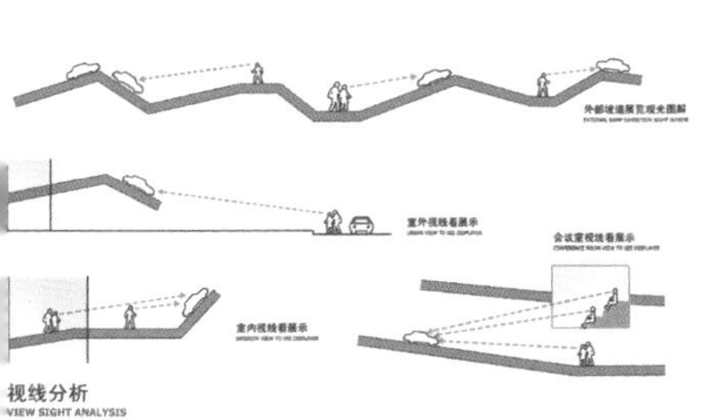

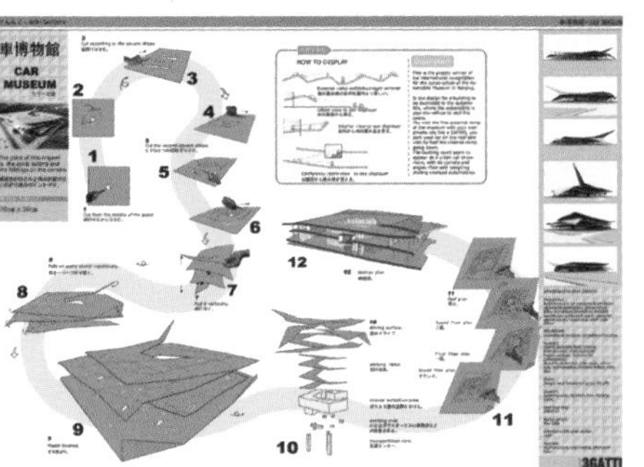

• *Automobile Museum in Nanjing (China), Schematic cross sections of viewpoints and folding principle.*
• *Aerial view of the museum and main entrance.*

3 Gatti Architecture Studio

ITALY – CHINA

The Automobile Museum in Nanjing: "Extreme" sensations and fluidity

In this project for an automobile museum, the desired result was a fluid perception of space. Here, there are no stairs or walls: the floors are cut and folded to form a single continuous plane.
The ramp is made of quick rises and falls that create an effect similar to a hilly landscape. This continuity sets up the route for visitors, who, as with a movie, follow the suggested route image by image. This varied but continuous landscape created by folds invites an exploration of new sensations.

3 Gatti Architecture Studio, head architect: Francesco Gatti, project leader: Summer Nie, contributors: Nicole Ni, Muavii Sun, Jimmy Chu, Luca Spreafico, Damiano Fossati, Kelly Han.

www.3gatti.com

Atelier Itoshi Abe

JAPAN

Yomiuri Media Miyagi Guest House, a folded ribbon

For this house, the architect tried to go beyond a confrontational relationship with nature and design a building that extended a forest space. The house is formed out of a 90-metre-long ribbon that is folded on itself in a double skin.
This in-between helps blur the boundaries between inside and outside. The ribbon encompasses the interior spaces, and its exterior folds generate all kinds of interactions with the surrounding terrain. The ribbon mirrors the topography of the site and turns it into an warped interior space, which is conceived as a second landscape. Six boxes containing the building's functions, such as the bathroom, have been inserted in this space in a grotto-like arrangement.

www.a-slash.jp

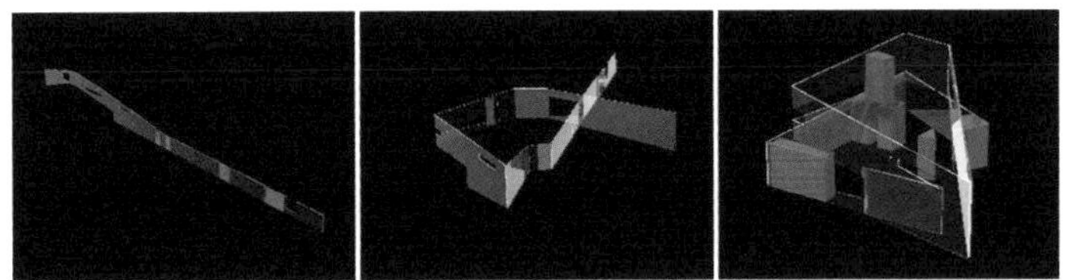

• *Design of the house's volume through folding of a ribbon connected to various functions.*
• *Outside and inside views of the holiday home located in Zao, Katta-gun, Japan, 1995-1997, surface area 170 m² (1,830 sq ft).*

• *Inside view of the loggia.*

"A piece of paper that weighs only a few grammes is capable of supporting a load of books that is two to three hundred times its own weight! A cylindrical shell made from folded paper needs buttresses to absorb outwards pushing, but its ability to carry a load is much higher than that of pleated sheet roofing, and it can easily reach 400 times its own weight."

Mario Salvadori, Comment ça tient? *éditions Parenthèses 2005, Eupalinos collection.*

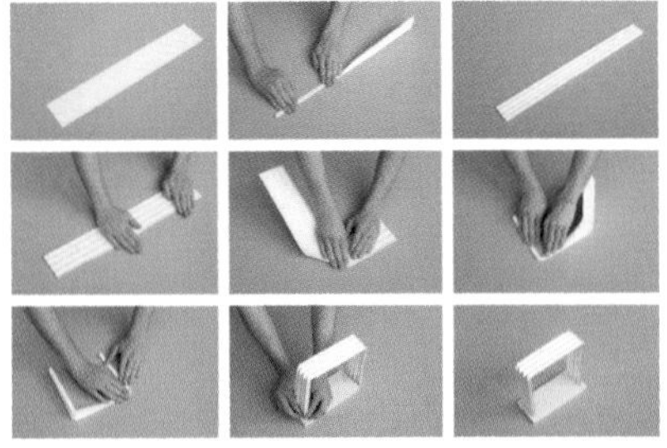

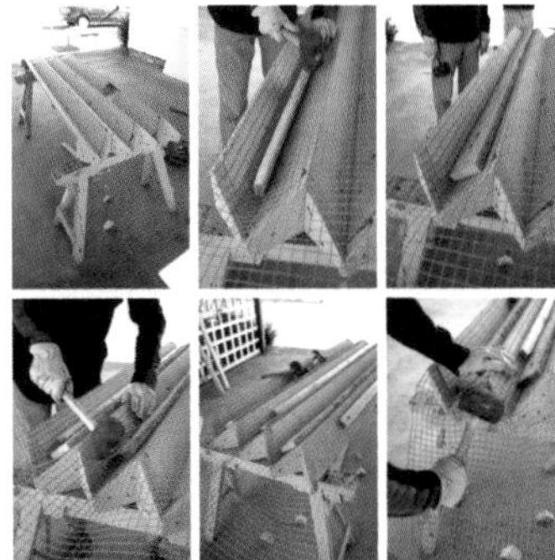

• *Sequences in the shaping of the mesh modules on a wooden template and using a mallet.*

Christopher Mullaney

AUSTRALIA

Origami Coop

Chris Mullaney is a young architect who received his training at the University of Newcastle, Australia. He is based in Sydney. *Chicken Coop* was his first experience of a project based on folding. When designing the coop, his goal was to eliminate the primary structure, which is generally the basis of this type of cage. Folding allowed him to reduce manufacturing, maintenance and waste costs. To achieve his aim, Chris tested out many folds on paper. The base material used is simply the galvanized wire mesh used in standard coops. Thanks to an ingenious folding principle, Chris developed a self-supporting system that is economical in terms of materials.

The coop can accommodate ten hens. A door on a pivot is made of folded wire, which also saved on jambs within the frame. A plywood shelter that is also inspired by folding has been designed in a way that minimizes material wastage. For example, the rectangle resulting from the cutting of the door was recut and "folded" into two to form a canopy. And the chicken coop has an egg collection system that makes inspection and collection easier.

The choice of the wire mesh is related to its durability, its transparency and the protection that it offers against predators (for this purpose, it is inserted into the ground to a depth of 30 cm). The great quality of this piece of architecture is precisely its use of a single material, which the architect has sought to exploit to the full. This brilliant idea of using chevron folding as a principle for rigidity and assembling the walls was based on the observation that traditional coops use many materials in their structure.

www.chrismullaney.com.au

LOCALARCHITECTURE Bureau d'architecture Danilo Mondada Shel (IBOIS, EPFL)

SWITZERLAND

© Milo Keller

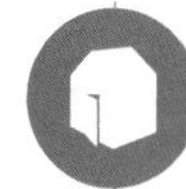

Temporary Chapel for St-Loup

In the summer of 2007, the group of architects comprising LOCALARCHITECTURE and the Bureau d'Architecture Danilo Mondada won a competition to renovate the motherhouse of the Deaconesses of St-Loup. During the works, the community had a pressing need for a temporary solution to allow it to conduct its daily worship.
LOCALARCHITECTURE'S architects, with their experience in construction projects based on wood, suggested a collaboration with IBOIS*, whose current research on folded structures seemed particularly appropriate for this project. Together, they developed a structure of cross-laminated timber panels based on origami geometry. Interpreting the traditional space of Protestant churches, the architectural project offers a series of folds that punctuate the interior volume.
The gable facades are made of textiles with coppery reflections that let in light. A frame made up of peaks and diagonals creates two facades and recalls the structure of a stained glass window. Created using engineered wood of different thicknesses, the structural panels of different sizes were cut using a CNC saw. The joints are strengthened with sheet metal. A bituminous seal covers the entire structure. The outer skin consists of panels of 3-ply wood.

Remarks from Robert-Grandpierre of LOCALARCHITECTURE *and Hani Buri, November 2014.*

- www.localarchitecture.ch
- www.ibois.epfl.ch
- "Origami - folded plate structures," Hani Buri (thesis no. 4714; presented at the EPFL in 2010).

© Milo Keller

© Milo Keller

• Outer skin made up of wood panels with 3 folds and gable facades in textiles that allow light to pass through.
• The peaks and diagonals of the frame create the two facades, calling to mind the structure of a stained glass window.
• Folds punctuate the external volume.

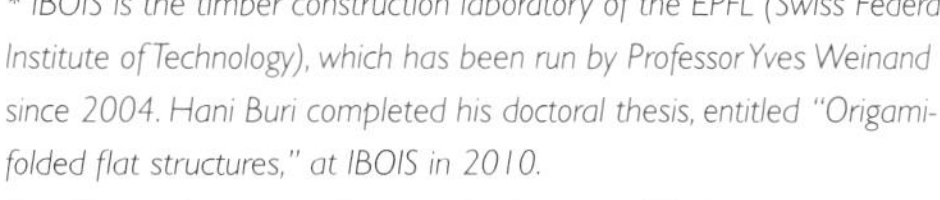

** IBOIS is the timber construction laboratory of the EPFL (Swiss Federal Institute of Technology), which has been run by Professor Yves Weinand since 2004. Hani Buri completed his doctoral thesis, entitled "Origami-folded flat structures," at IBOIS in 2010.*
Yves Weinand and Hani Buri are the founders of SHEL.

Archiwaste

FRANCE

The Archiwaste collective (Rupert Maleczek, Chloé Genevaux and Guillaume Bounoure) developed, in collaboration with the Institute of Design | unit koge. Structure and Design, University of Innsbruck, a 10-metre-high (33 ft) tower built entirely out of cardboard. The project was part of the exhibition *Carton Plein*, held at the Cité de l'architecture et du patrimoine in Paris in 2009. A retrospective of the collective's work was also exhibited. Archiwaste's architectonic folding works made from cardboard or polypropylene are based on an optimization of forms and the reappropriation of "poor" materials, such as those used in packaging. If the usefulness an beauty of what we overlook and reject every day were revealed, then a circular economy could come into being.

Cardboard is used here owing to its specific qualitie and it is pushed to its limits.

The project was designed and constructed in partnership with teachers and students from the KOGE unit under the direction of Professor Eda Shaur and her assistant Rupert Maleczek. The form of this project, installed in the central void of a spiral staircase in the Cité Chaillot, stems from the requirements given by the security commission for the exhibition. The structure, which was prefabricated in Austria, was transported to Paris in a small vehicle, with the foldable elements stored fla and therefore occupying only a very small amount of space.

• *Cardboard tower, a collaboration between Archiwaste and Institute of Design | unit koge. Structure and Design, University of Innsbruck, Austria, designed by R. Maleczek.*

he tower was digitally modelled and optimized ased on the idea of a simple fold creating "a unity etween materiality, space and structure." Standing : 10 m (394 in) tall, and comprising 96 elements ıd 300 bolts, it weighed only 280 kg. The folds ere cut at a specific angle with a CNC milling ıachine in the layers of the plates of 28 mm (1 1/8) corrugated cardboard; two layers of cardboard emained intact to strengthen the hinge. Assembly as carried out in a day by turning the tower in the entre of the spiral staircase, which helped to avoid ıe need for any scaffolding.

- www.archiwaste.com
- www.archispass.org
- www.citechaillot.fr
- www.koge.at

P

Coll-Barreu

SPAIN

'he characteristic ceted facade of the ilding.
Partial view of the uble facade.
Internal volume of the rium.

The facade of a public building: folds as a second skin

Architect Juan Coll-Barreu chose to give a folded form to the facade of his building in order to meet the major technical demands of the project's site. This public building is home to the health administration service in Bilbao's city centre. According to Juan, folding, as a form of distortion, makes it possible to adapt the facade as a "system" in response to the given criteria—for example, to incorporate user needs or the atmosphere of the city. The design process was a long one. Unlike other designers, the architects in this case worked directly on computer in 2D and 3D: Juan prefers to start out from an "abstract idea defined by the computer rather than making real models." For him, a digital model is a method of expression starting from the sketches, which is a sign of the evolution of professional practices.

During the design phase, there were digital models for the aluminium and glass external facades, the concrete floors and the internal facade, all of which had to coincide! They consulted specialized engineering companies, but none wanted to run the risk of designing the facades in detail for the execution. They therefore developed in-house proficiency in Dassault Systèmes' Catia software package and defined a very specific model themselves, in order to obtain the calculations for the structure of the facade and production of this folded form and all its details. They were therefore able to optimize the connecting principles, calculate expansion and so forth, which allowed them to make the complex joinery with the company that they hired. After a first successful sample, the construction process took place without any problems!

This type of double facade offers temperature-regulation functions by allowing the circulation of air, and it also provides protection from the sounds and smells of the street.

Interview with Juan Coll-Barreu Architects, 2014.
Juan Coll-Barreu and Daniel Gutiérrez Zarza, Bilbao.

www.coll-barreu-arquitectos.com
www.3ds.com/fr/produits-et-services/catia/

Gramazio and Kohler

SWITZERLAND

Public toilets in Uster: the anti-tag fold

Sarah Schneider is project leader at Gramazio Kohler. She has a strong interest in manufacturing technologies: "We seek to oversee designs to find intelligent ways to produce complex components." For this project, a public washroom in a park, research involving folded models centred on the way to create overlapping surfaces that create an interplay of light and shadow. In this case, the facade is in a difficult environment, and so the holes in the mesh can prevent graffiti. The strips are made from 1.5-2 mm (1/16 in) thick lacquered aluminium, making them difficult to destroy. These facade components hang on a backing structure and can be changed individually. The project's requirements led to this folded design. The architects started out from folded paper models to get an idea of the construction method, and they then used the potential of parametric design to determine the overall facade in 3D and integrate the changing requirements during the project. This innovative method of design is particularly suited to folding. They then found a manufacturer and completed a scale sample so that the client could check the finish. The colours were chosen in order to fit in with the other existing buildings in the park.

Interview with Sarah Schneider, 2014.

www.gramaziokohler.com

- *Paper model.*
- *Folding of the aluminium elements.*
- *In situ prototype.*

F.A.D.S Fujiki Studio KOU::ARC

JAPAN

Aqua-scape

"This architecture that floats on water was built by us in the summer of 2006. Architecture until now has been hard, heavy and immobile.
Yet when I think about the architecture of the future, I think about softness, lightness and mobility. This project is a prototype created out of this idea.
This architecture consists of plastic materials that are soft to the touch and that have no skeleton, a bit like a jellyfish.
Applying the traditional technique of origami to the folding of flexible plastic materials allows structures created in this way to independently support themselves.
In addition, through the weaving of 1 m x 4 m (39 x 158 in) elements, it is possible to build large structures. Following the failures of many tests, I focused on seeking a structure whose form gave it strength. The final form is obtained by folding the surface of a cylinder."
Aqua-scape was produced for the *Echigo-Tsumari Art triennial* exhibition, which took place in 2006 in Tokamachi, Niigata Prefecture. The city of Tokamachi is known for its silk fabrics and kimonos.

Remarks from Ryumei Fujiki, December 2014.

www.fads-design.jp
www.ns.kogakuin.ac.jp/~wwd1034/Home.html

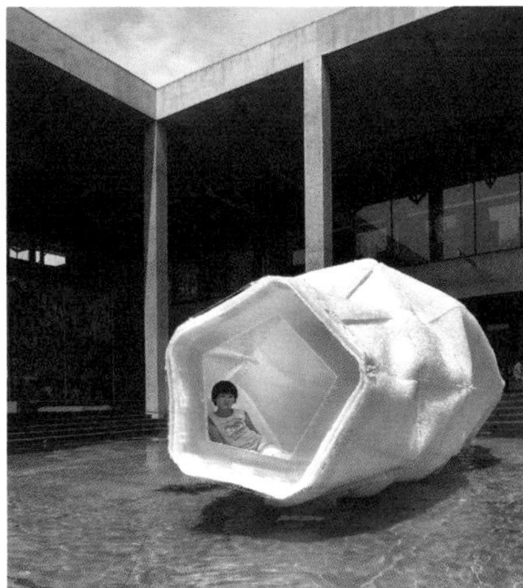

- *Making the pavilion.*
- *Multiposition compartment.*
- *Full view of the cocoon.*

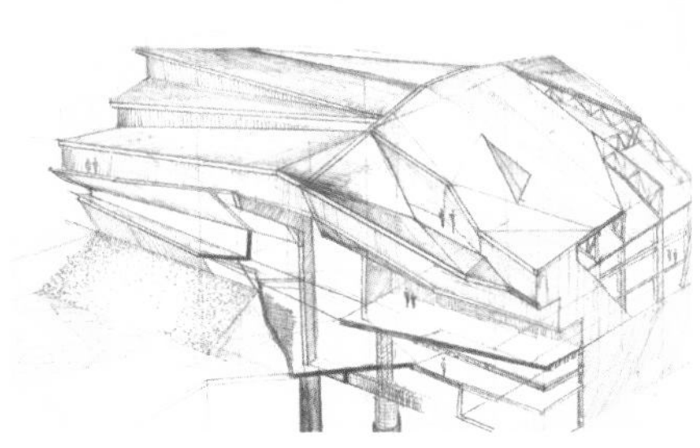

Broissin

MEXICO

Roberto Cantoral cultural centre

"Transforming floors into walls and then ceilings always brings out a strong emotional response in both building users and me. The facade was created out of a pentagram that starts to lose its shape with the harmony of musical notes: there are five slabs, which, from left to right, fold in tribute to that moment when a composer transforms a piece of paper into music.
Although not folded in the truest sense, the pillars of the facade are cast in concrete in forms that follow the geometry of folds. Inside, the concert hall is also folded, but partly for acoustic reasons in this case. The building envelops you, and its form transforms into music."

Remarks from Gerardo Broissin Covarrubias, December 2014.

www.broissin.com

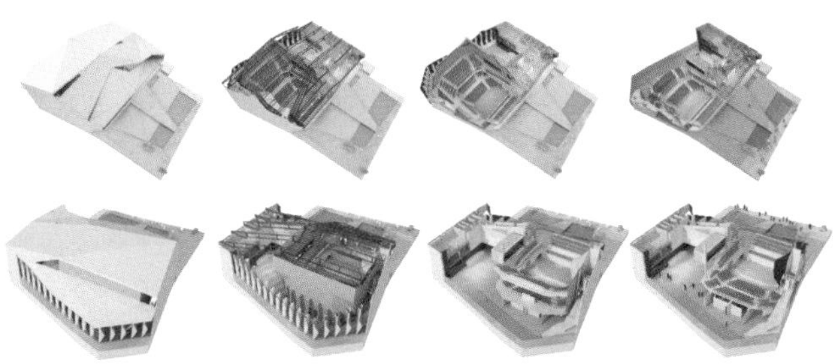

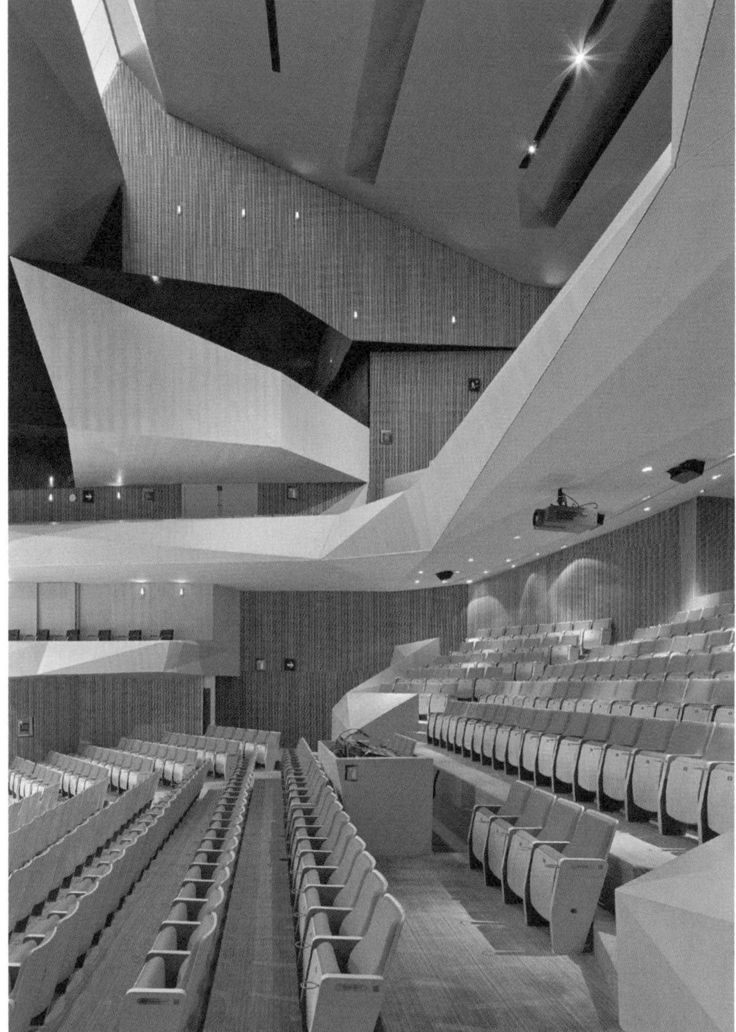

• *Sketch.*
• *Laying of panels.*
• *Organization diagram.*
• *The folded walls contribute to the hall's acoustic correction.*

• *Inner view of the folded facade.*

1

• *The pavilion consists of 95 modules and weighs about 100 kg. The internal surface area is about 7 m² (75 sq ft). This temporary pavilion is built from 2 mm (1/16 in) thick Miniwell sheets (a very rigid corrugated cardboard).*
The roof and the facade are suspended with hangers, a solution that has parallels with Lego and makes the house easy to assemble and adjust. The flexible design of the house allows it to be stretched out over several hundred metres if need be.

Mattias Lind / White arkitect

SWEDEN

Chameleon Cabin

Mattias Lind, an architect and partner at White arkitekter AB, designed a home made entirely from paper—*Chameleon Cabin*—that changes appearance as a chameleon changes depending on the angle under from which it is viewed. We usually see architecture while we are moving, and in this project folds helps to create a kinetic effect. By printing pictures of black and white marble on the facade, the architect wanted to ennoble the modest material that paper is. For the interior, he chose a bright yellow to create a warm atmosphere that also contrasted with the exterior's more discreet black and white. Mattias expects buildings that use paper will develop in the future, especially as the material is renewable. Parametric design with new digital design and cutting tools creates new opportunities to solve complex problems.

Remarks from February 2015.

www.white.se/en/project/298-chameleon-cabin

• *Deployment steps of the* Rolling Bridge.

Heatherwick studio

ENGLAND

Rolling Bridge

This pedestrian bridge crosses the Grand Union Canal at Paddington Basin in London. It rolls up on itself to allow boats to pass. The goal was to ensure that movement itself gave the bridge an extraordinary feature. The *Rolling Bridge* opens up by slowly unrolling. From a circular sculpture on the edge of the canal, it turns into a conventional straight bridge.

www.heatherwick.com

Make Architects

ENGLAND

Canary Wharf Kiosk,

when folding is "open" for business

Make is a studio of architects and designers founded by Ken Shuttleworth in 2004. It designs and executes projects involving unconventional spaces and buildings of all types.
This team's creations are amazing and innovative. Their business ethic is based on social responsibility and economic and environmental relevance.
These two folding kiosks built in the centre of London for Canary Wharf Group Plc were part of an ice sculpture festival that took place in January 2014. These mobile structures that look like sculptures were prefabricated in the studio and delivered to the site by crane. The front of the booth is composed of plywood panels protected by a sealed membrane on the underside and on the surface by engineered panels with an aluminium powder finish. This ingenious system of panels articulated by hinges is manipulated using a motorized system of pulleys and counterweights. When it is closed (and therefore protected from external elements), the rectangular box opens up through retraction in a manner similar to a flower. This system amazes many passers-by and fits in with a point of sale's need to be visible.
This project, which won in the temporary spaces category at the New London Awards, illustrates the potential of folding to create transformable architecture.

www.makearchitects.com

People's industrial design office / People's architecture office

CHINA

These two industrial design and architecture studios were founded by Zangfeng, James Shen and Hezhe in Beijing, China, in 2010. They have explored folding structures in several projects (*Pop-up Habitat*, *Dumpling Chair* and *Tricycle House*).

In China, there is no private ownership of land, and so the *Tricycle House* suggests a future that embraces the temporary relationship between humans and the land that they occupy. In a crowded Chinese city, the *Tricycle House* is quite affordable for a single person. Parking spaces are used as living spaces at night, and traffic jams are made acceptable because living and travelling go hand in hand.

"The design process started with folded paper models. We then created scale prototypes by folding honeycomb polypropylene. These materials are easily accessible and manipulable, and for this reason we were able to develop this design in a fairly short space of time. In parallel, we created 3D models. From these, we generated flat cutting patterns, which were used to make prototypes.

Polypropylene can be folded many times without losing its strength. The house can therefore open outward and extend like an accordion to enlarge the space and connect to other homes. We also took advantage of the pliability of the material to design the furniture inside. The furniture folds, going from a bed to a dining table and then to a counter. And the sink, stove and bathtub can fold into the wall. The structure contains no metal; it is made entirely of plastic."

www.peoples-products.com

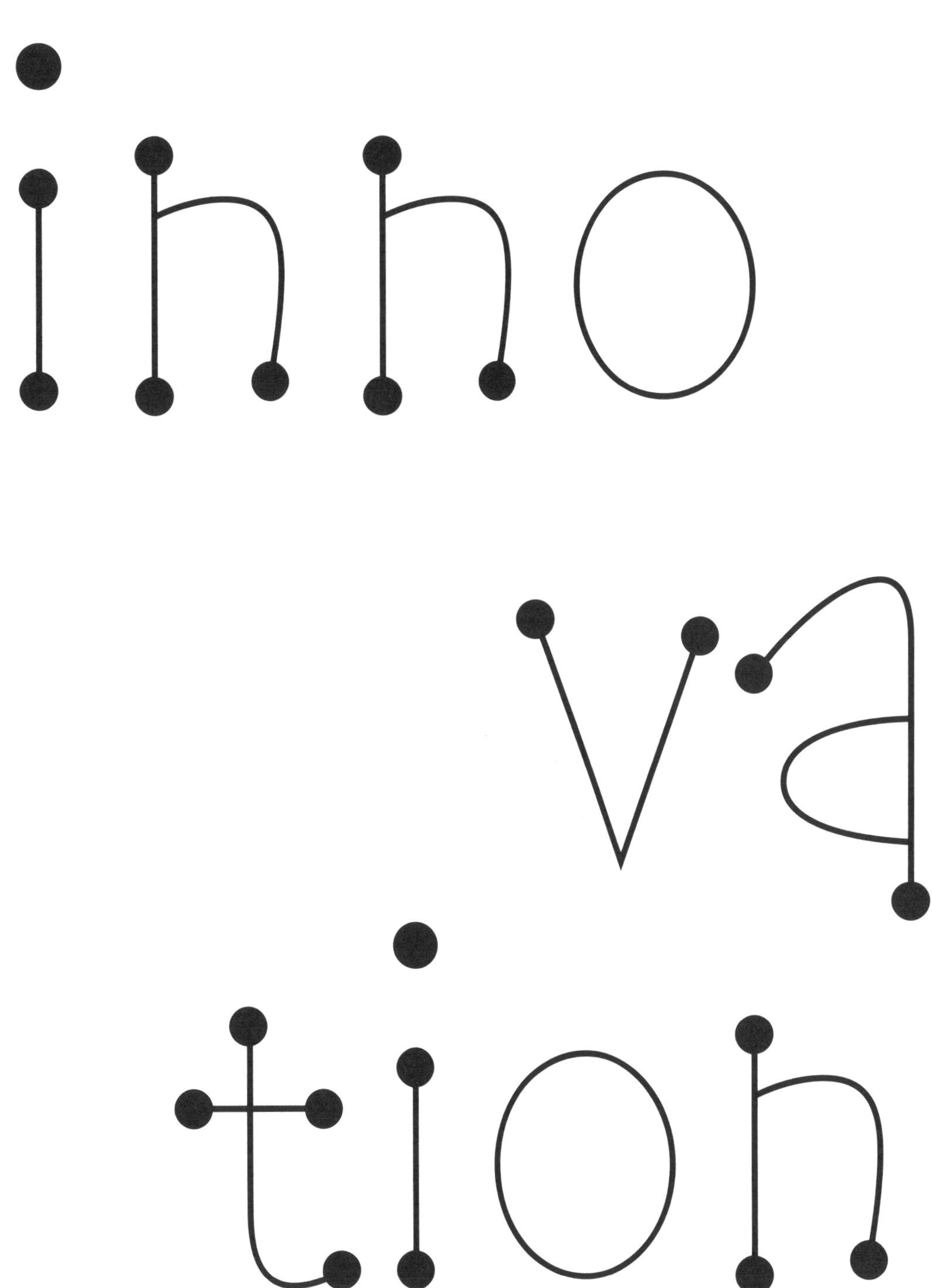

Kaleidome, *Otto Ng / Laab Architects,*
ong Kong, 2015.

SEARCHING IS NOT FINDING

Folding is a field of investigation for research, an area that involves providing answers to a problem through an investigation plan.
Although research sometimes leads to industrial applications, patents and so forth, these are not its primary objective. Enhancing the community's overall knowledge of the subject under study must come first. Innovation is made possible though knowledge. Once an innovation has been developed by researchers for a range of applications, it is transferred to industry as technology for the development of expertise that is useful for the production of goods and services.

Scientific research on folding may focus on folding techniques, the production of new materials or the geometry of folds and their mathematical modelling. It is therefore capable of providing solutions to questions related to miniaturization or intelligent and animated objects.
Origami as a variable geometry can also be a potential form of innovation in the logic of a virtual system as a program, without necessarily manifesting itself in a dramatic way. Folding is a form of renewal!
Whether it takes the form of the push towards nanotechnologies, the management of space or DIY, when it comes to renewing modes of production, folding never ceases to amaze us.

• *Eric Olsen,* The Pleated Bucket.

• *Jun Mitani,* Relief of Wave, *diagram, 3D model and paper folding.*

Origami computer modelling tools have been developed to simulate the transition from a flat surface to a three-dimensional one. Valley- and mountain-fold lines are drawn on the starting surface, and the software then calculates the gradual transformation of the planes in space through folding.

There are also tools that specialize in unfolding, in which the starting surface is a three-dimensional volume that can be unfolded to obtain patterns.

Tools developed for folding:

✏ Tomohiro Tachi: Rigid Origami Simulator, Origamizer, Freeform Origami. www.tsg.ne.jp/TT/origami/

✏ Jun Mitani, straight folds: ORIPA, curved folds: ORI-REF, ORI-REVO, ORI-REVO-MORPH www.mitani.cs.tsukuba.ac.jp/origami_application/

✏ RobotFold: KingKong, plugin simulation of folds for the 3D software Grasshopper® - Rhinoceros®, IO robotics simulation plugin and Unicorn: www.robofold.com/make/software/king-kong-folding-software

Tools developed for unfolding:

✏ Pepakura by (C) Tama Software Ltd: http://www.tamasoft.co.jp/pepakura-en/

• *RobotFold, folding simulation for a metal sheet through two robotic arms.*

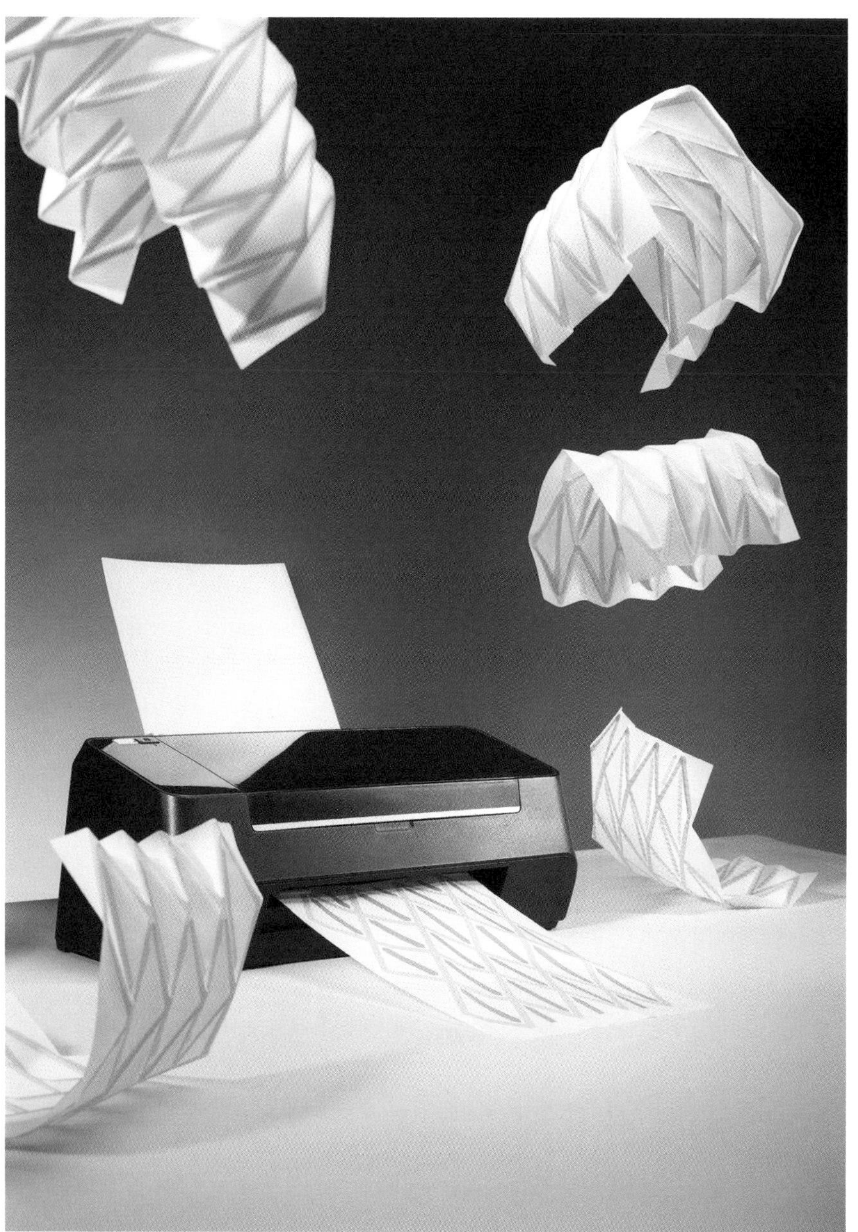

• Hydro-Fold, *a special printing technique that transforms a simple sheet of paper into a three-dimensional structure.*

Christophe Guberan

SWITZERLAND

Hydro-Fold: *wet folding*

Christophe Guberan is a product designer and, above all, a researcher who is interested in the process of flat folding and "active" materials. Folding using moisture is the result of a research process whose end is the research itself. *Hydro-Fold* emerged from a study project and a simple observation: a wet mark on copy paper.

Hydro-Fold entailed injecting water into inkjet printer cartridges to generate folds through the thickness of the wet lines and the curving of the fibres. Other than research, there was no application for this experiment. Today, Christophe is called upon to speak at prestigious universities such as MIT, and he collaborates in the development of futuristic projects. He imagines things like partitions contained in a liquid that would take their form when the package is opened, chairs that could be thrown into a pool to store them, or even an outfit that takes shape as dancers sweat during a routine. For this engineering researcher, folding is about research both into shaping materials and into light, which "draws the object through the edge of the fold."

Interview with Christophe Guberan, October 2014.

- www.christopheguberan.ch/Hydro-Fold
- www.ecal.ch/fr/1206/formations/bachelor/design-industriel/projets-workshops/hydro-fold
- www.web.mit.edu/

Patrick Jouin

FRANCE

One Shot Stool: when a prototyping tool becomes a production tool

Patrick Jouin is the founder of a dynamic and multidisciplinary agency made up of designers, architects and interiors experts. Through the quality and scope of his production, this French designer has become one of the driving figures of contemporary design.

For designers, folding begins with an idea: they often try to fold projects. To begin with, there's a big page with concepts and constraints. And little by little, they fold them over one another, to obtain a folded thing: the project. They try to put hidden things in the "folds" of the project: these are intentions that can be poetic or delicate. They are often not explicit, but these are the most important ones.

Patrick's style isn't particularly geometric; he is attracted to supple forms, though ones that always maintain a certain solidity. According to Patrick, this is where folds provide the right answer.

One Shot follows on from a previous project (2004) called *Solid Stool 1*, which was made using new rapid prototyping tools: stereolithography and selective laser sintering. But the final object was expensive because of the volume, as the possibilities of the machine had not been sufficiently exploited to build these mechanisms and forms that were impossible to assemble in any other way. So Patrick's team sought to make with the same volume of sintering allowed by the tool not one, but thirteen or fourteen stools.

It was in this context of rapid changes in technology and the cost of 3D printing of objects that the first series project was produced by the agency. The manufacturer MGX offered to release it in 2006, and then there was the *Bloom* lamp in 2008, which was based on the same principle.

Interview with Patrick Jouin, February 2015.

www.patrickjouin.com
www.mgxbymaterialise.com/designers/designer/detail/detail/14)

• One Shot
stool and its clever unfolding.

• *RoboFold Studio, panorama.*
• Sartorial Tectonics Paneling System *in collaboration with Andrew Saunders US, for UPenn, Robotic Smoked Lattice, USA 2013/4.*
• Stathis Lagoudakis, *polished aluminium work.*

RoboFold

ENGLAND

An innovative implementation of curved folds

Gregory Epps is an architect and the founder of RoboFold. During his studies at London Metropolitan University, he discovered by chance that it was possible to fold a curve. He initially did this on paper, using a compass to draw an equilateral triangle, and then on metal to make sculptures. He set about exploring these forms, whose beauty and simplicity appealed to him. Then, wanting to design a bike, he had the idea of applying this technique rather than using a mould to produce the curved forms that he sought for his frame.

To achieve the right folds, he had to use software. As there wasn't really any at this time, he decided to code it himself. Folds produced manually on paper could not be reproduced so easily on metal sheets: he had to find an industrial process. Gregory became interested in car design, which leads the way in the serial production of objects through the automation of production lines. After observing the possibilities of robotic arms used for many tasks that have spatial implications (five axes), he had the idea of reproducing the movement of the robots' hands. There is iteration between the analysis of movements and sequences in the early phases and the robotic programming. This type of design, known as parametric design, allows early manufacturing constraints to be taken into account (for example, compensation of angles related to the strength of materials, rupture thresholds of folds and elasticity) in order to integrate them into the design of the shape of the corresponding flat pattern.

The team has developed the King Kong software package, the plugin IO robotics simulation and Unicorn, which allow architects to simulate the process of manufacturing and folding of geometries with the extravagant shapes that are used in designs today. Previously, it was difficult to make the connection between the form and the fabrication of complex objects. This process allows a direct link between the two. This type of "bridge" approach is a clear sign of an evolution—through recently accessible advanced technology—towards a form of "micro" industry that is more specialized, localized and agile.

The team is working on the manufacture of a small mobile production unit, and it has also developed a prototype of a micro robot for small prototyping, which DIY 3D printing enthusiasts will love. These new interfaces between man and machine open ingenious perspectives for also developing metal moulds with curved folds (with a smooth surface to the metal) for casting pieces made using concrete or carbon-fibre reinforced resin, or for plastic injection. In the near future, thanks to this type of robotic folding process, everyone might be able to locally and inexpensively produce spare parts that are needed using plans or a "scan" of the object to be reproduced.

Interview with Gregory Epps, January 2015.

www.robofold.com
www.robots.io.com

• *RoboFold,* Arum for Zha, *Venice Biennale, 2012*

Eric Olsen

USA

The Pleated Bucket, *a basket for transporting water*

Eric Olsen is an architect and professor at Woodbury University in Los Angeles, California. *The Pleated Bucket*, also known as the Solar Water Disinfecting Tarpaulin, was developed as a prototype in 2008. The project sought to respond to problems related to drinking water. The goal was to formulate an answer on the scale of the individual rather than on the scale of a city or a community. Eric Olsen became interested in custom infrastructure. He has created a flexible pleated tank to contain, transport and purify water using the sun's heat and UVA rays. This project was inspired by folding in nature; and in particular the way in which desert organisms retain water. The Saguaro cactus was a particular source of inspiration. Its wrinkled skin contracts during the dry season and stretches during the rainy season in response to the availability of water. Folding gives a structure to the pleated bucket and allows it to adapt to varying volumes of water. It can be compacted into a small volume when it is empty in order to make it easier to carry, or it can be stretched over a large surface to expose the water to the sun in order to disinfect it.
The top layer is made from transparent polyethylene to let the rays of the sun pass through, and the bottom layer is made from rubberized nylon fabric, which reflects radiation.
The first prototypes were manufactured with plastic and hot glue to test the performance of the folds. Subsequent prototypes were developed using CNC machines and software. The patterns were laser cut and manually welded with radio frequency welding equipment.

Remarks from Eric Olsen, November 2014.

www.superficialstudio.com

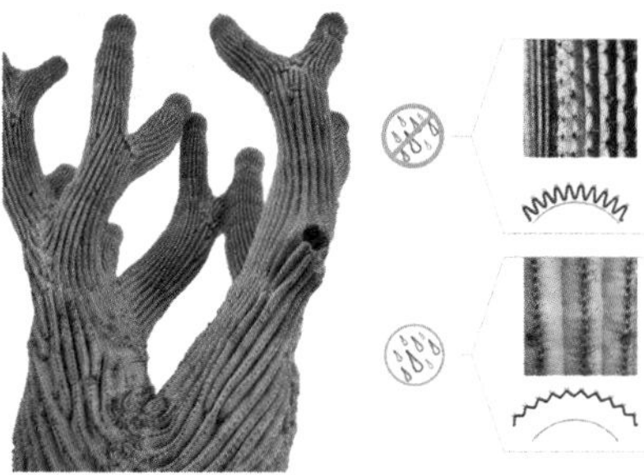

• The Saguaro cactus and its special morphological adaptation response to the presence of water.
• The design of the pleated tarpaulin allows its contents to be evenly distributed, and it can extend as needed while also having a large fill capacity of up to 20 l of water.

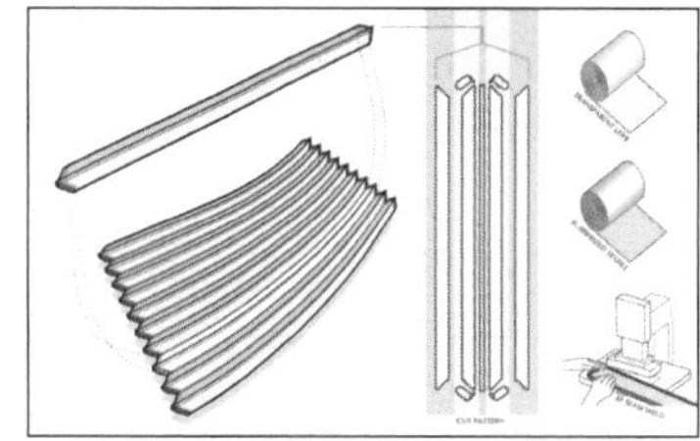

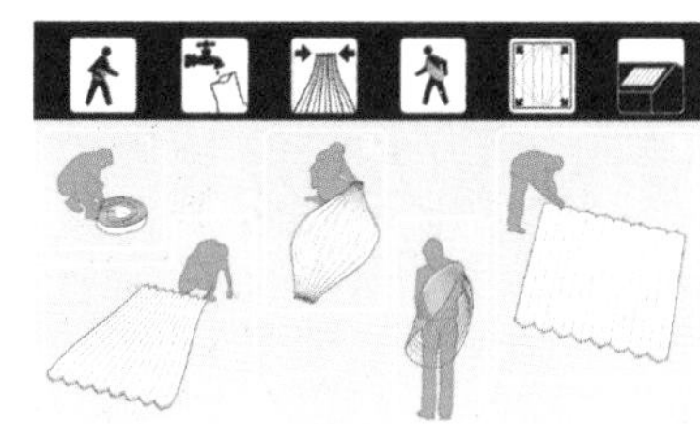

• Manufacturing of the tarp by laser cutting and high-frequency welding.
• Versatility of use and ease of storage.

This flying object is made based on a kaleidocycle, a sort of crown composed of tetrahedrons. The development of this flexible solid involves isosceles triangles.

ANIMATED AND "INTELLIGENT" OBJECTS

Festo

GERMANY

Smartinversion, ***a folded drone***

Since the beginning of the 1990s, Festo's activities have focused on the subject of bionics—the transposition of natural phenomena into the world of technology. The modern world moves in a straight line from A to B, or turns in circles—translation and rotation. The third method of propulsion, inversion, deploys its interior outwards. But until now, it had existed only in theory and models. *SmartInversion*, developed by Festo, is the first free-levitating propulsion device that moves through "inversion." An unidentified flying object moves silently and gracefully, several metres above the ground. An articulated chain of transparent prisms endlessly turns inside out. It contracts, closing into a compact structure, and then reopens in the next instant, deploying its interior outwards. It hangs in the air and on it, and creates a propulsion movement through rotation. It is a fascinating sight for the observer, though his mind doesn't want to accept what he sees because it doesn't understand it. It must be said that such a thing had only existed until now in theory or in the form of a model. It is an inversion propulsion device.

So that they can freely levitate in the air, the prisms are filled with helium. Carbon-fibre rods form an ultra-light frame, which is surrounded by a gastight membrane. The fascinating structure rotates by virtue of three servo motors that cause the linking axes to move forwards or backwards in accordance with the propulsion phase. *SmartInversion* has a very simple smartphone control system that uses Festo's specially developed software.

Press release excerpts.

www.festo.com/en/smartinversion

M.C. Escher kaleidocycles, Doris Schattschneider, Wallace Walker, 1992

Otto Ng / Laab Architects

HONG KONG

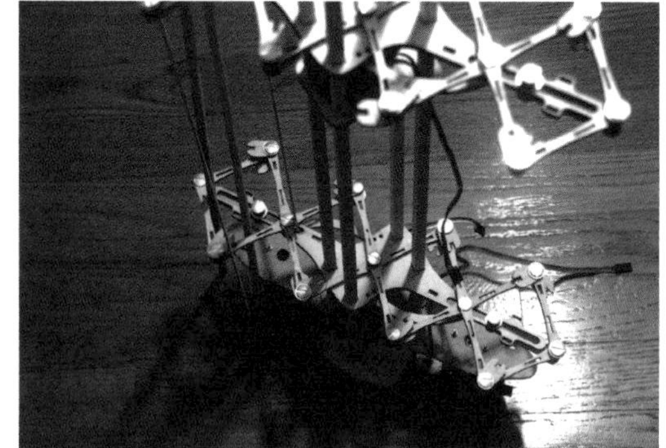

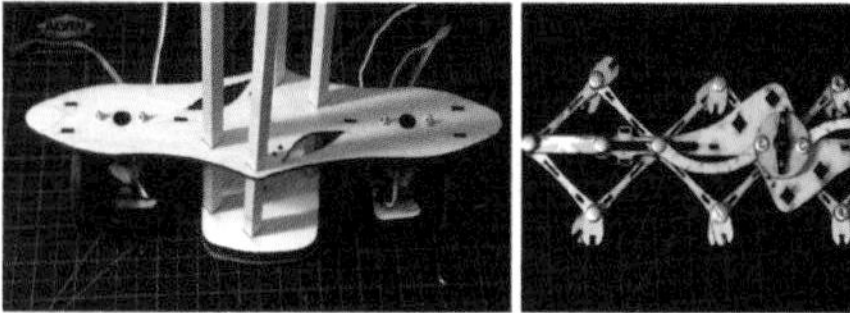

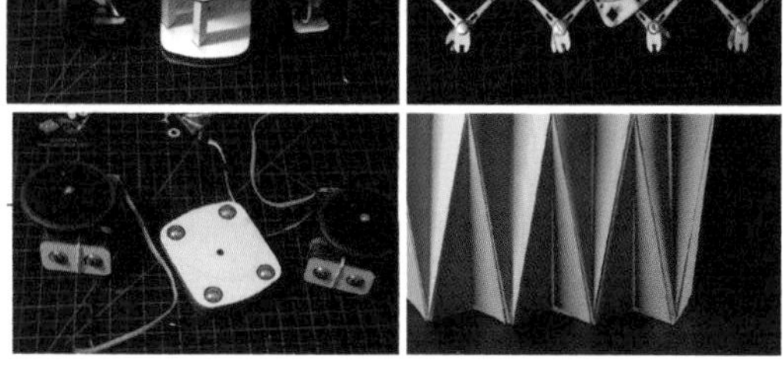

• Wallbot, *manufacturing sequences.*

Wallbots

Laab is a studio whose practices are very innovative: 99% of its projects are built, which is rare for architects. The reason for this achievement is that this team of about 20 people has its own "lab." They produce their own digital and interactive constructions to meet various orders, including interior design projects, installation art and architecture.

Otto is an architect who is in charge of design development for Laab, an assistant professor, and a very inventive young man. His interest in origami is twofold. From the architect's point of view, it's a way to turn inexpensive 2D materials into 3D components. And when it comes to robots, it can be used to produce transformations.

When he was a student at MIT, as part of the University of Toronto's RAD (Responsive Architecture at Daniels) lab, Otto developed a project called *Wallbots*. It is a system of mobile walls that interacts with the user of the space to adapt to his or her changing needs.

The walls set limits, the idea being to create a wall that can change the configuration of a room.

The device comprises a chevron fold made from transparent polypropylene and wood, and it moves using two synchronized engines at the top and bottom of the wall. Sensors and a "brain" (an Arduino-type programmable controller) allow the entire room to become "smart." This type of experimental installation really prefigures the environment that we will live in tomorrow.

Wallbot's robotic walls can stretch and go from 1 m to 1.50 m (39 to 59 in), and they are able to move and connect with each other through magnetization and infrared sensors.

The *Wallbot* project, which was originally a prototype, will undergo new developments at the robotics lab that will soon be installed in the studio. Laab is currently working on an art installation in a park: a kaleidoscope with flowers inside it. Mirror-sheet faces are folded to achieve the kaleidoscopic effect. Once again, for these inventors of the modern world, folding is both a means of expression and a source of inspiration.

Remarks from Otto Ng, cofounder of Laab Architects, February 2015.

www.laab.pro
www.web.mit.edu/
www.arduino.cc/

• Wallbot, *a robotic partition-wall system for reconfiguring spaces.*

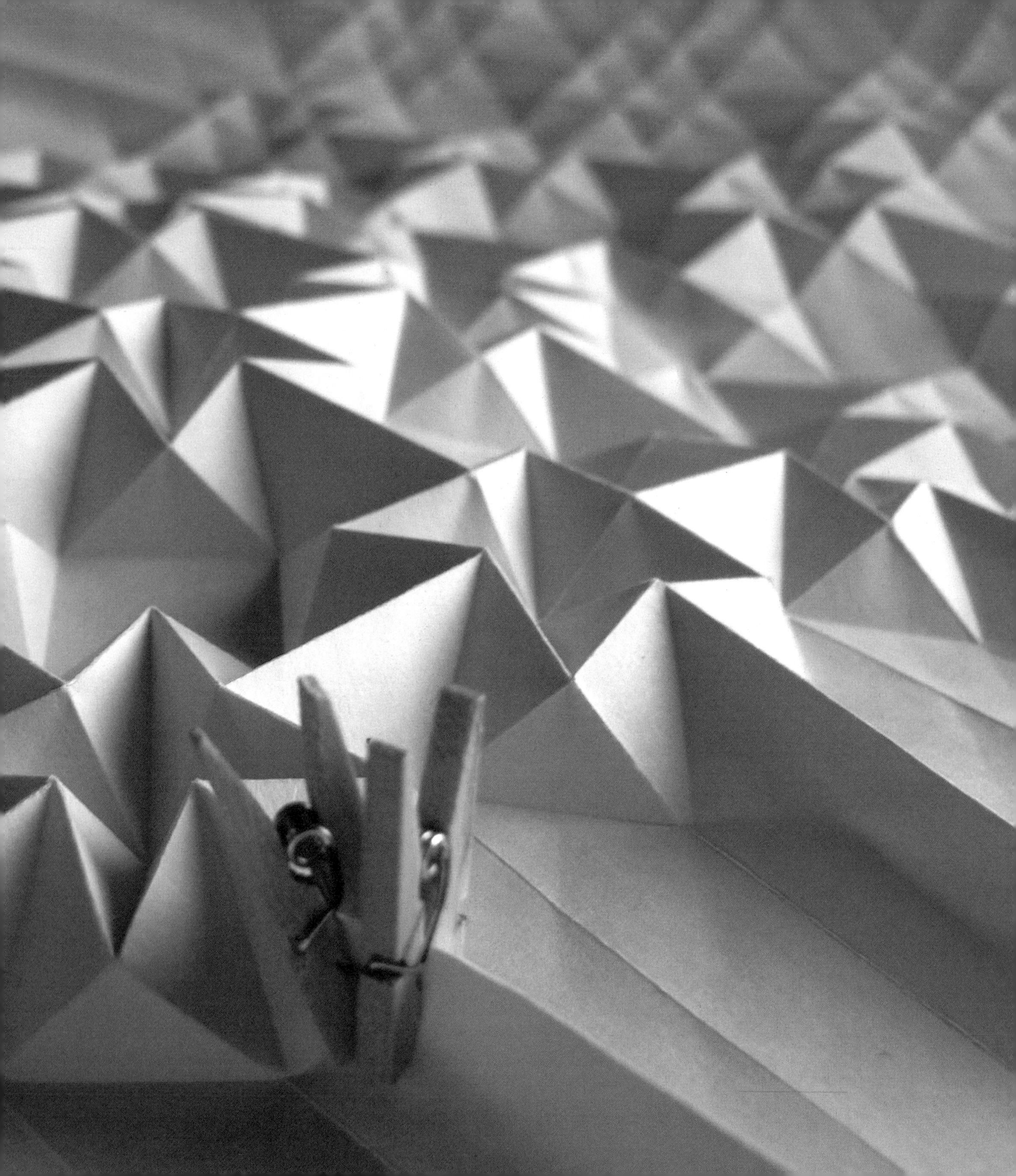

Models to fold

Ilan Garibi, folds of the Molecules light, *in collaboration with Ofir Zucker & Aqua Creations.*

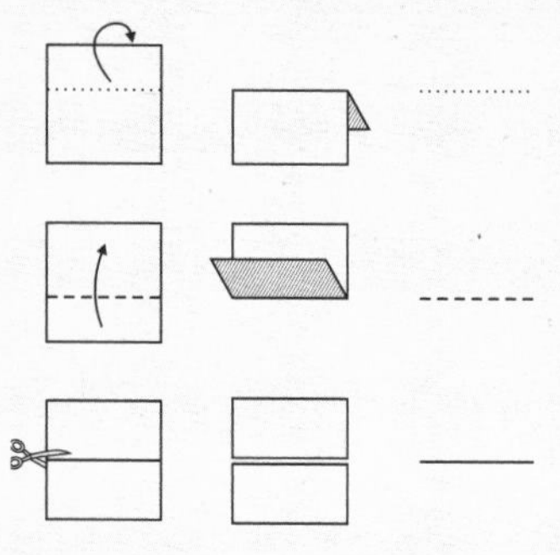

• *Folding symbols:*
Mountain fold, valley fold and cut.

Warning! The models presented on these pages may not be reproduced for the purposes of commercial use under penalty of prosecution. Any use or dissemination other than for private purposes expressly requires the authors' permission.

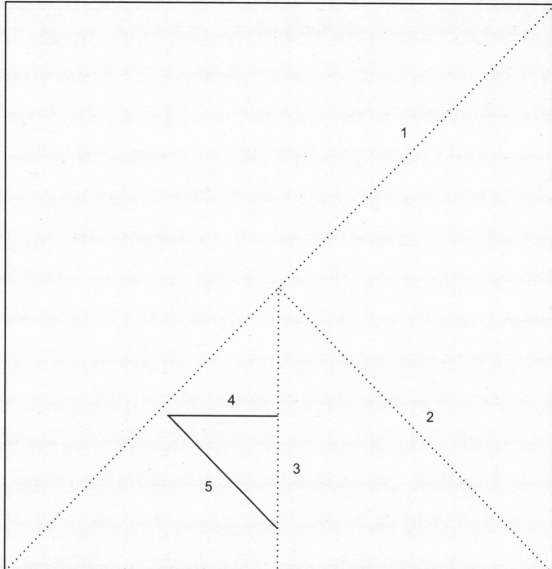

***Origami* Several folds, one cut,** *created by J.-Ch. Trebbi (level: easy).*
A trick widely performed by magicians in the last century was, after completing a clever folding routine, to make a single cut with a pair of scissors and in so doing make a form appear. The mathematicians Erik and Martin Demaine have sought to extend this application to all forms (see p. 34).
Here, there are two simple models: a small square in a large square and a 6-point star. Fold the sheet according to the order of the numbers, keeping them visible and obeying the mountain or valley folds.
Warning: for the small square, do not cut to the edge, respecting the limits of the cutting line indicated in bold.

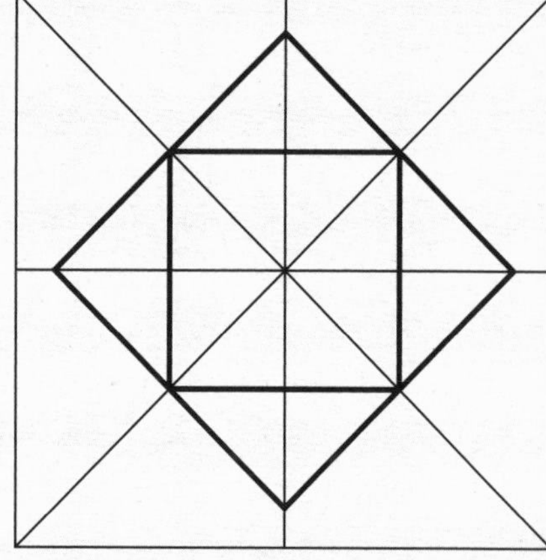

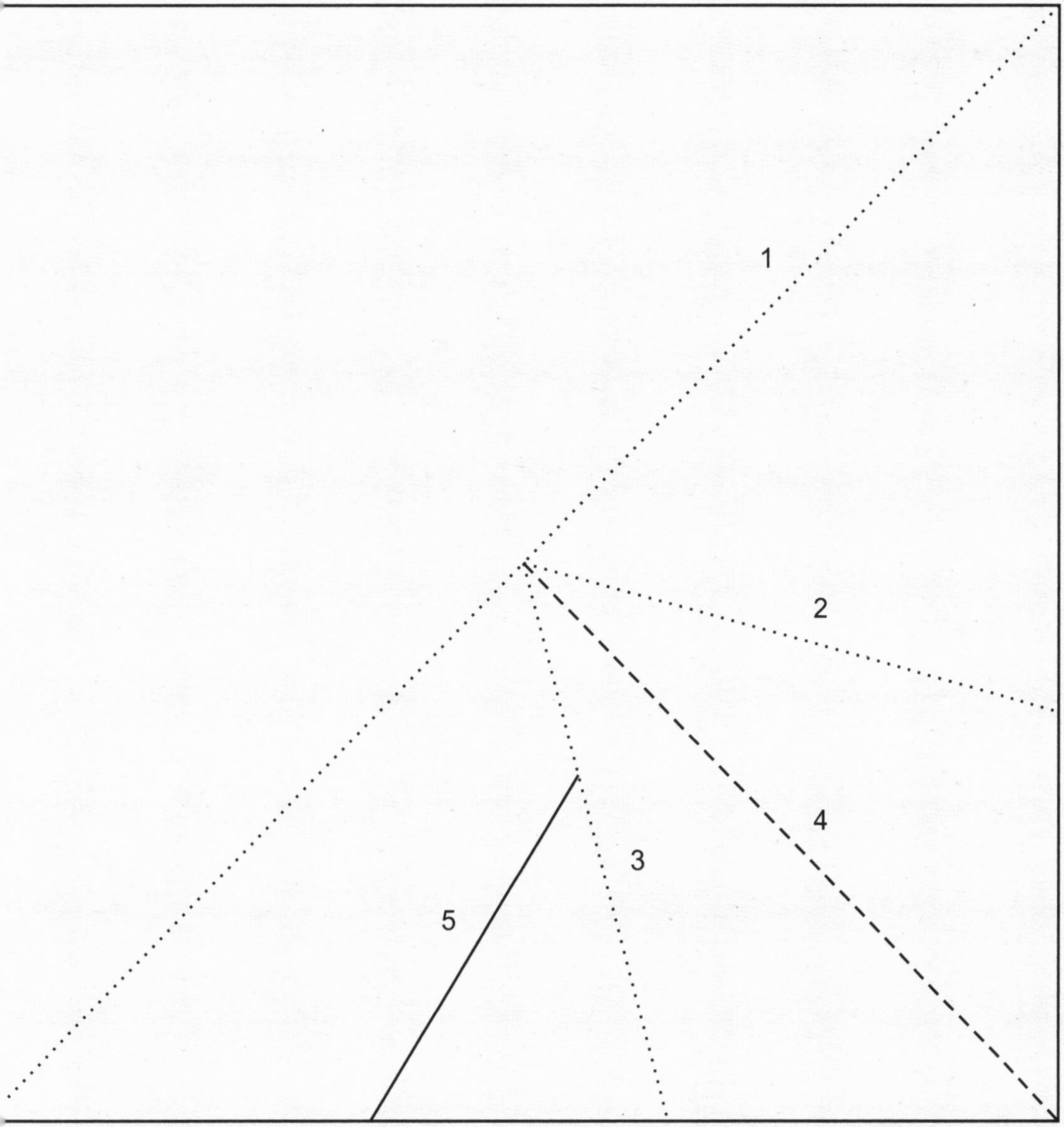

1

2

4

3

5

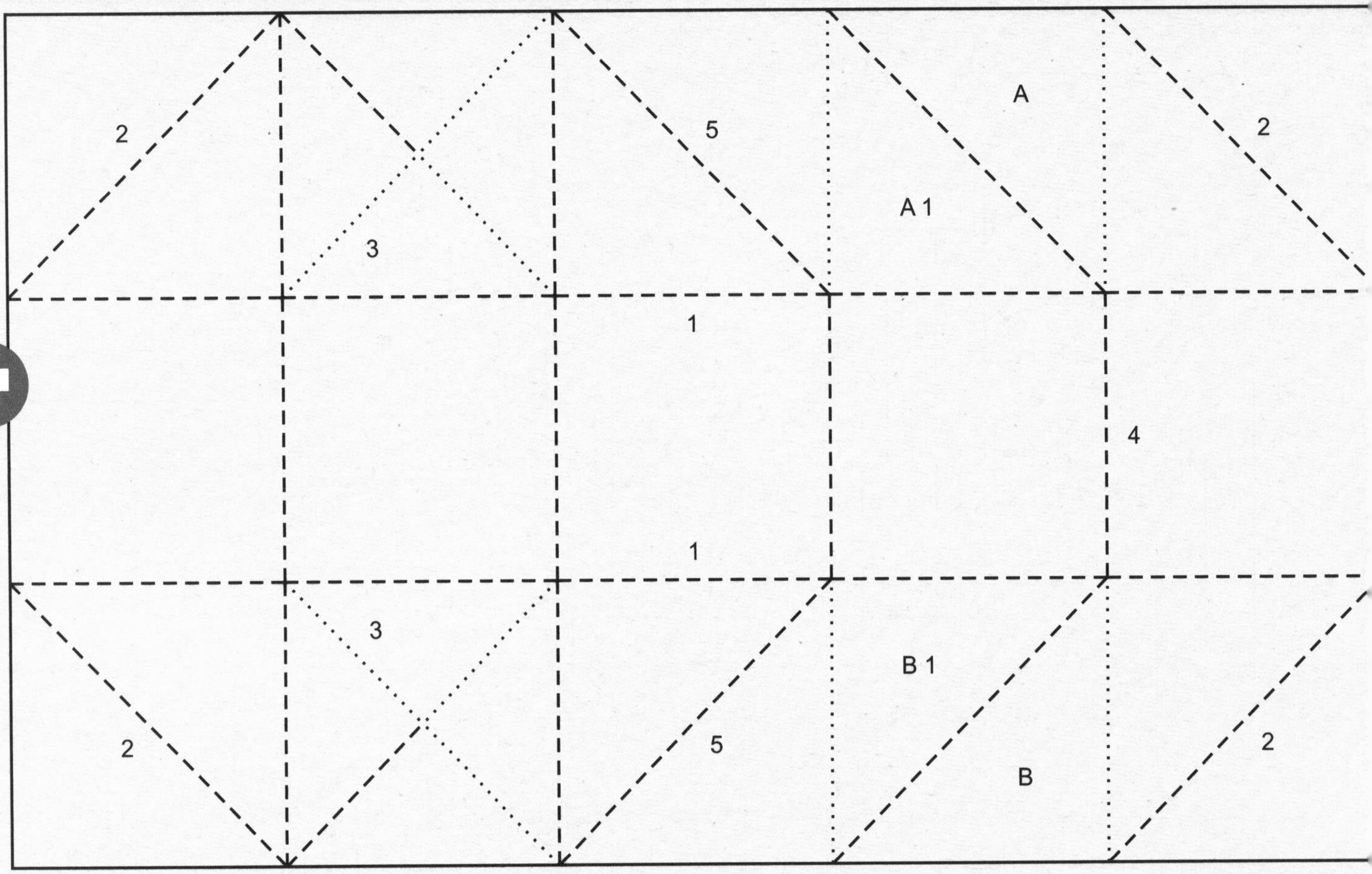

2 5 A 2

A 1

3

1

4

1

3

B 1

2 5 2

B

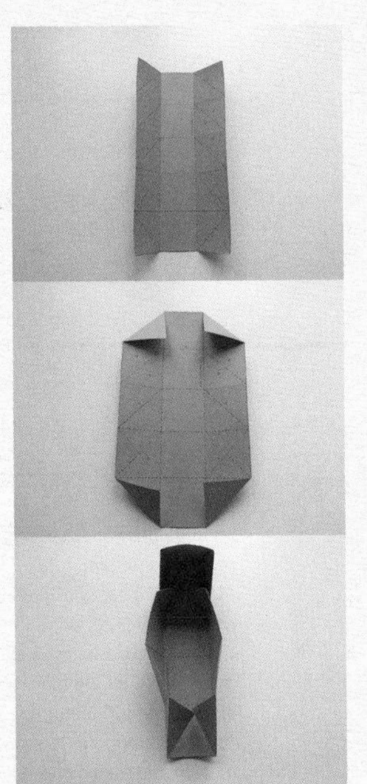

• **Mode. Mystery cube box,** *created by J.-Ch. Trebbi (level: intermediate).*
An exercise in folding around a cube for a small jewellery box.
160 g card.
Mark all the mountain and valley folds. Hold the short side strip toward you.
Fold down the longitudinal folds (1) and then start folds (2) and diagonal (3), bringing them to the centre.
Implement the folds in a symmetrical way.
A base for the cube will be formed.
Fold (4) and (5) while folding down the triangular faces A on A1 and B on B1.
The shaping of the box comes about through the valley folds (5), and the blocks are made by inserting the naturally opposite faces.

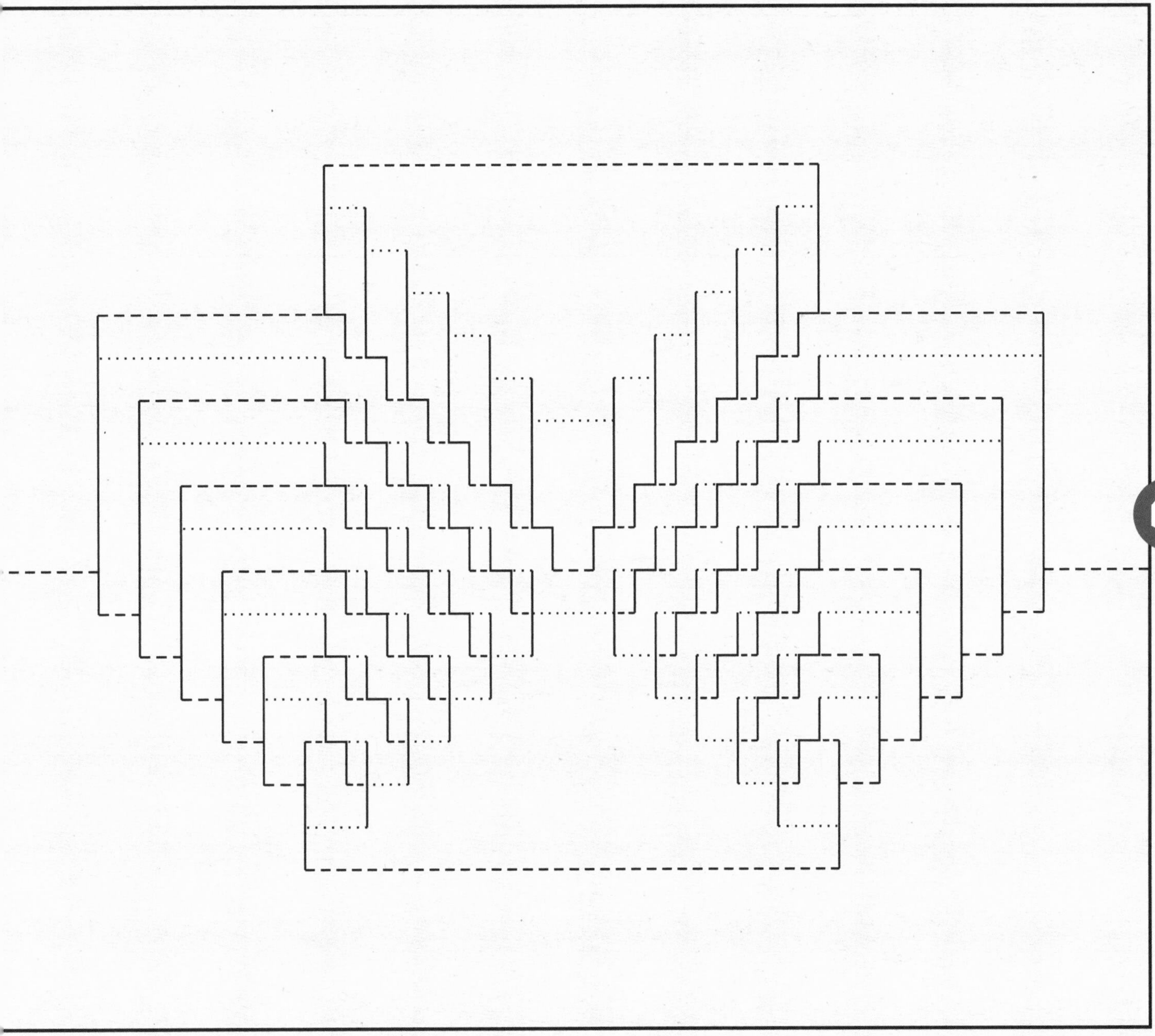

• Architecture. Double staircase, *created by J.-Ch. Trebbi (level: expert).*

An origami architecture pop-up card featuring an interplay of light and shadow.

Make a photocopy of everything, and place the sheet on a cutting board.

Cut at all of the heavy lines, mark valley folds with the tip of a stylus, and then the mountain folds. For good support, use card of between 200 and 250 g/m².

Pay attention to the direction of the fibres of the paper; the median fold should always be perpendicular to the direction of the fibres.

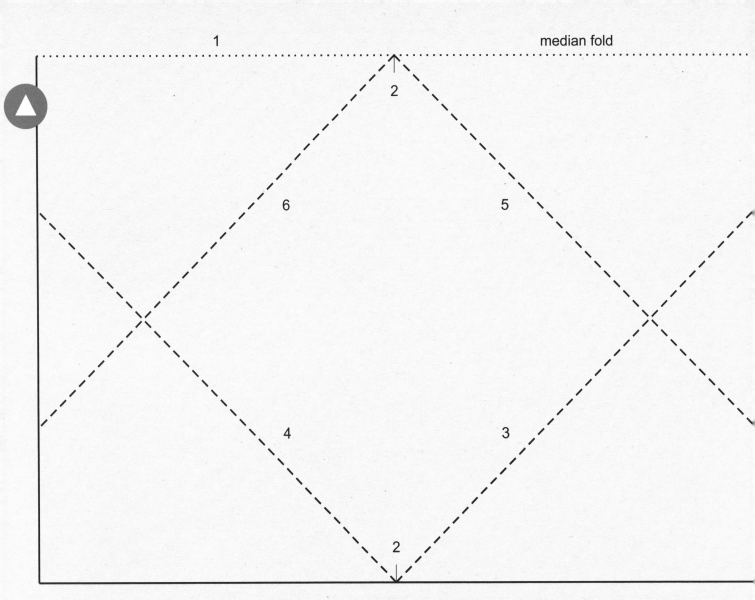

1 median fold

2

6 5

4 3

2

• ***Origami*. Folded letter,**
traditional model (level: easy).
Fold model adapted from a love letter from Benjamin Constant to Juliette Récamier in 1815.
Through folding an A4-size letter we produce a 10.5 x 10.5 cm (4 1/8 x 4 1/8 in) square ready for sealing. (see "Lettres d'Amour," Albin Michel, 1996.) J-J Delalandre Coll.
Fold the sheet in two to produce the median fold (1), then lightly mark the middle (2) of the large sides.
From points (2) fold down the tips according to the numbers.

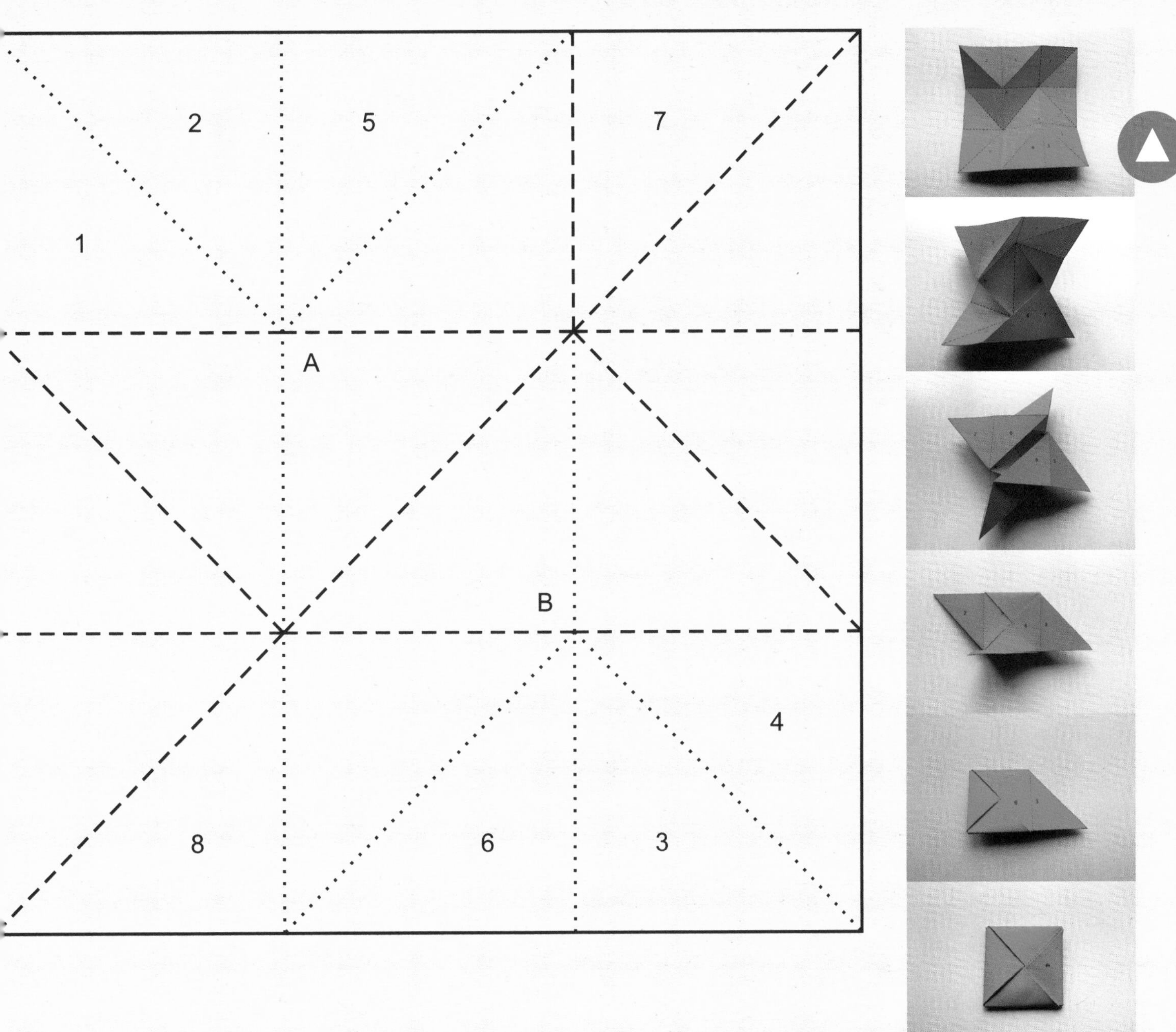

Origami. **Menko,**
aditional model (level: easy).
modular origami envelope, often made from
vo sheets of various colours; here the model
equires a single sheet.
lark all mountain and valley folds.
inch the mountain folds of faces (1)-(2) and
3)-(4), bringing them to the centre.
twisting phenomenon will arise, with the
diagonal valley fold only serving this purpose.
Moving points A and B aside and flattening
them, the blades of the mill are achieved. To
close the Menko, *simply slide face (7) under*
(6) and (8) under (5).
Turn the sheet and slide the last 2 points.

• ***Décor. Wall sculpture,***
Knot creation (level: easy).
A full-colour wall decoration based on the juxtaposition of paper pyramids of various sizes. Cut out the desired number of pyramids in 160 to 200 g paper.
Fold and glue the tabs to create the shape.
Attach to the wall with adhesive putty or double-sided adhesive.

✏ Aline, Alexandra and Cyrielle,
authors of Knot magazine
www.knot-magazine.com

✏ www.tetedange.canalblog.com/archives/2012/10/19/25374123.html

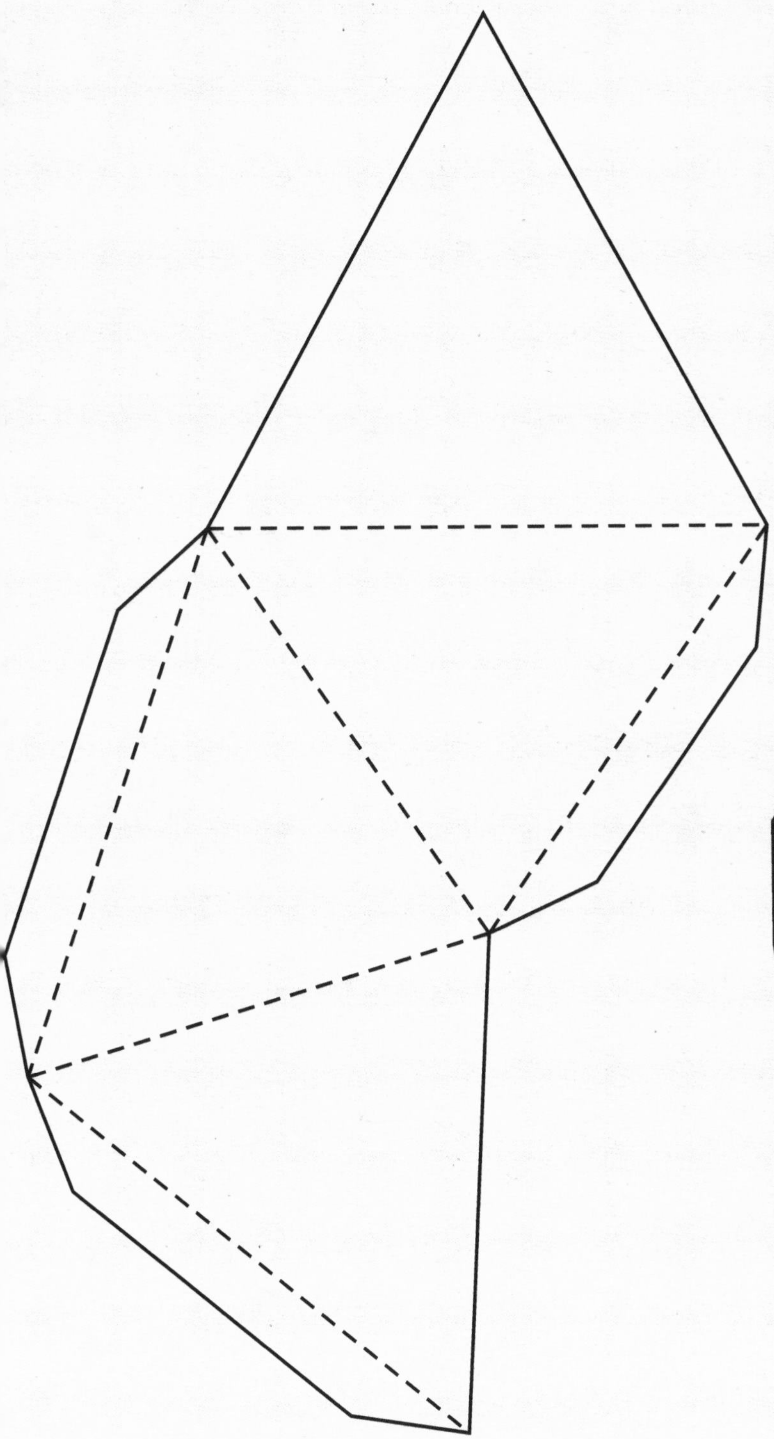

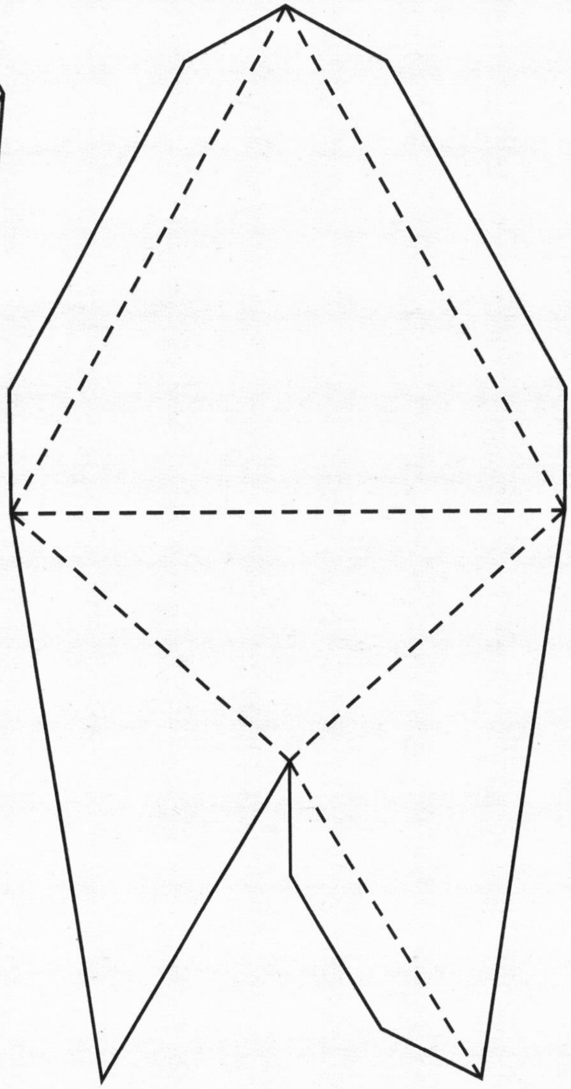

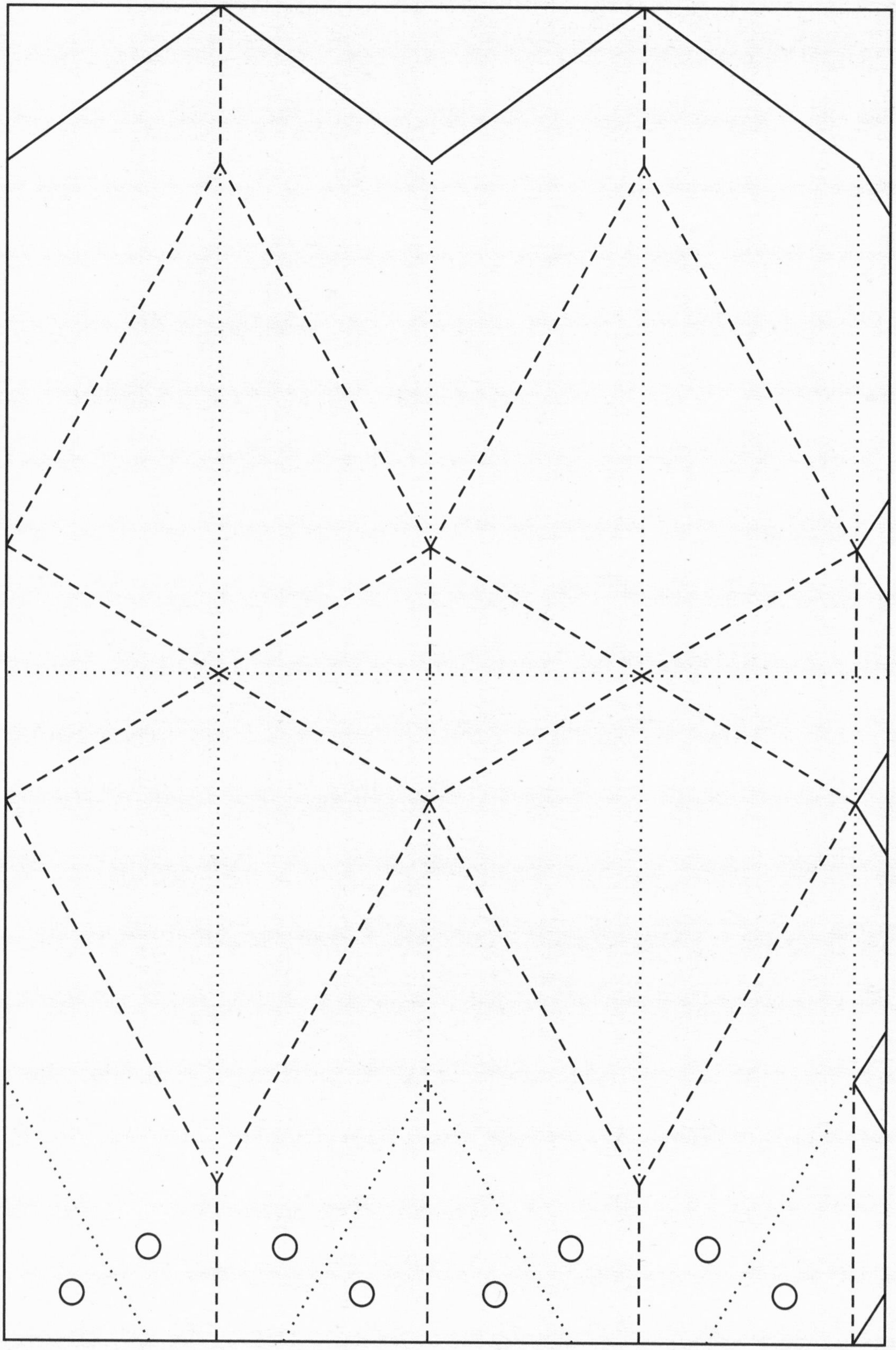

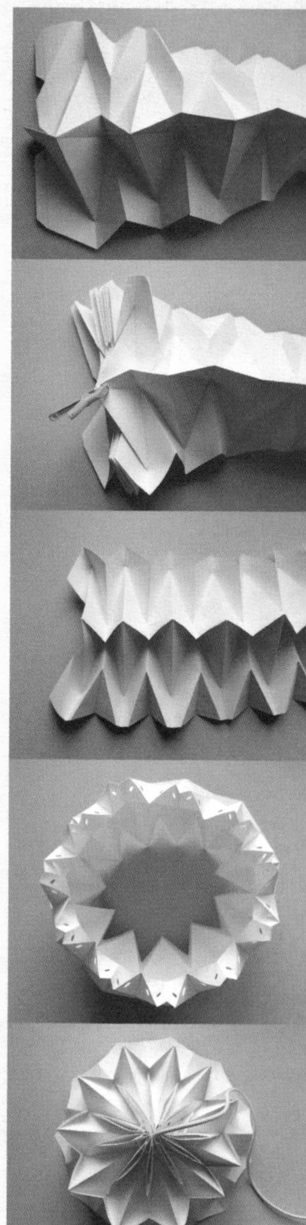

• ***Lighting.* Star Lamp,**
created by J.-Ch. Trebbi (level: intermediate).
Created on a single 1 m x 27 cm (39 3/8 x 10 5/8 in) sheet. 160 g card.
The lamp consists of 11 9 cm (3 9/16 in) wide modules. The diagram shows two end modules with tabs.
Mark all mountain and valley folds.
Fold the horizontal mountain fold over the whole length, then unfold the sheet.
Shape all of the model's folds.
Refold the central mountain fold and pinch the diamonds.
Shape the modules, with the help of pincers to hold them.
Once half the length has been finished, repeat for the other end.
Turn over and then mark the mountain folds with points.
Glue the end tabs, starting with the central ones of the diamond.
Pass the fastening cord through the upper part.
Attach the socket and use an 11 w cold energy-saving bulb.

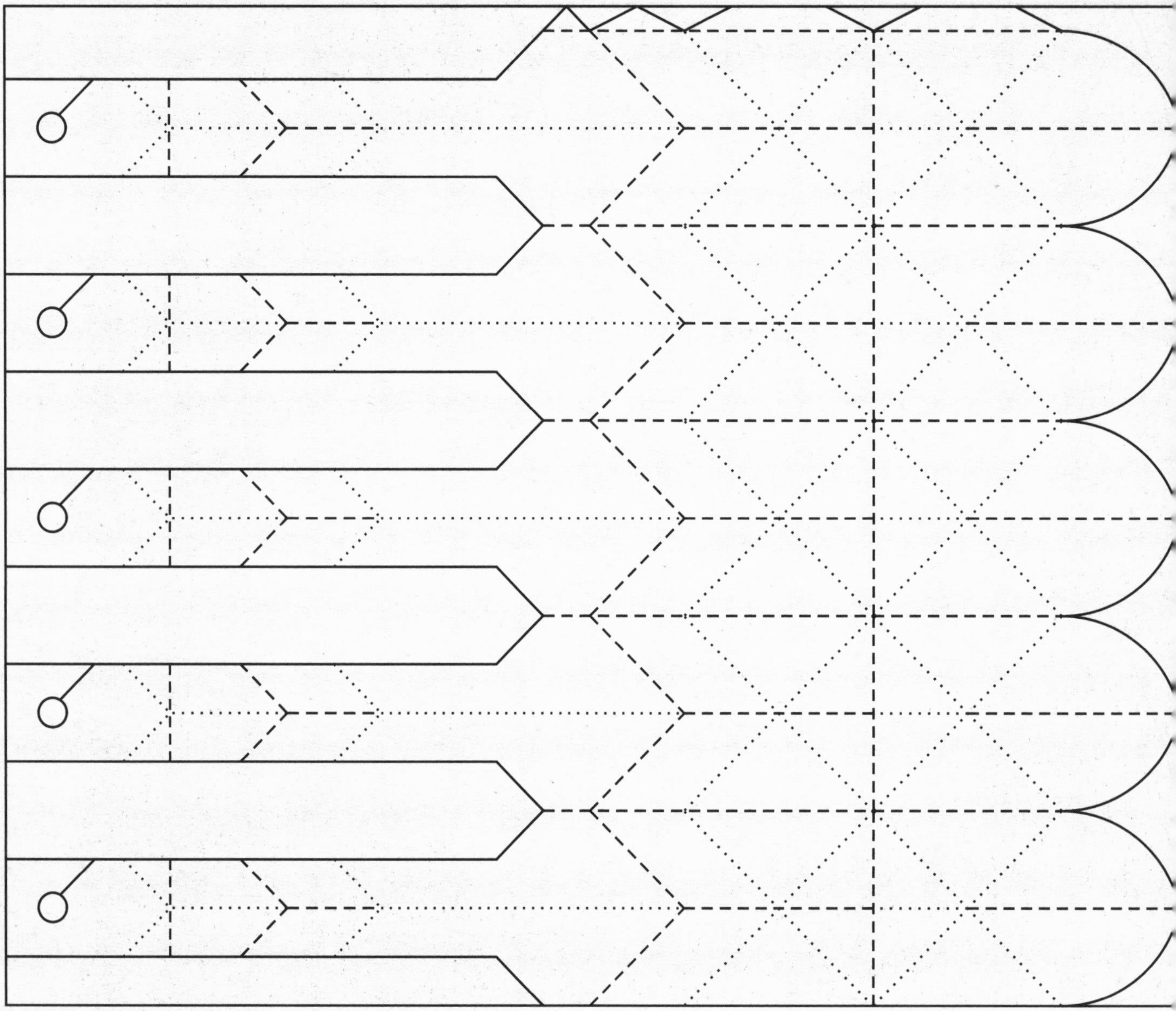

• **Lighting. Corolla**, *created by J.-Ch. Trebbi (level: expert).*
The folding of this petal lamp is based on the technique of chevron folds and includes a reversal of folds that is somewhat tricky.
To be made on a single sheet of 80 cm x 50 cm (31 1/2 x 19 11/16 in) 160 g card.
Dimensions: 34 cm (13 3/8 in) in diameter, height of 27 cm (10 5/8 in).
Make 2 copies of the design in double size (because the model has 10 petals.)
Cut out the contours and punch the circles for the cable to pass through.
Mark all mountain and valley folds.
Shape of all vertical valley folds.
Shape the folds of the small triangles at the top.
Shape the diagonal folds by putting your hands behind the sheet.
Form an accordion by tightening each module against the other without worrying about the nature of the folds, but while folding the lower petal.
Once this operation has been performed on the whole piece, unfold everything and then begin shaping module by module according to the line representation.
Attach the socket and use an 11 w cold energy saving bulb.

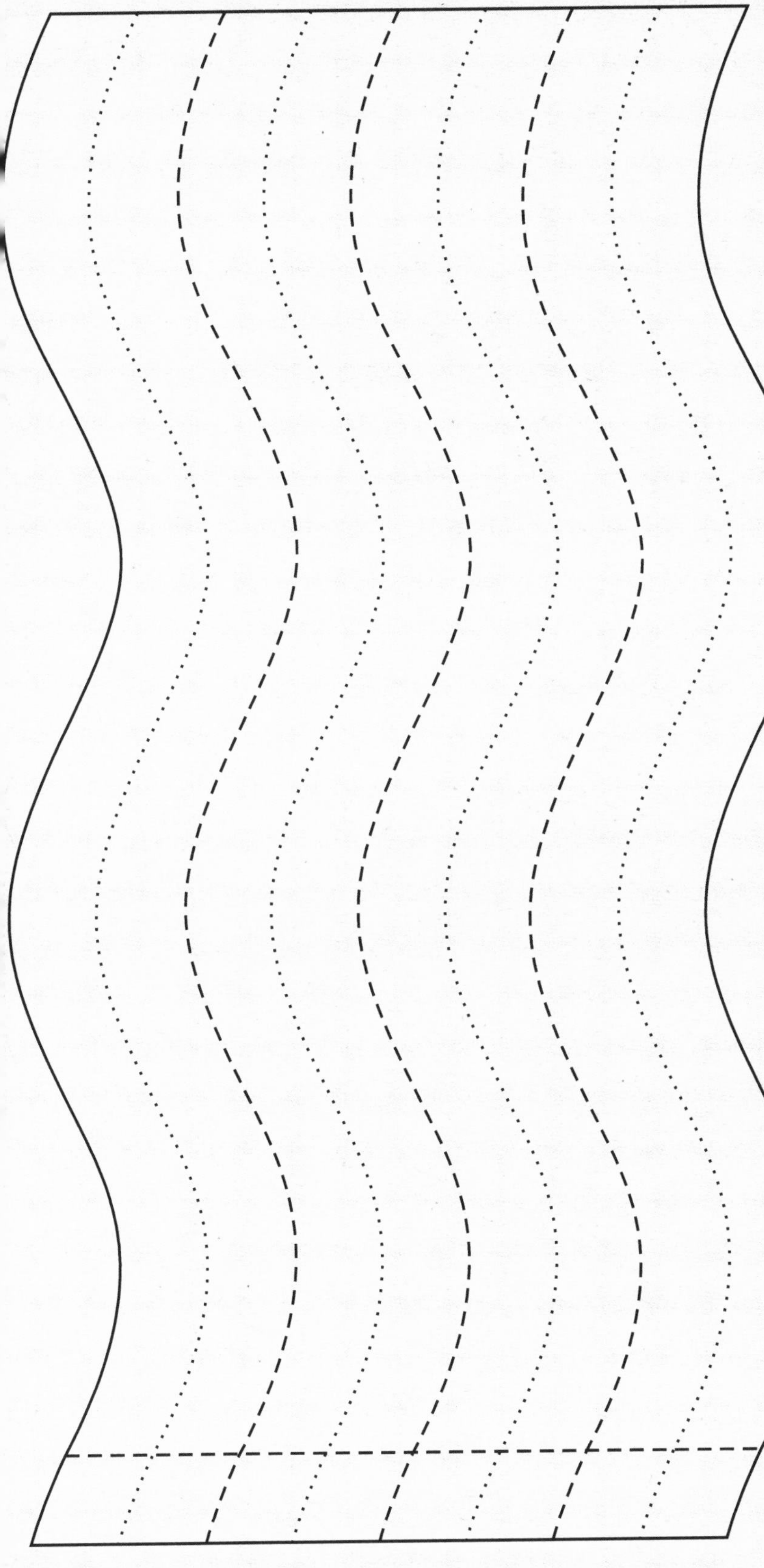

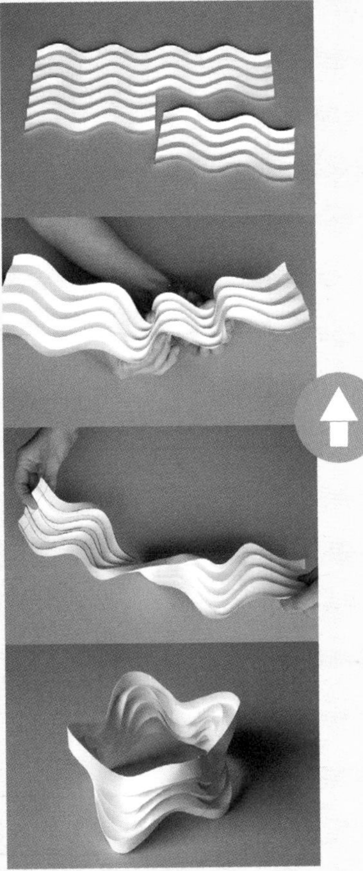

• **Prospective. Wave**, *created by Brigitte Parousel as part of an artist's residency at RobotFold, 2014. (level: intermediate)*
A fundamental exercise in curved folding on 250 g Bristol paper. As with previous models, mark all mountain and valley folds.
Start with a mountain fold and then a valley fold, and repeat mountain and valley alternately.
For the valley folds, it is easier to turn the paper over.
Once this process is finished, firmly tighten everything to mark the folds well.
The field of experimentation is now open to your creativity.

Composition of folds

FOLD TYPE

STRAIGHT FOLD

CURVED FOLD

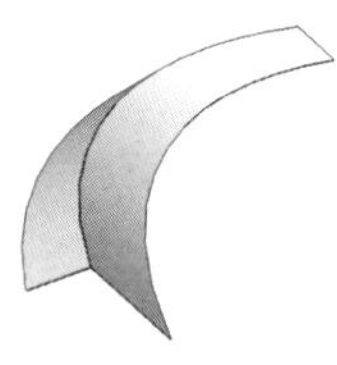

• *At the level of the fold, there are two scenarios: a fold following a straight line or a curve. A curved fold creates rounded faces.*

NUMBER OF FOLDS FORMING AN INTERSECTION (OR NODE)

1 FOLD (NO NODE)

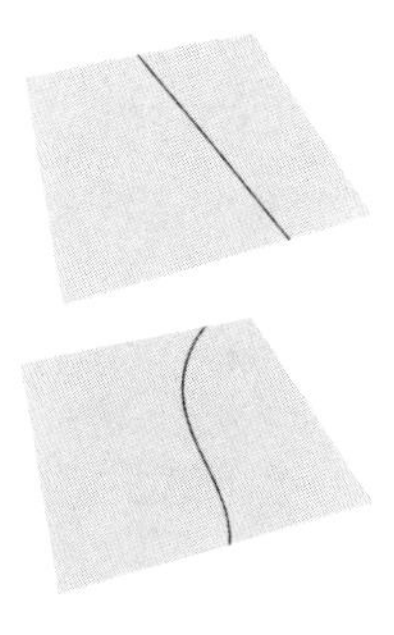

2 OR 3 FOLDS

4 OR MORE FOLDS (GATHER)

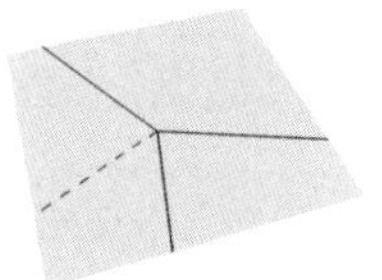

• *The number of folding lines meeting at a point determines the whether a model can be refolded flat, its mobility and the flatness of the faces.*
A gather (through four folds) allows the folding to be turned around, while maintaining flat faces in the case of straight folds.

ORGANIZATION OF THE FOLDS

PARALLEL

RADIATING

GROWING

OTHERS

• *According to the number of intersections on the sheet and their layout, folding acquires increasing complexity.*

"The edges of the polyhedron correspond to the rectilinear generators of the curved surface. Each situation of rectilinear folding can therefore be made to correspond to an associated curvilinear folding"
Jean-Marie Delarue, Plis, règles géométriques et principes structurants. *École d'architecture de Paris-Villemin, 1997.*

SHAPING DIAGRAMS

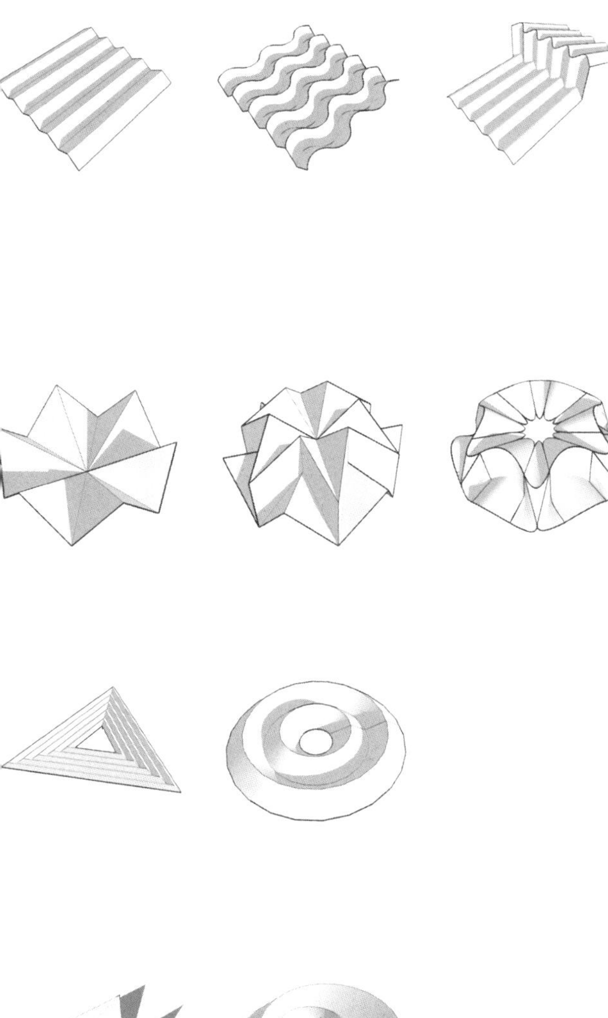

EXAMPLES

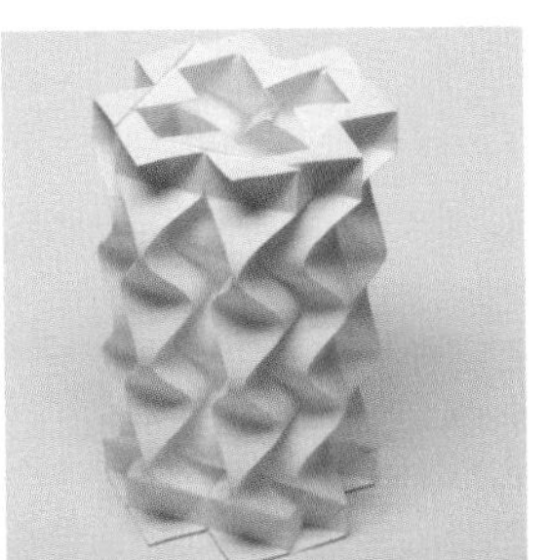

• Alain Chevalier, Pesanteur, coloured folds, personal exhibition, 2003.

Bibliography

BUCHNER Tilman, *Kinematics of 3D Folding Structures for Nanostructured Origami*, PhD thesis, Massachusetts institute of Technology, 2003.

BURI Hani, *Origami-folded plate structures*, PhD Thesis, École polytechnique fédérale de Lausanne, Laboratoire de construction en bois, 2010.

BURI Hani, WEINAND Yves, *Origami aus Brettsperrholz*, DETAIL Zeitschrift für Architektur + Baudetail, N° 10, p. 1066-1068, 2010.

DELARUE Jean-Marie, *Morphologie*, UPA1, Paris, 1978.

DELARUE Jean-Marie, *Faltstrukturen*, in IL N°27, Natural Structures, 1980.

DELARUE Jean-Marie, *Pliage*, Institut de recherche en morphologie structurale, Paris, 1980.

DELARUE Jean-Marie, *Plis, Règles géométriques et Principes structurants*, École d'architecture Paris-Villemin, Paris, 1992.

DELARUE Jean-Marie, *Morphogenèse*, Paris-Villemin, Paris, 1997.

DELARUE Jean-Marie, "Le pli, source de formes et de sens," in *Les Cahiers de la recherche architecturale, imaginaire technique* n°40, p. 39-46, éditions Parenthèses 1997.

DELEUZE Gilles, *Le Pli, Leibniz et le Baroque*, Collection Critique, 1988.

DEMAINE Eric, O' ROURKE Joseph, *Geometric Folding Algorithms, Linkages, Origami, Polyhedra*, Cambridge University Press, New York, USA, 2008.

DUREISSEIX David, "An Overview of Mechanisms and Patterns with Origami," *International Journal of Space Structures*, vol. 27, n° 1, 2012.

ERMAKOV Andrey, *Origami, School of Masters*, 2012.

FLODERER Vincent, *Crumpling*, exhibition catalogue, Galerie Freising, Munich, Germany, 2008.

GJERDE Eric, *Origami tessellations, Awe-Inspiring Geometric Designs*, A K Peters, Ltd., 2009. Wellesley, Mass.: A K Peters, 2009.

JACKSON Paul, *Pliages et Découpages*, Manise, Paris, 1996.

LYNN Greg, *Folding in architecture*, Chichester, West Sussex, Hoboken, NJ, Wiley-Academy, 2004.

Mc ARTHUR Meher, LANG Robert J., *Folding paper*, Tuttle Publishing, 2013.

MEADOWS Fiona, *Mini Maousse, Archipetit*, éditions Alternatives, Paris, 2010.

RUTZKY Jeffrey, PALMER Chris K., *Shadowfolds*, Kodansha international, 2011.

SALVADORI Mario, *Comment ça tient?*, collection Eupalinos, éditions Parenthèses, 2005.

SCHMIDT Petra, STATTMANN Nicola, *Unfolded, paper in design, art, architecture and industry*, Basel, Birkhäuser, 2009.

TACHI Tomohiro, *Generalization of Rigid Foldable Quadrilateral Mesh Origami*, in Proceedings of the International Association for Shell and Spatial Structures Symposium 2009, vol. 50, p. 173-179, Valencia, Spain, 2009.

TACHI Tomohiro, *Rigid-Foldable Thick Origami*, presented at the Origami Fifth International Meeting of Origami Science Mathematics and Education, vol. 4, p. 253-264, 2011.

TREBBI Jean-Charles, *L'Art du pli*, éditions Alternatives, Paris, 2008.

VASSEUR Nadine, *Les plis*, Paris, Seuil, 2002.

VYZOVITI Sophia, *Folding Architecture*, BIS Publishers, Amsterdam, 2003.

VYZOVITI Sophia, *Supersurfaces*, BIS Publishers, Amsterdam, 2006.

\cknowledgements

olishing this book has required the involvement of many participants, and more than 120 designers thusiastically agreed to participate in this new editorial adventure. We are very pleased to present their ented creations here. All receive our warmest and most sincere thanks.

i Hiltunen – Formosis - Alain Chevalier - Alexander Rehn - Alexandra Verschueren - Amila Hrustić - idrey Ermakov - Anne Bouin - Archiwaste - Arturass - Atelier Itoshi Abe - Bedy and Sarah Angold - Bernard rault - Broissin Architectes - Camille Trouvé, Compagnie Les anges au plafond - Cartonlab, Nacho Bautista iz - Charlène Fétiveau - Charlot et Compagnie, Charles Macaire - Claudio Colucci and Dominique Serrell - ıristian Renonciat - Christiane Bettens - Christiane Bongardt and Michale Kolodzie - Christophe Guberan - ıristopher Mullaney - Christy Oates - Coll – Barreu - Damien Daufresne - Daimonds Pučko, Pioes Sia - elphine Huguet - Different + Different, Cyril Jouve and Adrien Camp - Dohyuk Kwon - Douwe Jacobs, Tom outen, Bieke Groenink, Flux Furniture - Edwige Chatoux and Jacky Pineau, Musée Ponts-de-Cé - Elisa Strozyk - FL, Yves Weinand and Hani Buri - Eric Gjerde - Eric Olsen - Erik and Martin Demaine - F.A.D.S, Fujiki Studio d KOU::ARC - FFIL, Claire Batardière - Flora Gotticelli - Freyja Sewell, Ness Furniture - Guactruck, Michealle enee Lee - Giang Dinh - Goran Konjevod - Gramazio and Kohler, Gramazio Fabio Matteo, Sarah Schneider - egory Epps and Brigitte Parusel - Héloise Piraud and Antoine Bécognée, Well Well Designers - HSH architects - n Garibi – Kaza - Industrial Origami, Bernie Mabrey - Issey Miyake - Jean-Claude Correia - Jean-Paul and ance Moscovino - Jie Qi - Joel Cooper - Julie Bénédicte Lambert - Jule Waibel - Julien Gritte - Jun Mitani - nior Fritz Jacquet - Klemens Torggler - Knot - Kunsulu Jilkishiyeva - L. Peraza Curiel, M. Garcia, D. Huet, P. unez Mardones - Laura Papp - Li Hongbo - Liya Maison - Local architecture, Antoine Robert-Grandpierre, lien Barras - Lucie Dorel - Luisa Robinson - Maartje Nuy and Joost van Noort - Madjid Esfini - Make chitects - Makoto Yamaguchi - Maori Kimura - Marcel Robelin - Mashallah Design, Hande Akcayli, Murat ocyigit, Linda Kostowski and Rozi Rexhepi - Materialise - Mathias Lind - White arkitecter AB - Matthew ardiner - Mauricio Velasquez Posada and Claudia Fernandez Silva - Mika Barr - molo - Nervous System - ormal Studio, Eloi Chafaï and Jean-François Dingjian - Ofir Zucker - Oricrete - Otto Ng - Laab Architects Patrick Jouin - Patrick Crossonneau - Paul Jackson - People's industrial design - Polly Verity - Ran Amitai nd Gilli Kuchik - Rebeca Gieseking - Richard Sweeney - Robert J. Lang - Robert van Embricqs - Robofold, Gregory Epps, Emma Epps, Brigitte Parusel - Sandra Backlund - Sarah Angold Studio -Sarah Kelly - ascha Akkermann - Poissonmobile Design - Sasha Roudet – Quinoa - Sébastien Cordoleani - Sentou - Studio, Véronica Posada - Sophie Guyot - Stefan Weber - Steven Leprize and Eric Demeyer, Arca - Studio Glow - Studio Oooms - Suzan Weitzman Conway and Jessy Yingbo Zhang - Thomas Diewald - Thomas Hillier - Tobias Labarque - Tomohiro Tachi - 3 Gatti architecture studio - Victor Coeurjoly - Vincent Floderer - Youwwow, Maartje Nuy and Joost van Noort - Yoshinobu Miyamoto.

or their support, participation and advice:
Alain Saillard - Alejandra Carranza - Ann Nilsson, White arkitect - Antoine Durot - Anton Zancker - Artemide, Marie-Océane Vaur - Carol Moukheiber, RAD - Chris Tucker - Colleen Kong - Daniela Gnad - liane Torggler-van Saanen - ENSCI, Antoine Durot - Fabienne, Stéphane and Julien Berthomier - Institute of Design unit koge, Structure and Design, University of Innsbruck / Archiwaste, Ruppert Maleczek, Thierry Berthomier and all those involved in the Tour en carton, Fiona Meadows, Myriam Feuchot, and the Cité de Architecture et du Patrimoine - Fanny Mercier - Jacqueline Townsend and Ruth Daniels, Heatherwick - James Shen - Janka Horvath, Kaza - Jean-Jacques and Mireille Pertusot - Klein Sun Gallery, New York, Elizabeth Misitano - Marielle Savoyat, Antoine Robert-Grandpierre and Julien Barras - Mathilde Tournoux - Monique Robelin - Paula Navarrete R. - Patrice Aoust and Gérard Aimé - Pierre Staudenmeyer, Galerie Mouvements Modernes - Sabine Puget Galerie - Sarah Schneider - Stephanie Forsythe, molo - Ryumei Fujiki - Thomas Moulis - Tim Mullaney - Knot.

As well as all the photographers listed in the photo credits.

For the wonderful production team:
Sabine Bledniak - Pierre Beaucousin - Cécile Lebreton and Denis Couchaux.

Special thanks go to:
Charlotte Gallimard - Marie-Christine Guyonnet - Frédérique Le Lous Delpech - Jean-Marie Delarue - Martine Cébron - Denis Trebbi - Nicole Charneau-Trebbi - Lucile Reverchon and Baptiste Hernandez.
Members of the MFPP (Mouvement français des plieurs de papier), and in particular:
Alain Joisel, Yves Clavel, Alain Georgeot, Claudine Pisasale, François Dulac, Michel Grand, Raymonde Bonnefille, Jean-Jacques Delalandre, Viviane Berty, Barth Dunkan, Taki Girard, Naomiki Sato.

• *Erik & Martin Demaine*, Earthtone Series, *papier aquarelle Mi-Teintes, 2012.*
• *Richard Sweeney*, Fluid dynamic, *papier, adhésif, 2013.*

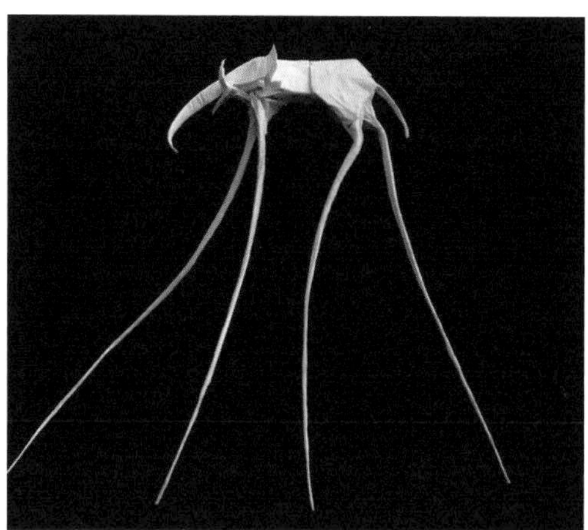

• *Victor Cœurjoly,* La Bête-Dali.

The Art of Folding vol. 2
New Trends, Techniques and Materials
Original title: *Un nouvel art du pli*
Authors: Jean-Charles Trebbi, Chloé Genevaux, Guillaume Bounoure
Translator: Tom Corkett
ISBN: 978-84-16504-64-0

Promopress is a commercial brand of:
Promotora de prensa internacional S.A.
C/ Ausias March, 124
08013 Barcelona, Spain
Tel.: 0034 932451464 / Fax: 0034 932654883
info@promopress.es / www.promopresseditions.com
Facebook & Twitter: Promopress Editions @PromopressEd
First published in English: 2017
Cover design: spread: David Lorente with the collaboration of Noelia Felip.
Front cover images: top *WW02* chair by Nuy Van Noort, p. 99; bottom right public building that houses the health administration services in the centre of Bilbao by Coll-Barreu Architects, photograph by Aleix Bagué, p. 136; bottom left *So Plicature* collection by Sophie Guyot, photograph by Hugo Juillard, p. 71.
Back cover images: top *Rising Furniture* by Robert van Embricqs, p. 109; bottom *molo benchwall* by molo, p 103.
Endpapers: Christophe Guberan (p. 150); Studio Nuy van Noort (p. 99); Polly Verity (p.36); Normal Studio (p. 96); HOID (p. 76); Charlène Féticeau (p. 56); Erik and Martin Demaine (p. 34); Robert van Embricqs (p. 109).

Printed in Bosnia and Herzegovina

Photo credits

P. 2 tl: Eric Joisel; p.2 ml: Paul Jackson; p. 2 bm: Mauricio Velásquez Posada and Claudia Fernández Silva, Geomorphos; p. 2 bl: FFIL; p. 3 tl: molo; p. 3 tl: Flux Furniture; p. 3 bm: Broissin Architectes; p. 3 bl: Eric Olsen; p. 4 tl: Guillaume Bounoure; p. 5 br: Jean-Marie Delarue; p. 6. pp: Vincent Floderer; p. 8 tl: Richard Sweeney; p. 8 ml: Kunsulu Jilkishiyeva; p. 9 tr: Stefan Weber; p. 9 br: Victor Coeurjoly; p. 10 tl: Eric Joisel; p. 10 ml: Robert Lang; p.10 bl: Victor Coeurjoly; p. 11 tr: Mauricio Velásquez Posada and Claudia Fernández Silva, Geomorphos; p. 11 br: Paul Jackson; p. 12 tl: Daimonds Pucko / Pioes Sia; p. 12 ml: Andrey Ermakov; p. 13 tl: Hauser & SPIN; p. 13 tr: Charlène Fetiveau; p. 13 bl: Maori Kimura; p. 13 mr: Make Architects; p. 14 pp: Richard Sweeney; p. 17 tr: François Dulac; p. 17 mr: Denis Trebbi; p. 17 bm: Yves Clavel; p. 18 tl: Makoto Yamaguchi, Origami house; p. 18 ml: Alain Joisel; p. 18 bl: Yves Clavel; p. 19: Makoto Yamaguchi, Origami house; p. 20 and p. 21: Giang Dinh; p. 22: Li Hongbo / Klein Sun Gallery; p. 23 tr: Junior Fritz Jacquet; p. 24 tl and br: Joel Cooper; p. 25 tl, ml and bl: Robert J. Lang and Kevin Box; p. 26 tl and bl: Madjid Esfini; p. 27 tl and br: Andrey Ermakov; p. 27 tr: Vincent Floderer; p. 28: Kunsulu Jilkishiyeva; p. 29: Victor Cœurjoly; p. 30: Christiane Bettens; p. 31: Eric Gjerde; p. 32: Goran Konjevod; p. 33: Paul Jackson; p. 34: Erik and Martin Demaine; p. 35: Jun Mitani; p. 36 tr, mr and br: Polly Verity; p. 37 tl, bl: Stefan Weber; p. 37 tr and br: Rebecca Gieseking; p. 38: Richard Sweeney; p. 39 tl: Chloé Genevaux; p. 40 tl: Bertrand Michau; p. 40 ml: Christian Renonciat; p. 40 bl: Damien Daufresne; p.41 tr, br: Patrick Crossonneau; p. 42: Anne Bouin; p. 43: Denis Trebbi; p. 44 br and tr: Jean-Jacques Pertusot; p. 45: Jean-Paul Moscovino; p. 46 pp: Alain Chevalier; p. 48: Yoshinobu Miyamoto / Hermes / LUXPRODUCTIONS.COM; p. 49 tl, tr, tm, bl: Alain Chevalier; p. 50: Eric Grundmann; p. 51: Camille Chalain; p. 52 tm: Hato Hino, Coonyang production; p. 52 ml and bl: Julien Gritte; p. 53: Brian Mayton; p. 54: Delphine Huguet; p. 55 tl and bl: Ilan Garibi; p. 55 cl: Ofir Zucker; p. 55 tr: Ofir Zucker & Ilan Garibi; p. 56 and p. 57: Charlene Fetiveau; p. 58 tr: Lisbeth Salas: p.58 br: Juan Pablo Quintero / Marc García-Durán Huet; p. 59: Guactruck - Michealle Renee Yu Lee; p. 60 and p. 61: Véronique Huyghe; p. 62: Otto NG; p. 63: KAZA; p. 64 pp: Jule Waibel; p. 66: Ilan Garibi; p. 55 tl: Mauricio Velásquez Posada and Claudia Fernández Silva; p. 67 br: Gonacas; p. 68 tl and ml: Musée des coiffes et des traditions; p. 69 tl, tm, bl: Susan Weitzman Conway; p. 70 tl, pp and p. 71 tm, bm, mr: Hugo Juillard, pH studio; p. 72 tr and mr: Bernard Dubois; p. 73: Mika Barr; p. 74 tl, bl: Jule Waibel; p. 75 tl: Tom Ziora; p. 75 bl and r: Jule Waibel; p. 76: HOID; tr and p. 77 tr, br: HOID; p. 77 tl: Jacob Hopkins; p. 78: Mauricio Velásquez Posada and Claudia Fernández Silva; p. 79 tr and mr: Irfan Redzovic. p. 80 tl, tr: Laura Papp; p. 81: FFIL; p. 82 tr, br and p. 83 tl: Maori Kimura; p. 83 tr and tm: Quinoa; p. 84 tl: Studio OOOMS; p. 85 tr, tl and br: Nervous system; p. 85 bm: Jessica Weiser; p. 86 tl, tr, bm, mc: Sarah Kelly - Saloukee; p. 87 tl, bl, br: Sarah Angold Studio; p. 88 pp: Daimonds Pucko / Pioes Sia; p. 90 and P. 91 tl, bl: Claudio Colucci and Dominique Serrell; p. 92 tr, mc, br: Industrial Origami; p. 93 tl, bl, br: Daimonds Pucko / Pioes Sia; p. 94 tl, mc, bc, br: Ran Amitai & Gilli Kuchik; p. 95 tr, mc and bl: Tobias Labarque; p. 96 tr: Normal Studio; p. 97 tl and bl: Different & Different; p. 98 tl, bl: Douwe Jacobs - Tom Schouten Flux Furniture; p. 99 tr: Studio Nuy Van Noort; p. 100 tr, mc, br, and p. 101: CartonLab; p. 102 pp and p. 103: molo; p. 104 tr, mc, br, and p. 105 tl, mr: ARCA, Steven Leprizé and Erick Demeyer; p. 105 bl: Fondation EY/Adrien Daste; p. 105 br: Damien Keller; p. 106 tl, mc, and br: Sébastien Cordoleani; p. 107: Sascha Akkermann; p. 108 tr: BZW Studio; p. 108 bm: Elisa Strozyk - Studio Been; p. 109 tl, bl, br: Goran Turnsek; p. 110 tl, tr, bl: Christy Oates; p. 111: Alexander Rehn, Designstudio; p. 112 and p. 113 Thomas Diewald. p. 114 tl, bl, br: Freyja Sewell; p. 115: avincze_torggler; p. 116 tl: Editions Artemide; p. 117 pp: Photo by Hiroshi Iwasaki © Miyake Design Studio; p. 118 tr, br: Formosis, Aki Hiltunen; p. 119 tm, ml, bl and bm: Arturass; p. 120 tl: Luisa Robinson; p.120 tr: Hive; p. 121: Studio-glow; p. 122: Charlot et Compagnie; p. 123 tl: Si Studio, Verónica Posada; p. 124 pp: Thomas Hillier; p. 126 tl: 3 Gatti Architecture Studio; p. 126 mc: Yoshinobu Miyamoto; p. 127: Yoshinobu Miyamoto; p. 128 bl: Thomas Hillier; p. 129: 3 Gatti Architecture Studio; p. 130 pp and p. 131 tr, mr, br and bl: Shunichi Atsumi; p. 132 tm: Christopher Mullaney; p. 133: Milo Keller; p. 134 tl and p. 135: Rupert Maleczek. Institute of Design | unit koge. Structure and Design, University of Innsbruck.; p. 136 pp and p. 137 tl, bl: Aleix Bagué; p. 138 tl, tr, tm, bl: Gramazio & Kohler; p. 139 tl, tr and br: Ryumei Fujiki; tl, tr and bl: Broissin Architectes; p. 140 br: Paúl Rivera; p. 141 pp: Paúl Rivera; p. 142 t and m: Rasmus Norlander; p. 142 bl: Stephen Speller © Heatherwick studio; p. 143: Make Architects; p. 144 and p. 145: People's industrial design office / People's architecture office; p. 146 pp: LAAB, Hong Kong; p. 148 br, bl: Eric Olsen; p. 149 tl, ml and bl: Jun Mitani; p. 150: Christophe Guberan; p. 151: Thomas Duval; p. 152 tl: Hugh Gilbert; p. 152 ml: RoboFold; p. 152 bl: Stathis Lagoudakis; p. 153 pp: Matthias Urschler; p. 154: Eric Olsen; p. 155: Festo; p. 156, 157: Otto NG / LAAB; p. 158 pp: Ilan Garibi; p. 162,163,164,165,168,169,170: Denis Trebbi; p. 166: Aline Caron and Alexandra Clamart; p. 171: Brigitte Parousel; p. 173 tm: Gramazio & Kohler, tr: Jun Mitani; tm: Eric Gjerde, Denis Trebbi; mr: Christiane Bettens, Richard Sweeney; bc and br: Jun Mitani; p. 174: Alain Chevalier; p. 175 tr: Erik & Martin Demaine; p. 175 br: Richard Sweeney; p. 176: Victor Coeurjoly.

Every effort has been made to identify and contact the copyright holders of images. If any errors or omissions have occurred, the publisher would be happy to be contacted by any copyright holders of images used in this work so that amendments may be made to credit them in future editions.
Technical pictographs: Guillaume Bounoure. Models for folding and diagram infographics: Denis Trebbi.